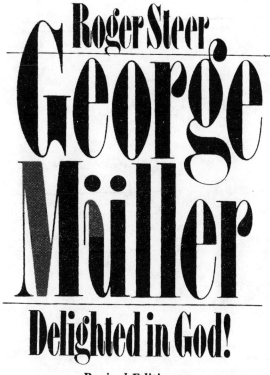

Roger Steer

George Müller

Delighted in God!

Revised Edition

Harold Shaw Publishers
Wheaton, Illinois

ISBN-13: 978-0-87788-304-3

Library of Congress Catalog Card Number 81-52600

First printing, August 1981
Second printing, January 1985
Third printing, October 1987

144915995

'Delight thyself also in the Lord; and he shall give thee the desires of thine heart' (Psalm 37:4).

'I know what a lovely, gracious, bountiful Being God is, from the revelation which he has been pleased to make of Himself in his Holy Word; I believe this revelation; I also know from my own experience the truth of it; and therefore I was satisfied with God, I delighted myself in God; and so it came, that He gave me the desire of my heart . . .'

George Müller, April 1874

To
the Memory
of my Father who
first told me about
George Müller

PREFACE

This is a revised and abridged version of the hardback edition first published in November 1975. Eight years have passed since I first became intrigued with the George Müller story, and I am now more than ever convinced that it is one of the most remarkable episodes in the history of the Christian church as well as a powerful answer to twentieth-century scepticism. The work which Müller established still flourishes and this edition includes a new chapter in which I have tried to capture the atmosphere in the modern family-group Homes.

I am grateful to those who helped in the task of revision. My wife Sheila worked through the first edition and successfully persuaded me to spare the reader a good deal of inessential material. Beverley Lawson readily agreed to type the new chapter. Jack Rose and Joe Cowan, upon whom Müller's mantle now falls, kindly talked to me about the work today and their plans for the future. Gordon and Ann Smith conducted me around the new Day Care Centre, and Bill and Sheila Dodd welcomed me to Tilsley House for a delightful weekend with Pauline, Beverley, Amelia, Sarah, Rowena, Erica, David, Robert, Paul, Mark, Shaun and Jason.

South Mimms   ROGER STEER
October, 1980

Contents

1	Prussian Playboy	*page* 11
2	'Constrained by the Love of Jesus'	18
3	England, 1829	28
4	Training by the Teign	36
5	The Bell Tolls	48
6	A Visible Proof	57
7	'Whose is the Gold and the Silver'	66
8	A Change of Air	76
9	'A Bank Which Cannot Break'	85
10	Looking to his Riches	98
11	A Just Complaint	111
12	Stronger Through Turmoil	122
13	Müller's Secret Treasure	134
14	When the South Wind Blew	151
15	Indescribable Happiness	165
16	'No Place Ever Seemed So Dear'	175
17	Letter to Yangchow	192
18	Safe to Glory	207
19	Return to the Rigi	215
20	To the White House	226
21	Simply by Prayer	239
22	The Scent of Honeysuckle	248
23	Loved by Thousands	263
24	Admiring His Kindness	276
25	Precious Prospect	283
26	A Final Assessment	295
27	Eighty Years On	313

CHAPTER ONE

Prussian Playboy

Half a century earlier, Wolfenbüttel's medieval castle had been the favourite residence of the dukes of Braunschweig-Wolfenbüttel; by the early nineteenth century, although the royal visitors had departed, the little seventeenth-century town nestling in the hills of Lower Saxony had lost none of its charm. In one of the half-timbered buildings, clustered around the castle, a police officer looked up from his desk. Two soldiers stood guard over a handsome Prussian youth. The officer began his interrogation.

'What is your name?'

'George Müller.'

'Age?'

'Sixteen.'

'Place and date of birth?'

'Kroppenstaedt, Prussia, September 27th 1805.'

'Is it true that you have been living in style at Wolfenbüttel, and that you are unable to pay the innkeeper?'

'Yes it is, but . . .'

'Is it also true that you spent last week at another hotel near Brunswick, living in similar luxury, and that when asked for payment you were forced to leave clothes as a security?'

There was little that Müller could say in his defence. It was true that he was penniless, and in debt. After three hours of questioning, and with no indication as to when he could expect a trial, the two soldiers marched him away—to prison.

December 18th 1821: George Müller looked at the cell where he was to spend his first night in prison. It was small and dark: lit only by a narrow window covered with large iron bars. Thick wooden partitions divided it from adjacent cells. The heavy door was bolted and locked: there was little chance of escape. That evening, Müller received some meat to eat with his bread, but he loathed the smell of it and left it untouched. This must have offended the chef, for there were no more special favours. On the second day he was treated to the same menu as his fellow-prisoners: for lunch, water and coarse bread; for dinner, vegetables but no meat—and, beginning to feel distinctly underfed, he ate a little.

Müller was locked in his cell day and night. He was given no work and no exercise. In order to help pass the time, he asked the keeper for a Bible, but his request was refused. On the third day he ate all his food, and after the fourth, would always have been glad of more.

Some time elapsed before he discovered that there was another prisoner in the cell next to him. He shouted through the thick wooden partition and discovered that his neighbour had been imprisoned for stealing. The governor decided to allow the two prisoners to share Müller's cell and they then spent their time describing their adventures. Warming to his task, Müller began to invent stories which impressed his friend immensely.

After about ten or twelve days, the two prisoners disagreed and for day after day, they refused to speak to each other. In the silence, Müller began to reflect on his life.

His earliest memory was of January in 1810 when, at the age of four, his family had moved from Kroppenstaedt to Heimersleben where his father was appointed collector of taxes. Before his tenth birthday, he had begun to steal government money from his father; and he remembered the day when his father had scored a tactical victory. Suspecting his son, Herr Müller had counted a small sum and placed it in the room where he was. Left alone for a while, George had taken some of the money and hidden it in his shoe. His father returned and counted the money; George was searched and found out. He remembered being punished on this and other occasions, but recalled that his reaction to being found guilty of mischief was usually to consider how he might do the thing again more cleverly, so as not to be detected.

Herr Müller had hoped that George would become a clergyman. not that he might serve God, but in order that he should have a comfortable living. There in his cell, George reflected on his five years at the cathedral classical school at Halberstadt; and remembered—with some shame—the Saturday night, some two years previously, when his mother had died. Not knowing of her illness Müller had played cards until two on the Sunday morning. Then, having quenched his thirst at a tavern, he had toured the streets, half drunk, with some friends.

He remembered that on the following day he had attended the first of a series of confirmation classes. On returning to his rooms, he found his father waiting to take him to his mother's funeral. Later he wrote:

This bereavement made no lasting impression on my mind. I grew worse and worse. Three or four days before I was confirmed (and thus admitted to partake of the Lord's supper), I was guilty of gross immorality; and the very day before my confirmation, when I was in the vestry with the clergyman to confess my sins, . . . I defrauded him; for I handed over to him only the twelfth part of the fee which my father had given me for him.

With nothing to disturb the routine of life in the cell, and with neither prisoner showing any inclination to communicate, Müller continued to reflect on the past. He had taken his first communion in Halberstadt cathedral on the Sunday after Easter 1820. That afternoon and evening, in search of quiet, he had stayed at home while the young people who had been confirmed with him were out and about. He had resolved to turn over a new leaf, and spend more time studying. But his resolution was soon broken and his behaviour had grown worse rather than better.

In the twenty months that had elapsed since his confirmation he had spent some of his time studying, but a great deal more time playing the piano and guitar, reading novels, drinking in taverns, making resolutions to improve, but breaking them almost as fast as they were made.

On January 12th 1822, Müller's recollections were interrupted by the welcome sound of the unbolting of his cell door. It was the keeper of the prison.

'You are wanted at the police office. Follow me, please.'

The commissioner told Müller that his father had sent the money which was needed for his travelling expenses, to pay his debt at the inn and for his maintenance in prison. He was therefore free to leave at once.

Herr Müller celebrated his reunion with his son by severely beating him. He took him home to Schoenebeck, near Magdeburg, where he had held another government appointment since the summer of 1821. George tried desperately hard to regain his father's favour. He began to tutor pupils in Latin, French, German grammar and arithmetic. He progressed in his own studies, became popular with everyone—including, after a time, his father. But, as he later admitted: 'All this time I was in heart as bad as ever; for I was still in secret habitually guilty of great sins.'

When he was just seventeen, Müller commenced studies at the gymnasium (pre-university school) at Nordhausen, one of the oldest towns in Prussia. Despite his enthusiasm for study, and occasional attempts to reform himself, Müller frequently disgraced himself at Nordhausen. One of his great failings was still an inability to make ends meet; he had contracted debts that he had no means of repaying. On one occasion, after receiving an allowance from his father, he purposely showed the money to some of his friends. Then, he carefully damaged the locks of his trunk and guitar case. A few minutes later he ran into the director's room with his coat off, and announced, breathlessly, that his money had been stolen.

Everyone was wonderfully sympathetic. Some of his friends kindly clubbed together and managed to give him as much money as he had lost, while his creditors agreed to extend their loans. However, the director—older and wiser—was suspicious and never fully restored George to his confidence. And for his part, Müller never again felt at ease in the presence of the director's wife, who had been like a mother to him during an illness caused, as he admitted, by his 'profligate and vicious life'.

Müller's great ambition was to enter Halle, the famous university founded in 1694 by elector Frederick III of Brandenburg who later became King of Prussia. It had been closed by Napoleon in 1806 and 1813, but it was reestablished in 1815 and strengthened by a merger with the old University of Wittenberg. It was recognised as one of the principal seats of Protestant theology in Europe, and also had faculties of law, medicine and philosophy.

He entered Halle in the Easter of 1825, when he was nineteen. The town is built on a sandy plain on the right bank of the River Saale. The inner town is old; it has a market square in the centre overlooked by a fine medieval town hall, and the Gothic *Marienkirche*—where Handel learnt to play the organ. Just west of the market square was the *Tal* where the town's famous salt springs rose.

On arrival at Halle, he made another resolution to change his course of life for the better. This time he was in earnest. He knew that in his present state no parish would ever choose him as its pastor. And even if he were accepted, he would need a good knowledge of divinity to obtain a comfortable living, which in Prussia depended on the standard of a man's university degree.

Almost at once, his resolution came to nothing. The freedom of university life offered too many temptations, and George Müller yet again found it impossible to manage money. He was forced to pawn his watch, some of his linen and his clothes; he began, once more, to borrow extensively. He felt utterly miserable: worn out by his constant, but unsuccessful, attempts at self-improvement.

It was in one of Halle's taverns (where he once drunk ten pints of beer in a single afternoon), that he thought he recognised a young man from his old school at Halberstadt. They had not been close friends, for Beta had been quiet and serious, but it occurred to Müller that if he struck up a close friendship now, it might help him to lead a steadier life. He picked his way across the crowded *Bierkeller* and shook the old timer warmly by the hand:

'Beta! How are you? How nice to see you after so long!'

'George Müller! I hardly recognised you.'

Beta welcomed the friendship because he thought it would enliven his social life.

At this time, Müller had a passion for travel. He suggested to his friends that they should make a trip to Switzerland.

'But we have no money, and no passports.'

Müller was not deterred. He persuaded his companions to forge letters from their parents which entitled them to passports. He took charge of the financial side and arranged that the group pledged all they could—particularly books—in order to obtain the necessary funds for the expedition. The party, which included Beta, left Halle on August 18th 1825.

They travelled to Erfurt and then westward to Frankfurt and south via Heidelberg, Stuttgart and Zürich to the heart of Switzerland. There before them, nestling between steep limestone mountains and a rising mist was Lake Lucerne. There was no railway then, but they climbed the Rigi and the view took Müller's breath away. He looked at the great promontories which thrust themselves into the lake: Bürgenstock, Seelisburg and away to the south-west Pilatus, all so irregular but magnificent. 'Now,' he thought, 'I have lived!'

They travelled home via Lake Constance and then east to Ulm and medieval Nuremberg in Bavaria, arriving back in Halle on September 29th. None of Müller's friends discovered that the man they had trusted with their money had cleverly arranged things so that he himself paid far less towards the cost of the trip than any other member of the party.

CHAPTER TWO

'Constrained by the Love of Jesus'

One Saturday afternoon, about the middle of November 1825, Müller and Beta were out for a stroll in Halle. As they talked, Beta grew serious.

'For some weeks I have been attending a meeting on Saturday evenings at the home of a Christian.'

He paused, wondering what George's reaction would be.

'And what happens at this meeting?'

'They read the Bible, they sing, they pray, and someone normally reads a sermon.'

'I should like to go with you, this evening.'

'I am not sure you will enjoy it.'

George had made up his mind: 'I am most anxious to go.'

'Then I will call for you this evening.'

Müller felt that at the meeting he might find something for which he had been searching all his life. But he felt sure that Herr Wagner, at whose home the meeting was held, would not welcome him. On arrival, he apologised for coming. Herr Wagner smiled: 'Come as often as you please; house and heart are open to you!'

He ushered George and Beta in to join the rest of the gathering and they sat down. They sang a hymn and then Herr Kayser—later to become a missionary in Africa with the London Missionary Society—knelt down and asked God to bless the meeting. Müller had never before seen anyone on his knees; he had never himself knelt to pray.

Herr Kayser read a chapter from the Bible and then a printed sermon. Prussian law, at that time, made the extempore exposition of Scripture an offence unless an ordained clergyman were present. At the end of the sermon, they sang another hymn and Herr Wagner closed the meeting with prayer. While he prayed, Müller thought, 'I could not pray as well, though I am much more learned than this man.'

The meeting made a deep impression on Müller. He felt strangely happy. As they walked home, he said to Beta: 'All we have seen on our journey to Switzerland, and all our former pleasures, are as nothing in comparison with this evening.'

It was the turning point of his life; and that night he lay peaceful and happy in his bed.

The next day and on several days during the following week, Müller returned to Herr Wagner's house to study the Bible with him and another Christian. Writing about this time later, he wrote:

It pleased God to teach me something of the meaning of that precious truth: 'God so loved the world, that He gave His only begotten Son, that whosoever believeth in Him should not perish, but have everlasting life.' I understood something of the reason why the Lord Jesus died on the cross, and suffered such agonies in the Garden of Gethsemane: even that thus, bearing the punishment due to us, we might not have to bear it ourselves. And, therefore, apprehending in some measure the love of Jesus for my soul, I was constrained to love Him in return. What all the exhortations and precepts of my father and others could not effect; what all my own resolutions could not bring about, even to renounce a life of sin and profligacy: I was enabled to do, constrained by the love of Jesus. The individual who desires to have his sins forgiven, must seek it through the blood of Jesus. The individual who desires to get power over sin, must likewise seek it through the blood of Jesus.

In January 1826, six or seven weeks after becoming a

Christian, Müller decided that he ought to become a missionary. The more he prayed about it, the more it seemed to be the right decision. He decided to go home to seek his father's permission which would be required by the German missionary societies. His father was angry. He told his son that he had spent large sums of money on his education in order that he could spend his last days with him in a parsonage. And now this prospect had come to nothing! He told Müller that he would no longer consider him as his son; and then, suddenly, Herr Müller began to weep, and begged him to reconsider. But George's mind was made up, and he felt that God gave him the strength to remain steadfast to His call.

Müller returned to Halle, and although he still had two years of study ahead at the university, he made up his mind never to take any more money from his father. It seemed wrong to do this, now that his father had no prospect of seeing him become what he had wished—a clergyman with a good living.

Müller was now faced with the problem of how to live without his father's support. Would he be able to honour his resolution? It soon became clear that he would. For a number of events followed—the first of many during his remarkable life—which demonstrated to Müller, and later to the world, that 'there is no want to them that fear Him' (Psalm 34:9).

It came about in this way. Shortly after he returned from visiting his father, several Americans arrived in Halle to study, three of whom were lecturers in American colleges. Their problem was that they did not understand German. However, Halle now had a new Professor of Divinity, a Dr Tholuck, who recommended to his new colleagues that one of his students should teach them the language. The Americans were delighted at the suggestion, and Dr Tholuck told them that George Müller would be the best man for the task. 'These gentlemen, some of whom were believers, paid so handsomely for the instruction which I gave them, and for the lectures of certain professors which I wrote out for them, that I had enough and to spare. Thus did the Lord richly make up to me the little which I had relinquished for His sake.'

Müller now embarked upon the task of proclaiming his new-found faith with the energetic dedication which was to become such a characteristic of his life. He circulated monthly about two hundred missionary papers in different parts of the country. He often stuffed his pockets full of tracts so that he could give them to people whom he met on his walks, and perhaps get into conversation with them. He wrote letters to his former friends pleading with them to turn to Christ. For thirteen weeks he visited a sick man and had the joy of seeing him become a Christian.

Not all his early efforts at personal evangelism were entirely successful. 'Once I met a beggar in the fields, and spoke to him about his soul. But when I perceived it made no impression upon him, I spoke more loudly; and when he still remained unmoved, I quite bawled in talking to him; till at last I went away, seeing it was of no use.' He came later to recognise the place of God's sovereignty in evangelism but 'yet so ignorant was I of the work of the Spirit, that I thought my speaking very loudly would force into him repentance towards God, and faith in the Lord Jesus'.

In August 1826 a schoolmaster who lived in a village about six miles from Halle asked Müller whether he would be prepared to preach in his parish where the elderly clergyman would be glad of assistance. Müller had never yet preached a sermon but decided that if he could commit a sermon to memory he might be able to help. It took him nearly a week to memorise the sermon and on August 27th 1826, in a chapel of ease at eight in the morning, he 'got through it, but had no enjoyment in the work'. At eleven he repeated the same sermon word for word in the parish church. Another service was planned

for the afternoon at which it was arranged that the
schoolmaster should read a printed sermon, as he often
did. However, suspecting that during the forty-eight
years the elderly clergyman had held his living the gospel
had never been preached in the church, Müller decided
to preach himself in the afternoon using the same
memorised sermon he had recited in the morning. But
when he stood in the pulpit to face his congregation,
something seemed to tell him to read from the fifth
chapter of Matthew's gospel and to make such comments
as came into his mind.

> Immediately upon beginning to expound 'Blessed are
> the poor in spirit . . .' I felt myself greatly assisted; and
> whereas in the morning my sermon had not been simple
> enough for the people to understand it, I now was
> listened to with the greatest attention, and I think I
> was also understood. My own peace and joy were great.
> I felt this a blessed work. After the service I left the
> aged clergyman as soon as possible, lest I should lose
> my enjoyment.

From then on, he preached frequently in the villages
and towns surrounding Halle. On Saturday evenings he
still visited and much enjoyed the meetings in Herr
Wagner's house. On Sunday evenings a group of
Christian students from the university met together, and
from the Easter of 1827 these meetings were held in
Müller's room, until he left Halle. On two occasions,
when his love for Christ had grown cold and he was
miserable, he opened his heart to his friends and they
prayed for him and brought him through.

In August 1827 the Continental Missionary Society in
England decided to send a minister to Bucharest. They
asked Professor Tholuck, at Halle, to keep his eye open
for a suitable man. Müller thought and prayed about it,
and was surprised to find that his father, formerly anta-

gonistic, did not disapprove of the idea. It seemed that this was the very opportunity for service he longed for and eventually he told Professor Tholuck that he would like to go.

As he waited to hear more details from London, he counted the cost of going to Bucharest and prayed earnestly about his future work. At the same time, oddly enough because it had nothing to do with the planned move to Bucharest, he developed a passionate interest in the Hebrew language and began to study it out of sheer enjoyment.

At the end of October 1827 an unexpected but welcome visitor turned up at one of the Sunday evening meetings in Müller's room. It was Hermann Ball, a missionary to Jews in Poland, whom he had first met in the Easter of 1826. He told Müller that for health reasons he would have to give up his work amongst the Jews. On hearing this Müller 'felt a peculiar desire to fill up his place', but did not think seriously about the matter in view of the Bucharest assignment.

In the evening of November 17th Müller called on Professor Tholuck. In the course of conversation, Tholuck said suddenly: 'Have you ever wanted to be a missionary to the Jews? I am an agent for the London Missionary Society which works amongst them.'

Müller was startled. He told Tholuck about Hermann Ball's visit, and his own recent passion for Hebrew.

'But it is surely not proper for me to think any more about the matter as I am going to Bucharest,' he said, and Professor Tholuck agreed.

Next morning, however, Müller felt that he had lost all his desire to go to Bucharest. This 'appeared to me very wrong and fleshly, and I therefore entreated the Lord, to restore to me the former desire for labouring on that missionary station. He graciously did so immediately. My earnestness in studying Hebrew, and my peculiar love for it, however, continued.'

Towards the end of November Professor Tholuck received a letter from the Continental Society. It said that owing to the war between the Turks and Russians, the committee had decided for the time being to abandon the idea of sending a minister to Bucharest where the armies were fighting. Tholuck once more asked Müller what he thought about becoming a missionary to the Jews. Müller wrote:

> After prayer and consideration, and consulting with experienced brethren, in order that they might probe my heart as to my motives, I came to this conclusion, that, though I could not say with certainty it was the will of God that I should be a missionary to the Jews yet, that I ought to offer myself to the committee, leaving it with the Lord to do with me afterwards, as it might seem good in His sight.

About the beginning of December 1827, Professor Tholuck wrote commending Müller to the committee in London.

Early in 1828 a new workhouse was established in Halle, where men convicted of minor offences were sent and made to work. Müller successfully applied to fill a temporary vacancy as chaplain to the inmates, while he waited to hear from London. This enabled him to preach to them twice on Sundays and once or twice in the week. He also took the men, one by one into a room 'to converse with them about their souls . . . I had at least some qualifications for ministering there; for I knew the state of those poor sinners, having been myself formerly, in all probability, a great deal worse than most of them, and my simplicity and plainness of speech they would not have found in every minister.'

Despite his many extramural activities, Müller successfully completed his university course at about Easter 1828. And it was a very different George Müller who graduated from Halle from the wayward and unhappy fresher who had arrived in 1825. Now his life had purpose, peace and joy; and if, with the passage of time, memories of Halle became dimmed, he would surely remember vividly that Saturday evening November 1825, when he had visited Herr Wagner's home and his life had been transformed.

In June 1828, Müller received a letter from the London Society for Promoting Christianity among the Jews (later to become the Church Mission to the Jews) of which Professor Tholuck was an agent. The committee decided to take him as a missionary student for six months on probation, provided that he would come to London. His immediate reaction to this news was bitter disappointment. He had spent most of his years since early childhood in study, and now longed to begin active Christian service.

But, on calmly considering the matter, it appeared to me but right that the committee should know me personally, and that it was also well for me to know them more intimately than merely by correspondence, as this afterwards would make our connection much more comfortable. I determined therefore after I had seen my father, and found no difficulty on his part, to go to London.

Just one obstacle remained, however, before Müller could obtain a passport for England. Every male Prussian graduate was required to serve one year in the army (rather than the more usual three years for the less educated) provided he was healthy. Müller had been declared fit for service when he was twenty but at his own request had had his service postponed until his course had been completed. However, it was well known that those who intended to become missionaries were often exempted. Some influential friends of Müller in Berlin therefore wrote to the King himself seeking his exemption. King Frederick William III, however, replied that the matter must be referred to the appropriate ministry and to the law, and that no exception was to be made in Müller's favour.

The solution to this problem was unexpected: Müller became quite seriously ill. An eminent doctor prescribed tonics and wine, and a friend—an American professor— took Müller to the country near Berlin. 'As long as I was day after day in the open air, going from place to place, drinking wine and taking tonics I felt well; but as soon as I returned to Halle, the old symptoms returned.' The main symptoms seem to have been severe giddiness, weakness of the stomach, and a cold which Müller could not throw off.

Müller described his American friend as a believer whose love for Christ had grown cold. They went together to the famous Michaelmas fair at Leipzig, and then on to the opera, but Müller did not enjoy it. After the first act, for refreshment, he took a glass of iced water; after the second act he fainted. He recovered sufficiently to return to their hotel where he spent a comfortable night. 'This circumstance the Lord graciously used as a means of arousing me—and on my way home, I freely opened my mind to my friend about the way in which we had been going on.' At this the professor promptly revealed that when Müller had fainted at the opera, it had struck him that it was an awful place to die in! 'This was the second and last time, since I have believed in the Lord Jesus, that I was in a theatre; and but once, in the year 1827, I went to a concert, when I likewise felt that it was unbecoming for me, as a child of God, to be in such a place.'

On their return to Halle, Müller suffered a haemorrhage in his stomach which he attributed to the glass of iced water. For several weeks he remained very weak in

body but his spirits revived and his love for Jesus
returned.

In January 1829, a Christian major in the Prussian
army suggested that Müller should offer himself for army
service in the hope that while he was still so weak, he
would be rejected, and be able at last to go to London.
He was duly examined, and found unfit; it was thought
that he had a tendency to tuberculosis. One of the generals
of the Prussian army, in the absence of his adjutant, wrote
out the necessary papers himself which gave Müller a
complete dismissal for life from all military engagements.
The general, himself a devout Christian, took the opportunity to point out certain parts of the Bible which he
particularly advised Müller to bring to the attention of
Jews, especially the eleventh chapter of Romans. For
some time, Müller's health continued to be very poor
until, acting on the advice of a medical professor, he gave
up all medicine and his condition began to improve!

In February, Müller left Berlin for London, visiting on
the way his father at the house in Heimersleben where he
had spent his boyhood. At Rotterdam the ice had just
broken up on the river, and no steamers would dare venture out. However, after nearly a month's delay Müller
boarded a ship which was bound for England. On March
19th 1829 he arrived in London.

CHAPTER THREE

England, 1829

You could smell the spring in London in 1829. The City had hardly begun to invade the country north of Hyde Park Corner. Over four hundred acres of rough heathland north of Oxford Street had recently been made into a beautiful park for the Prince Regent by John Nash: they called it Regent's Park. Leading south from the Park to the Mall, where the Prince lived, Nash had designed and built Regent Street. As one of the Street's prominent features he had built a fine church with a circular Ionic portico: All Souls, Langham Place, just five years old when Müller arrived in London.

By 1829 Nash was occupied with the rebuilding of Buckingham Palace for George IV, but the King died the following year before the work was done. William IV preferred to live at St James's Palace and the young Princess Victoria, now living at Kensington, would not move into the Palace until after her Coronation in 1837. Müller was no doubt intrigued by the modern gas lamps which lit Pall Mall: a sign to all that London was the most advanced city in the world.

Müller eventually found some inexpensive lodgings—not in the fashionable west end—but in Hackney, said at that time to be a haunt of highwaymen. His great desire was to become fluent in English as quickly as possible, but most of his fellow students being German, opportunities to further this ambition were limited. It was in the country beyond Hackney that he spoke in English for the first time 'to a little boy . . . about his soul, thinking that he would bear with my broken English'.

Soon after his arrival in England Müller heard one of his colleagues talking about a wealthy Exeter dentist named Anthony Norris Groves. Groves, he was told, had given up his fifteen-hundred-pound-a-year practice, and planned to go as a missionary to Persia, with his wife and children, depending on God alone for his needs. 'This made such an impression on me,' Müller recorded, 'and delighted me so, that I not only marked it down in my journal, but also wrote about it to my German friends.'

Characteristically, Müller worked hard in London: for about twelve hours a day, mainly at Hebrew (which included memorising portions of the Hebrew Old Testament), Chaldee and the Rabbinic alphabet. As he worked, he would pray about the most minute matters: 'I looked up to the Lord even whilst turning over the leaves of my Hebrew dictionary, asking His help, that I might quickly find the words.'

In May 1829 Müller, who was then aged twenty-three, fell ill. He had been far from well when he left Germany, and the long hours of study took their toll in London. He felt sure he was dying; introspection set in but an inner happiness prevailed. 'It was as if every sin, of which I had been guilty, was brought to my remembrance; but, at the same time, I could realise that all my sins were completely forgiven—that I was washed and made clean, completely clean, in the blood of Jesus. The result of this was great peace. I longed exceedingly to depart and be with Christ.' But this departure was not to be just yet. After a fortnight's illness, his doctor announced that he was better. 'This, instead of giving me joy, bowed me down, so great was my desire to be with the Lord; though almost immediately afterwards grace was given me to submit myself to the will of God.'

Müller's friends advised him to go to the country for a change of air. He therefore made his first visit to South Devon, the county where he would later spend over two years, but this stay lasted for less than three months. It was at Teignmouth, in that summer of 1829 that Müller struck up a friendship that would last thirty-six years and change the course of his life.

Henry Craik was a Scotsman who, like Müller, was nearly twenty-four and who, also like Müller, had been converted while at university. After graduating with some distinction at St Andrews, he had moved to Exeter in 1826 to become private tutor in the home of Anthony Norris Groves—the dentist about whom Müller had been told in London. In Exeter Craik had led a course of Bible studies in a school-room at Heavitree before moving, in 1828, to Teignmouth. What really attracted Müller to Craik was 'his warmth of heart towards the Lord'; and both were at this time fascinated by the study of Hebrew.

While at Exeter Craik had been greatly influenced by Anthony Norris Groves, and it must have been from Craik that Müller first learnt more about this remarkable man and the equally remarkable circle of friends Groves had met in Dublin. In 1822 Groves, who at that time described himself as a 'high churchman', had begun an intensive study of the Bible and had come to regard the Scriptures alone as a sufficient source of spiritual growth. In 1825 he had written a tract entitled *Christian Devotedness* in which he set out the reasons why he thought that Christ was speaking *literal* truth, and meant to be understood as so speaking, when he used expressions such as 'Sell that ye have, and give alms,' (Luke 12:33) and 'Lay not up for yourselves treasures upon earth,' (Matthew 6:19). He argued for a return to the spirit and practice of the early church whose members 'sold their possessions, and goods, and parted them to all men, as every man had need' (Acts 2:45); this, he said, was as 'consonant with reason as it is with revelation'.

Groves then proceeded to practise what he preached: he and his wife had already given up first a tenth and then a quarter of their income and distributed it among the poor. Now they abandoned any idea of saving money or putting it aside for their children, and, reducing their expenses by simplifying their living, they gave away all the rest.

In preparation for missionary service, Groves had enrolled as an external student of Trinity College, Dublin, intending to take a degree in theology before ordination in the Church of England. It was in Dublin that he met the group of men who are now regarded as the founders of the 'Plymouth Brethren', although they had no idea they were founding a movement: indeed the last thing any of them would have wished to do would have been to add another denomination to what they saw as a sadly divided Christendom.

Groves' decision to go to Persia as a missionary had compelled Craik to seek alternative employment, and in the summer of 1828 he had been engaged by Mr John Synge, then living at Teignmouth, as tutor to his two sons. Synge's permanent home was at Glanmore Castle, near Dublin, and he was one of the circle with which Groves had been in contact in that city. Thus Müller must have gained from Craik and Synge a pretty full and accurate picture of developments in Dublin. Moreover Craik's and Müller's links with Groves continued and in Müller's case were to become particularly close.

A few days after his arrival in Teignmouth, Müller attended the reopening of Ebenezer Chapel and was greatly impressed by one of those who preached on this occasion. He recorded, 'though I did not like all he said, yet I saw a gravity and solemnity in him different from the rest'. After the service Müller made enquiries to find out more about this preacher and was invited to Exmouth, where he was staying, to spend ten days with him in the same house. Müller readily accepted the invitation and recorded that 'through the instrumentality of this brother the Lord bestowed a great blessing upon me, for which I shall have cause to thank Him throughout eternity'. Unfortunately we do not know who 'this brother' was; what is clear, however, is that the development of

Müller's thought during and immediately following his stay in Exmouth reflects the influence of his contacts with the early Brethren movement.

Müller felt that God was leading him to a 'higher standard of devotedness' than he had known before. His comments on this in his journal suggest that he had carefully studied and been impressed by Groves' tract *Christian Devotedness*: 'it ill becomes the servant,' he wrote, 'to seek to be rich, and great, and honoured in that world, where his Lord was poor, and mean, and despised'.

All in all he described the change which he experienced during his stay in Devon as being 'like a second conversion'. In a letter written many years later, Müller wrote of this time as follows:

I became a believer in the Lord Jesus in the beginning of November 1825 ... For the first four years afterwards, it was for a good part in great weakness; but in July 1829 ... it came with me to an entire and full surrender of heart. I gave myself fully to the Lord. Honour, pleasure, money, my physical powers, my mental powers, all was laid down at the feet of Jesus, and I became a great lover of the Word of God. I found my all in God ...

Müller returned to London in September, determined to share his new insights and enthusiasms with his colleagues. He organised a meeting every morning from six to eight for prayers and Bible reading, at which each man present explained what God had shown him from the Bible portion he had read. One of his fellow students, in particular, shared his enthusiasm for spiritual things. On several evenings, when Müller enjoyed particularly good times of communion with God he went to his friend's room after midnight and found him in a similar state. The two of them then continued in prayer together until one or two in the morning. Müller would then return to his room, but a few times he felt so full of joy that he hardly slept until six when it was time for him to meet his colleagues again for prayer and fellowship.

Müller believed that God had called him to preach the gospel, and was not prepared to wait until he became a fully qualified missionary before he began to work amongst London's Jews. He wrote his name and address on hundreds of tracts, and, as he gave them out, invited the recipients to come and talk with him about the things of God. He preached at favourite Jewish meeting points and regularly read the Bible to about fifty Jewish boys: he became a teacher in a Sunday School.

Towards the end of November 1829, Müller began to wonder whether he should continue his connection with the London Society for Promoting Christianity amongst the Jews. The feeling was growing in his mind that as a servant of Christ he ought to be guided by the Holy Spirit in his missionary endeavours and not by men. One of the requirements of the committee would be that he should spend the greater part of his time working amongst the Jews. It now seemed to him that the Scriptural plan for him, on arrival in an area, would be to seek out and work especially among the Jews, and to preach to Gentiles as well.

By December he had more or less made up his mind to write to the committee of the Society to make his views known to them. But, typically, he decided to wait a month longer to consider the matter so as to be sure he was taking the right course. Before making his final decision, he travelled again to Devon, intending to spend a short vacation there. As things turned out, however, he never returned to London as a student.

He planned to spend a fortnight in Exmouth and determined not to idle away his time. On the first morning he preached at Ebenezer Chapel on the difference between being a Christian and a happy Christian. Several of those present promptly asked him to speak again in the afternoon, which he did and took the opportunity to suggest a meeting in the chapel every morning at ten, when he would expound Paul's epistle to the Romans.

On the second day, after his first exposition of Romans, a devout Devonian approached him with a suggestion:

'I have been praying for this month past that the Lord would do something for Lympstone, a large parish where there is little spiritual light. There is a Wesleyan chapel, and I doubt not you would be allowed to preach there.'

Müller gladly took up the suggestion, and the next day, a Sunday, found him at Lympstone enjoying the rich smells of the mud-flats on the Exe estuary. He had no difficulty in obtaining permission to preach twice that day at the Wesleyan chapel in the village. On most days in the following week he held a meeting 'in a room with several ladies, for reading the Scriptures with them'; and preached in another village near Exmouth.

In view of these growing commitments he decided to write straight away to the committee in London so that while they were making up their minds about him, he could continue to preach. His letter set out what his views on missionary service were before he became connected with the Society and how they had since changed. He said that he owed them a lot for their part in bringing him to England, where he had been so blessed; and that he would be happy in future to serve them without any salary if they would allow him to go from place to place throughout England, as the Lord directed him, and to preach to nominal Christians as well as Jews. He would like to obtain his supplies of Hebrew Scriptures and tracts for the Jews from the Society.

In reply, he received a 'very kind private letter from one of the secretaries, who always had been very kind to me', plus an official letter which pointed out politely that the Society could not employ anyone who was unwilling to submit to its guidance, and that it could not therefore consider him a missionary student. If more mature reflection caused him to change his mind, the Society would gladly reconsider the matter.

Thus ended Müller's connection with the Society which he had come to England to serve. He did not attach any blame to the Society, and always appreciated the help it had been to him; but, at the same time, never regretted the break he had made. He was now free to put into practice his sincere belief 'A servant of Christ has but one Master' and to work whenever and wherever his Master directed him.

After three weeks in Exmouth Müller left for Teignmouth intending to spend ten days with the friends he had made there during his convalescence the previous summer. The journey from Exmouth to Teignmouth is not a long one as the crow flies: Exmouth lies just east of the estuary where the Exe meets the sea, and Teignmouth lies on the other side a few miles to the south-west. But for those, like Müller, unable to fly, the journey involves either a detour of nearly twenty miles to the lowest bridging point of the Exe at Countess Wear, or the use of a tiresome ferry from Exmouth to Starcross. However, the compensation for the weary traveller is the magnificent scenery. There is the fine view across the estuary to Powderham and the woods of Mamhead. And beyond, on the Haldon hills, Belvedere Tower already stood out, in 1830 as it does today, a landmark over much of Devon. This was the country which was to become familiar to Müller—not as he thought for ten days or so, but for the next two and a half years. Who would have expected that the young Prussian who had so recently been rejected by the army on grounds of health, and who spoke such broken English, would now make the West Country his home until his death at the close of the century? He travelled to Teignmouth with little more than five pounds in his pocket, no income and no employment. But it was in those two and a half years that George Müller began to learn the lessons which would fit him for the work that lay ahead.

CHAPTER FOUR

Training by the Teign

Teignmouth already had a long history as a small seaport, fishing and market town, when in the late eighteenth and early nineteenth century it became a fashionable seaside resort. Both Keats and Fanny Burney stayed there, among other notables. In 1827, a bridge was opened which linked the town to Shaldon, the charming village on the opposite bank of the Teign estuary where Henry Craik lived.

Almost immediately on his arrival at Teignmouth, a member of the congregation of Ebenezer Chapel asked Müller whether he would consider becoming their minister. Müller replied that he did not intend to put down roots at any one place, but to travel the country preaching as and where God directed him.

On his first evening in the area, Henry Craik asked Müller to preach for him at the Baptist chapel in Shaldon. In the congregation that night were three ministers: none of them liked the sermon. But a young lady who had been servant to one of them was converted after the service; Müller could not help reflecting that she had heard her master preach many times.

Müller preached every night that first week either at Shaldon or Teignmouth. Some of those who listened, who had been friendly to him in the summer, now turned hostile. Müller concluded, 'That the Lord intended to work through my instrumentality at Teignmouth, and that therefore Satan, fearing this, sought to raise opposition against me.' Nevertheless there were a number who responded to the gospel and became Christians in that first week.

Despite a degree of opposition, the pressure from a section of the congregation at Ebenezer Chapel for Müller to become their minister increased. And then, after twelve weeks, the whole congregation unanimously invited him to become their pastor. Müller accepted the invitation but made it clear that he would only stay with them for as long as he was sure that this was God's will. He had not given up his intention to go from place to place as God directed him. The congregation offered him £55 a year, a sum which they later increased as numbers grew. But this method of support was later abandoned as Müller's views developed. Although he lived at Teignmouth Müller began to preach regularly at Exeter, Topsham, Shaldon, Exmouth, Lympstone, Bishopsteignton, Chudleigh, Cullompton and Newton Abbot.

At about the beginning of April (1830) Müller went to preach at the select little town of Sidmouth and became involved in a conversation with three equally select ladies. The conversation turned to the subject of baptism and he was asked to give his opinion. Müller who had often spoken against believers' baptism, replied:

'I do not think that I need to be baptised again.'

One of the ladies who had been baptised as a believer said, 'Have you ever read the Scriptures, and prayed with reference to this subject?'

'No.'

'Then I entreat you never to speak any more about it till you have done so.'

Thus chastened, Müller made up his mind to examine the subject. Characteristically he read the New Testament from the beginning looking particularly at references to the disputed matter. He decided that believers only are the proper subjects for baptism, and that immersion is the scriptural pattern. He was especially struck by Acts 8:36–38 and Romans 6:3–5; some time afterwards he was baptised by Henry Craik, and almost all of his friends followed suit sooner or later.

Devon is a big county—about seventy-five miles from north to south—but news of the able young Prussian who had settled at Teignmouth was spreading rapidly. In the north at Barnstaple, a lawyer, Thomas Pugsley, had built a chapel and invited Müller to preach at the opening in June (1830). Müller accepted the invitation and two locals were converted. In fact almost every time Müller now preached there was a response.

In that summer of 1830 Müller decided that Ebenezer Chapel should follow the example of the Apostles in Acts 20:7 and observe the Lord's Supper every Sunday, although he admitted that there is no commandment to do so either from Christ or in the epistles. He decided, too, that it was scriptural, according to Ephesians 4, and Romans 12 etc., 'that there should be given room for the Holy Ghost to work through any of the brethren whom He pleased to use; that thus one member might benefit the other with the gift which the Lord has bestowed upon him. Accordingly at certain meetings any of the brethren had an opportunity to exhort or teach the rest, if they considered that they had anything to say which might be beneficial to the hearers.' Thus Ebenezer Chapel, with Müller as pastor, adopted a distinctively Brethren-style observance of the Lord's Supper.

Throughout that summer of 1830, Müller never refused an opportunity to visit Exeter. It was not only the beauty of the journey along the coast from Teignmouth to Starcross and then up the road by the Exe estuary to the county town that he enjoyed. The attraction lay at the end of the journey: Müller had fallen in love. He had never confined his admiration of the Groves family to Anthony, but extended it to the sister who had been left behind in 1829. Mary Groves kept house for a Mrs Hake, an invalid who ran a boarding school at Northernhay House. Müller was sure that it was better for him to be married, and prayed much about the choice of a life's partner. Miss Groves could hardly have been a more ideal answer to his prayers. She shared her brother's earnest devotion to her Lord, and fully supported him in his decision to trust in God for material supplies. According to Müller, she played the piano nicely and painted beautifully; and as for providing him with intellectual companionship, she had studied English grammar, geography, history, French, Latin and Hebrew. She could also—should he be interested—teach George a thing or two about astronomy of which she possessed 'a superior knowledge'. On August 15th he wrote asking her to be his wife; four days later he happened to be in Exeter, and called at Northernhay House. Mary accepted his proposal and they fell to their knees asking God to bless their marriage.

Another housekeeper was found for Mrs Hake, and the couple were married on October 7th. It was a simple wedding. They walked to St David's Church for the service which was conducted by the Rev. John Abbot. They then returned with their friends to Northernhay House and 'commemorated the Lord's death; and then I drove off in the stage-coach with my beloved bride to Teignmouth, and next day we went to work for the Lord'.

Soon after returning to Teignmouth, the newly-married couple decided that it was wrong for George to receive a set salary. His salary had been made up by pew-rents, and, as the better seats were more expensive, they now took the view that the system engendered unacceptable social discrimination and was contrary to the spirit of James 2:1–6. Therefore all pew-rents were abandoned and all seats made free. At the end of October Müller announced to the church that from then on he would give up his regular salary; he gave his reasons and read Philippians 4. A box was placed in the chapel with a notice saying that anyone who wanted to support Mr and Mrs Müller might put their offerings therein.

Müller also decided that from that time onwards he would ask no one, not even his fellow Christians in Ebenezer Chapel, to help him financially in any way. There would be no more 'going to man, instead of going to the Lord'. Müller admitted that this decision 'required more grace than to give up my salary'. But it was this decision, probably more than anything else, that makes the story of his life from this time so exciting. At this time also they decided to take literally Luke 12:33 'Sell that ye have, and give alms', and carry out the commandment.

Throughout their married lives the Müllers never disagreed about the principle or practice of these momentous decisions made at the commencement of their life together. Looking back on this period later Müller wrote, 'this has been the means of letting us see the tender love and care of our God over His children, even in the most minute things, in a way in which we never experimentally knew them before; and it has, in particular, made the Lord known to us more fully than we knew Him before, as a prayer hearing God'.

Bishopsteignton is an attractive village on a hill overlooking the Teign estuary with magnificent views over the river and Dartmoor beyond. A number of the congregation at Ebenezer Chapel lived in the village. From the Norman conquest it had belonged to the bishops of Exeter and traditionally was one of their richest manors. But two visitors to the village in November 1830 were not rich. It was nearly three weeks since the Müllers had given up their salary and they were reduced to about eight shillings. (For most of the nineteenth century, which was remarkably free from inflation, a farm labourer typically earned about ten shillings (50p) a week.) That morning they had asked God to give them some money.

They had to visit a lady member of the church who lived in the village. During the conversation, their hostess asked Müller, 'Do you want any money?'

'I told the brethren, dear sister, when I gave up my salary, that I would for the future tell the Lord only about my wants.'

She replied, 'But He has told me to give you some money. About a fortnight ago I asked Him, what I should do for Him, and He told me to give you some money; and last Saturday it came again powerfully to my mind, and has not left me since, and I felt it so forcibly last night, that I could not help speaking of it to brother P.'

Still thinking it better not to mention their circumstances, Müller changed the subject to other matters. When they left, the lady gave him two guineas.

The following week at Exmouth, when they were reduced to about nine shillings Müller prayed again for money and within thirty hours they were given £7 10s from three different sources. Müller commented on the first few weeks after their decision to ask God alone for funds '. . . admire the gentleness of the Lord, that He did not try our faith much at the commencement, but gave us first encouragement and allowed us to see His willingness to help us, before He was pleased to try it more fully.'

What some would no doubt call Müller's fanatical principles on the reception of gifts often led to amusing incidents. In March 1831, while staying at Axminster to preach, he was invited to spend a Sunday at Chard in Somerset. On that sort of occasion he was very reluctant to accept any gifts, as he was afraid to give the impression that he preached for money. After one service a member of the congregation tried to give him some money wrapped in paper, but Müller refused to accept it. However, Somerset people are not easily discouraged: this determined saint forced the paper into Müller's pocket and ran away. Another gentleman from Chard forced him to accept a sovereign, but only after a tussle.

At Barnstaple they developed some ingenious solutions to the problem of Müller's reluctance to accept gifts while

preaching away from Teignmouth. While Mr and Mrs
Müller were there in April 1831 they found a sovereign
in Mrs Müller's handbag which had been put there
anonymously. On their return to Teignmouth, when they
opened their case, an envelope fell out on to the floor. It
contained two sovereigns and threepence. The three-pence
had obviously been put in to make a noise when the case
was emptied.

When Müller gave up his salary he asked the responsible brethren at Teignmouth to open the box in
Ebenezer Chapel once a week. However, as these gentlemen either forgot to take it out weekly or were ashamed
to bring it to Müller in very small sums, it was usually
emptied once in three to five weeks. This was a problem
for the Müllers; Müller decided, however, to say nothing
about the matter, on principle. But for a while the practice
led to some narrow financial scrapes. One Saturday in
June 1831, Müller and Henry Craik returned from
Torquay where they had been preaching. The Müllers
had ninepence left. Müller prayed 'that the Lord would
be pleased to impress it on brother Y that we wanted
money, so that he might open the box'. Next morning at
breakfast the Müllers had just enough butter for a friend
and relative who were staying with them. They made no
mention of their circumstances, of course, so that their
visitors should not feel uncomfortable. After the morning
meeting, 'brother Y' quite unexpectedly opened the box
and gave Müller the contents—£1 18s 10½d, the equi-
valent of rather more than two weeks' wages. Poor brother
Y, who had evidently learnt his lesson the hard way, told
George that he and his wife had been unable to sleep the
previous night for worry that the Müllers might be in
need. Müller found it hard to conceal a smile.

Henry Craik's way of living was the same as Müller's
and this often deepened their friendship. On June 18th
he called on the Müllers and mentioned that he had only

TRAINING BY THE TEIGN

one and a half pence left. He later returned to their home having been given a sum of money and gave them ten shillings. They only had three shillings left themselves.

In July a shoulder of mutton and a loaf of bread was sent to the Müllers anonymously. They later discovered that there had been a false rumour that they were starving and that therefore an anxious friend had sent these provisions. The truth was that although in the early days they were often brought so low they had not even a penny left, or not enough money to buy more bread when the last of the loaf was on the table, they never sat down to a meal without nourishing food on the table. Müller conceded, however, that God sometimes used these false rumours to remind people of their needs.

On September 10th Müller was given £6 and recorded in his diary that in the previous month he had received £40 plus all sorts of gifts in kind. On November 16th, the Müllers were forced to pray for some meat for dinner as they had no money to buy any. After praying, they opened a parcel which had arrived from Exmouth. Among other things it contained a ham which was ample both for them and a friend who was staying with them.

Müller was not yet a hundred per cent fit. On Saturday afternoon, February 18th 1832, he suffered a haemorrhage in his stomach and lost a good deal of blood. He was not unduly alarmed. Next day on the Sunday morning, two brethren from Ebenezer who had heard of the occurrence called at the house to ask about Müller's arrangements for the day. Some of the brethren were in the habit of preaching in four neighbouring villages but they presumed that one of them would have to stay at Ebenezer to substitute for Müller while he remained ill. Müller asked them to call again in an hour when he would give them his answer. After they had gone, Müller prayed; and God gave him the faith to get up. He made up his mind to go to the morning service. Even walking the short distance to the chapel tired him out but he was able to preach and his voice was as strong and loud as usual. At lunch time, a medical friend called and pleaded with him not to preach in the afternoon as it might seriously injure him. Müller agreed that under normal circumstances it would indeed be foolish, but, he said, God had given him the faith to carry on. He preached again in the afternoon, after which his medical friend called again and begged him not to preach in the evening. But the doctor was no match for the faith of the stubborn Prussian; he preached yet again in the evening. After the service, he returned home and went straight to bed; the time had come when even he knew when enough was enough.

Next morning he rose early and spent a normally busy day. On the Wednesday, after attending a meeting in the morning, he walked the six miles with two friends to Newton Abbot and then rode to Plymouth. Strangely, this odd form of convalescence worked, for on the Thursday, he felt as well as he had before the haemorrhage. He wrote: 'I could not say, that, if such a thing should happen again, I would act in the same way; for when I have been not nearly so weak as when I had broken the blood vessel, having no faith, I did not preach; yet if it were to please the Lord to give me faith, I might be able to do the same, though even still weaker than at the time just spoken of.'

At this time, Müller frequently prayed with sick believers until they were restored. He would ask God, unconditionally, for the blessing of health; later in his life, he gave up the practice of asking unconditionally for this blessing. Nearly always, his prayers were answered, but on some occasions they were not. Müller drew a distinction between the 'gift' and 'grace' of faith. He believed that at this time of his life he was given in some cases the 'gift' of faith so that unconditionally he could ask and expect the answer. With the 'gift' of faith, Müller believed that he was able to do something which if he had not done, or had not believed, would not have been sinful. But with the 'grace' of faith, Müller believed a man could do something or believe something, respecting which he had the word of God to rest upon, and which if he had not done, or believed, would have been sinful. For instance, it would need the 'gift' of faith to believe that a seriously ill person would be restored, for there is no promise that he should be; but it simply needs the 'grace' of faith to believe that God will give us the necessities of life if we seek first the Kingdom of God and his righteousness, for this is promised in Matthew 6.

On April 8th 1832 Müller wrote in his diary:

'I have again felt much this day that Teignmouth is no longer my place, and that I shall leave it.'

Since the previous August he had begun to feel that his work at Teignmouth was done and that he should move. He found that wherever he went he seemed to preach with more power and enjoyment than at Teignmouth, which was the opposite to his experience in his early days in the town.

On April 13th Henry Craik, who was on a working visit to Bristol (attracting large crowds to Gideon Chapel to hear him) wrote to Müller inviting him to come and help him. He replied that he would come if he clearly saw it to be God's will. After preaching at Ebenezer Chapel on the evening of April 15th Müller announced to his flock that he might soon leave them. He reminded them of his warning when he had become their pastor that he would stay only as long as he felt it was God's will so to do. There was a lot of weeping; but Müller was by this time sure he knew God's will.

On April 19th, Müller preached the last of his regular weekly sermons at Torquay, and the following day left Teignmouth to join Craik at Bristol. Müller and Craik spent ten days together in Bristol, preaching in Gideon

and Pithay Chapels and also in a ship called the Clifton
Ark which had been made into a place of worship. Their
visit was an undoubted success and there were many
striking conversions; they felt sure that God was indicat-
ing His will for them to work in Bristol. On the evening
of April 29th they held a meeting at Gideon Chapel. It
was the last service of their visit and Henry Craik
preached. The aisles, the pulpit stairs and the vestry were
packed, and hundreds were turned away when no further
square inches could be found. They left Bristol the following day: dozens of people pressed them to return. One
man promised that he would rent Bethesda Chapel for
them at his own expense.

May 2nd found them back at Teignmouth.

On May 18th, while Müller was praying about Bristol,
a message arrived for him to visit Henry Craik. Craik
told him that the congregation of Gideon Chapel, Bristol,
had written accepting an offer the two men had made to
work amongst them under certain conditions which they
had laid down. These were: that they would preach and
work amongst them not according to a fixed pastoral relationship governed by any rules of the congregation, but
as they themselves interpreted God's will; that pew-rents
should be abolished; and that they would continue the
practice they had established at Teignmouth with regard
to their financial support.

On May 21st, Müller began to call in turn on each
member of the congregation at Ebenezer to say his fare-
wells. It was a trying day, with a lot more weeping. That
night he wrote in his diary: 'Were I not so fully persuaded
that it is the will of God we should go to Bristol, I should
have been hardly able to bear it.' The following day was
spent in similar fashion and was no less emotional for all
concerned.

On May 23rd, Müller left Teignmouth for Exeter with
his wife and father-in-law. Henry Craik followed the next
day. They arrived in Bristol on the evening of May 25th

1832. Just before they left Teignmouth they had been given £15 without which they could not have afforded to make the journey.

Müller had spent two years and five months at Teignmouth. When he arrived, the congregation of Ebenezer Chapel had numbered eighteen, when he left it numbered fifty-one. Both men had gained invaluable pastoral experience which would be stretched to the full as they worked amongst far larger congregations in Bristol; and both of them, too, had learned to depend on God alone for their needs. Müller was still only twenty-six when he arrived in Bristol and his maturity is perhaps one of the most striking features of the story so far; but he would need sterling character indeed to carry out the work God planned for him.

CHAPTER FIVE

The Bell Tolls

High above the Avon Gorge, where Bristolians enjoy
fresh channel breezes, a new foundation stone had been
laid eleven months before the Müllers came to Bristol.
But soon after Lady Elton had performed the ceremony
in June 1831 funds ran low and work on Brunel's daring
suspension bridge came to a temporary halt. In fact it
was not until after the designer's death in 1859 that the
bridge was completed carrying a new road nearly two
hundred and fifty feet above the Avon to link Clifton
with the suburbs at Leigh Woods and Failand.

Magnificent as they are, the high cliffs of the gorge had
the awkward habit of depriving a ship of wind; add to
this the hazards of the Avon's steep mudbanks and a
Bristol fog and you begin to understand why already by
the turn of the century the city had begun to lose its
place as England's second port to Liverpool with its miles
of easily accessible estuary. And then, in 1833, a year
after Müller's arrival, the emancipation of the West
Indian slaves dealt Bristol a blow which hastened the
decline of the city in the early Victorian era. Isambard
Kingdom Brunel, however, did much to maintain the
prestige of the city by his completion of the Great
Western Railway and his construction in Bristol of the
steam-ships 'Great Western' and 'Great Britain'.

After their arrival Müller and Craik spent nearly a
fortnight looking for lodgings. They paid eighteen shillings a week for two sitting-rooms, three bedrooms, 'coals
and attendance'. Craik lived with the Müllers at this
time.

By the end of June the way had become clear for Müller and Craik to work in the heart of Bristol at Bethesda chapel in Great George Street; this was in addition to their prior arrangement to work at Gideon Chapel in Newfoundland Street. Bethesda was large and modern, built a few years earlier by a group led by a seceding clergyman, Mr Cowan. The congregation, however, had recently broken up as a result of false teaching. The offer for Müller and Craik to take the empty building gave them an opportunity to build up a work on their own lines, as they interpreted Scripture. A local supporter provided the first year's rent, and they began to preach at Bethesda on July 6th 1832.

Recalling those early days at Bethesda, W. Elfe Tayler wrote (in 1866): 'They preached alternately—one Lord's day Mr Craik preached in the morning, and Mr Müller in the evening; the next Lord's day the order was reversed. From the first they attracted great attention; the chapel, especially at night, was crowded to excess. No doubt this was owing, in some degree, to certain peculiarities connected with their ministry. They are neither of them Englishmen—the one being a Scotsman, the other a German, with a strong accent and pronunciation.' Müller saw the funny side of this bonus attraction of his sermons; after one Bristolian was converted, he recorded that she came to hear him preach 'merely out of curiosity to hear my foreign accent, some words having been mentioned to her which I did not pronounce properly. Scarcely had she entered the chapel, when she was led to see herself a sinner.'

It was during July 1832 that Müller and Craik began the practice, which they never abandoned, of setting aside evenings when people could come to the vestry to talk with them individually. On the first of these evenings there were so many enquirers that the two pastors were there for well over four hours.

July 1832 was also the month that cholera broke out in

Bristol. By mid-August, the outbreak had reached hor-
rifying proportions and between two and three hundred
people met (at six a.m.) in Gideon Chapel to pray for
relief from the suffering.

On August 24th Henry Craik wrote in his diary: 'Our
neighbour, Mrs Williams, a few yards from us, was
attacked about three this morning, and died about three
in the afternoon. Her husband was also attacked and is
not expected to recover. The bell is incessantly tolling;
it is an awful time.' The same evening Müller recorded:
'Just now, ten in the evening, the funeral bell is ringing,
and has been ringing the greater part of this evening. It
rings almost all day ... If this night I should be taken
in the cholera, my only hope and trust is in the blood
of Jesus Christ shed for the remission of all my many
sins.'

Both men displayed courage throughout and carried on
their pastoral work undaunted, visiting many cholera victims day and night; throughout September the epidemic
showed no signs of abating.

In the midst of all this danger, Mary Müller was due
to have a baby. As labour began, she became very ill.
(Her illness was not connected with the epidemic.) Müller
spent a whole night in prayer; next day Mary gave birth
to a daughter. Despite everything, mother and child did
well. They called the little girl Lydia and she was in fact
their only child to survive infancy.

A week later Müller wrote:

Last night brother Craik and I were called out of bed
to a poor woman ill in the cholera. She was suffering
intensely. We never saw a case so distressing. We could
hardly say anything to her on account of her loud cries.
I felt as if the cholera was coming upon me. We com-
mended ourselves into the hands of the Lord when we
came home, and He mercifully preserved us. The poor
woman died today.

By the beginning of October, the epidemic had passed its peak and Müller and Craik were able to set aside a day for thanksgiving. Miraculously, only one of the members of Bethesda and Gideon had died during the course of the outbreak.

Craik's first wife had died young early in 1832 at Teignmouth. In October he remarried. For this reason, and as a result of the birth of Lydia, their first lodgings became too small. Just as they began to think about this problem, the house belonging to Gideon chapel was unexpectedly given up by the tenant. The church then offered it to Müller and Craik, and suggested that they should furnish it for them. The two men objected to this, fearing that it would be a financial burden. However, several of the brethren insisted, and Müller and Craik, having prayed over the matter, accepted the offer on condition that the furniture was very plain. The house was furnished, and Müller recorded that 'the love of the brethren had done it more expensively than we wished it'.

In May 1833, the two churches at Gideon and Bethesda met together for tea. It was the first of many such occasions and Müller loved them—not least because, as he said, 'they give us a sweet foretaste of our meeting together at the marriage supper of the Lamb'. The two congregations prayed together and sang, and Müller made it clear that 'any brother has an opportunity to speak what may tend to the edification of the rest'.

It was just twelve months since he had arrived in Bristol, and as he looked at the crowd gathered in the hall, Müller thought about the year that had passed. Bethesda already had sixty members; and nearly fifty new members had joined the congregation at Gideon. He knew of sixty-five people who had been converted under the preaching of Craik and himself. Many 'backsliders' had regained their first love for Christ and a number of Christians had been strengthened in their faith. Surely,

Müller thought, this was proof enough that it had been God's will for them to come to Bristol.

All this time Müller was living in the way to which he had become accustomed at Teignmouth—depending on God for his needs and those of his family. During his second summer in Bristol (1833), he carefully recorded his gifts both large and small:

> June 22. A brother sent a hat to brother Craik, and one to me, as a token of his love and gratitude, like a thank-offering, as he says. This is now the fourth hat which the Lord has kindly sent me successively, whenever, or even before, I needed one. Between August 19th and 27th was sent to us, by several individuals, a considerable quantity of fruit. How very kind of the Lord, not merely to send us the necessities of life, but even such things as, on account of the weakness of our bodies, or the want of appetite, we might have desired! Thus the Lord has sent wine or porter [beer] when we required it; or, when there was want of appetite, and, on account of the poverty of our brethren, we should not have considered it right to spend money upon such things, He has kindly sent fowls, game, etc., to suit our appetite. We have, indeed, not served a hard Master.

By the end of December 1833 over three years had passed since Müller's decision never to ask anybody for anything he needed, but to rely on God alone. In the first of those three years he had received just over £150, in the second nearly £200 and in 1833: £267 15s 8¼d— Müller's accounts never lacked precision!

In 1834 Müller and Craik founded the 'Scriptural Knowledge Institution for Home and Abroad', which still flourishes today despite its unimaginative title. The three aims of the Institution were first, to assist and establish

Day Schools, Sunday Schools and Adult Schools in which scriptural teaching was given; second, to distribute Bibles; and third, to aid missionary work. The last of these three objects is the most well known today: and the Institution currently sends well over £30,000 abroad annually.

In the first seven months of its existence, the Institution provided for about one hundred and twenty children to be taught in Sunday Schools, forty adults in an Adult School and over two hundred children to be taught in two Day Schools. One thousand Bibles and New Testaments were circulated and £57 was sent abroad to missionaries.

On March 19th, Mary Müller gave birth to a son whom they called Elijah—'My God is Jehovah'. For this reason, after living for nearly two years with the Craiks, George and Mary decided that they and Lydia and Elijah should live in a house of their own. Thus on May 15th they moved into No. 21 Paul Street, an end of terrace house in High Kingsdown. The house was solid but not beautiful. Nine steps led up to the front door on the first floor above a basement; there were four storeys in all. At the back of the house was a small garden which Müller was to use for prayer and meditation. In the eighteenth century Kingsdown had been a much sought-after suburb of the city, popular with merchants made wealthy by the slave trade. But by Müller's day it was considered less desirable and had become a little scruffy. The Müllers received several substantial sums to help with furnishing the new house and also some carpeting.

Two diary entries in the autumn of 1834 show that Müller's personal needs were still well provided for: 'September 18. A brother, a tailor, was sent to measure me for new clothes. My clothes are again getting old, and it is therefore very kind of the Lord to provide thus. September 25. A brother sent me a new hat today.'

At the end of 1834 Müller recorded that his income had been nearly £230 and that he had received gifts in kind worth about £60. Bethesda chapel now numbered one hundred and twenty-five and Gideon, one hundred and thirty-two. Of these, over one hundred souls had been converted under Müller and Craik's preaching.

Müller spent a few months in Germany early in 1835 staying mostly at Heimersleben with his father and brother. Herr Müller was keen to hear about political and social affairs in England which his son had scarcely mentioned in his letters—so much so that his father asked whether it was forbidden in England to send letters abroad dealing with such matters. By the middle of April Müller was back at Bristol to find Henry Craik suffering from a throat infection and unable to preach. In May Craik travelled to Devon for a change of air.

June 1835 was a sad month for the Müllers—especially for Mary. On the 22nd she lost her father, and on the 26th their son Elijah, now fifteen months old, died of pneumonia. Müller wrote:

My prayer last evening was that God would be pleased to support my dear wife under trial, should he remove the little one; and to take him soon to Himself, thus sparing him from suffering. I did not pray for the child's recovery. It was but two hours after that the dear little one went home. The eldest and the youngest the Lord has thus removed from our family in the same week. My dear Mary feels her loss much, yet is greatly supported.

It is not clear why Müller did not pray for Elijah's recovery. According to his distinction between the 'gift' and 'grace' of faith, this was the sort of situation where, early in his Christian life, he sometimes received the 'gift of faith'—that is he felt able to ask God unconditionally for the blessing of health. It appears that on this occasion he did not feel able so to do. On the day before Elijah died Müller simply recorded in his journal, 'The Lord's holy will be done concerning the dear little one.' And several years later, he wrote: 'When the Lord took from me a beloved infant, my soul was at peace, perfectly at peace; I could only weep tears of joy when I did weep. And why? Because my soul laid hold in faith on that word: "Of such is the Kingdom of Heaven." Matthew 19 : 14. Believing, therefore, as I did, upon the ground of this word, my soul rejoiced, instead of mourning, that my beloved infant was far happier with the Lord, than with me.'

Financial worries followed these losses. Early in July Müller wrote: 'Our taxes are due, and may be called for any day, and for the first time we have no money to pay them, as we were obliged, on account of our late afflictions, to spend the money which we had put by for them. May the Lord in mercy provide.' Two anxious days followed before Müller could record: 'I was enabled today, by the free-will offerings through the boxes, and by what I had left, to pay the taxes before they were called for. How kind of the Lord to answer my prayer so soon.'

Craik returned from Devon in mid-August but was still unable to speak very much, despite a considerable improvement in his general health. Müller himself was now suffering from a stomach disorder. He wrote: 'I feel very weak, and suffer more than before from the disease. I am in doubt whether to leave Bristol entirely for a time. I have no money to go away for a change of air. I have had an invitation to stay for a week with a sister in the country, and I think of accepting the invitation, and going tomorrow.' Two days later he wrote: 'Today I had £5 given to me for the express purpose of using change of air.' Shortly afterwards he received another £10 for the same purpose.

At the beginning of September Müller travelled with Mary, Lydia and one servant whom they now employed, to Portishead where he settled down to read Foxe's *Book of Martyrs*, feeling too weak for talking, walking or writing. The book refreshed him; and as his strength returned he took to horse riding in the country. However, he soon began to feel depressed and bored with 'having for my chief employment eating and drinking, walking, bathing and taking horse exercise . . . I would rather be again in the midst of the work in Bristol, if my Lord will condescend to use His most unworthy servant'.

Later Müller discovered that the person from whom he was hiring his horse had no licence, and decided that as a Christian he could ride the animal no longer. On the same day he received a pressing invitation from friends in the Isle of Wight to stay with them at their house in Niton near Ventnor; funds, however, were too low to enable the whole family to make the journey. But the next day Müller unexpectedly received over £6 which was owing to him and a letter containing a present of £2—more than enough for the trip.

Before retiring to bed on September 29th Müller felt able to pray, for the first time during his illness, that God would restore his health. He wrote in his diary, 'I now long to go back again to Bristol, yet without impatience, and feel assured that the Lord will strengthen me to return to it.' At the end of another week, he was able to record, 'My strength has been during the last days increasing, but I feel still the symptoms of indigestion. I have been able to speak several times at family prayer, and to expound the Scriptures to the school children, without suffering in consequence of it.' On October 15th (1835) they returned from the Isle of Wight to Bristol; Müller was fit again and about to embark on the great adventure of faith which would make him famous.

CHAPTER SIX

A Visible Proof

What an excellent example of the power of dress young Oliver Twist was! Wrapped in the blanket which had hitherto formed his only covering, he might have been the child of a nobleman or a beggar—it would have been hard for the haughtiest stranger to have fixed his station in society. But now that he was enveloped in the old calico robes, which had grown yellow in the same service, he was badged and ticketed, and fell into his place at once—a parish child; the orphan of a work-house; the humble half-starved drudge; to be cuffed and buffeted through the world—despised by all, and pitied by none.

Oliver cried lustily. If he could have known that he was an orphan, left to the tender mercies of churchwardens and overseers, perhaps he would have cried the louder.

Thus, in *Oliver Twist* (1837), Charles Dickens drew the British public's attention to the desperate plight of orphans. The book levelled a series of charges against the Poor Law Amendment Act of 1834, which *The Times* in 1836 attacked as, 'that appalling machine . . . for wringing the hearts of forlorn widowhood, for refusing crust to famished age, for imprisoning the orphan in workhouse dungeons and for driving to prostitution the friendless and unprotected girl'. The main aim of the new act was to stop the benevolent Allowance Systems—under which labourers' wages were supplemented to subsistence level by contribution to the Poor rate—by abolishing relief to the able-bodied outside the workhouses. No able-bodied

man would receive assistance unless he entered a workhouse; the workhouses themselves were to be, in the words
of Edwin Chadwick 'uninviting places of wholesome re-
straint'. Conditions in the workhouses became a social
disgrace; and the children 'imprisoned' within their walls
became quickly demoralised by the decrepit, insane and
handicapped adults who also lived there.

Leah and Harriet Culliford lived in Bristol in 1835:
Leah was five and Harriet nine. The girls' parents were
poor and—like so many of their contemporaries—had
fallen victim to tuberculosis. Medical science was power-
less to help: the future for poor Leah and Harriet was
grim. If they could expect little from the State to com-
pensate them for the loss of both their parents, the attitude of the public was, in general, equally unsympathetic.
Dickens' charge that orphans were 'despised by all, and
pitied by none' is well illustrated by a letter which
appeared in the *Bristol Mirror and General Advertiser* on
Saturday, June 23rd 1849:

'The Begging Nuisance'

. . . It was only a day or two ago I was returning from
Bristol, when I saw a woman—whom, from the number
of children she had about her, I should imagine an Irish
woman—exposing to public gaze a leg and foot in the
most loathsome state of disease, and this, too, in one of
the principal thoroughfares in Bristol—Park Street!
There is also a little girl I see almost daily, with a
wooden leg, who, to convince you she is not an im-
postor, shows you the stump of her amputated limb.
This little girl I think one of the most hardened beggars
I ever came into contact with. She seems to know the
tactics of the police quite as well as the Superintendent
himself, for, if you tell her you will give her in charge
of the first policeman you meet with, she will laugh, as
much as to say—'You may, if you can meet one', and
still importune. Now, Sir, I need not say what distres-

sing effects such sights as those cited above may have upon females in a certain critical state of health, not to say a word about the disgust excited in all. To say the least wherever the fault is, the inhabitants and visitors of a fashionable place like Clifton, and the wealthy citizens of the second city in England, should be able to take their recreation without having their nerves and senses shocked by such shocking and revolting sights ... Allow me to subscribe myself, dear Mr Editor. A CONSTANT READER

Clifton, June 20th 1849

It is not possible that such a harsh attitude to poverty can have been typical in the first half of the nineteenth century; but the fact that the editor printed the letter without comment is surely significant.

If the State did little, and the public were unsympathetic, what could Leah and Harriet—and their many contemporaries in a similar plight—expect from charitable institutions? In 1835 orphanages supported by private charity were rare. Dr Barnardo founded his first home in 1866, and Spurgeon followed in 1867; the National Children's Home was founded in 1869 and Mr Fegan began his work in 1870. (Both Barnardo and Fegan were members of the Brethren.) The Church of England Children's Society (then 'Waifs and Strays') began in 1881. But in 1835 private orphan homes were regarded as revolutionary experiments.

In the whole of England and Wales it is possible to trace a dozen orphanages which date back to the 1830s or earlier. They were all small and there was none in Bristol. Eight of the orphanages were in London and the other four in the Home Counties. But even if the Cullifords had lived in this area they would still have been ineligible for nearly all the homes. In the first place, they would have been barred for reasons of expense. Only one of the twelve homes—in Southwark—was intended for destitute children and required no payment; the other eleven homes stipulated that admission was by election by subscribers or by purchase of annual or life subscriptions. The cost of a life subscription ranged from about £100 to £250. Secondly, the Cullifords would have been barred from most of the homes on grounds of class. For instance, the British Orphan Asylum made it clear that it was for 'children of middle-class parents . . . who in their life time were in a position to provide a liberal education for their children', and the Royal Asylum of St Anne's Society advertised itself as existing to help children of 'parents who have seen better days, and have moved in a superior station in life'. The Infant Orphan Asylum at Wanstead, Essex, was prepared to accept children from all parts of the British dominions, but only 'children who are respectably descended'. Its prospectus boasted that 'of the children on the foundation many are the orphans of clergyman, officers and professional men'. In fact 'no candidate is admitted whose parents have not filled respectable positions in society and, *ceteris paribus*, its eligibility is proportionate to the former respectability of its family'. The London Orphan Asylum made it clear that 'Children of domestic or agricultural servants and of journeymen tradesmen are ineligible.' Many of the homes refused to accept children who were in any way diseased or deformed; some refused those who could not read, and a number barred children whose parents had at any time received parish relief. Once again, the only institution which made no restrictions on grounds of class or creed was the Southwark home which had been founded in 1830. Maintained by the funds of Bridewell hospital it had room for five hundred children from any part of the United Kingdom. The minimum age for entry was twelve.

But even this forward-looking institution could do little to alleviate what had become one of Britain's major social problems. It was a problem, however, which in the closing months of 1835 began increasingly to occupy the thoughts of one citizen of Bristol. While a student at Halle in 1826, Müller had lodged for two months in one of the great orphan houses built by the German Professor A. H. Franke in the late seventeenth century. He never forgot the experience; and late in 1835 he was particularly reminded of Franke's work. Müller's diary contains the following entries:

> November 20. This evening I took tea at a sister's house, where I found Franke's life. I have frequently, for a long time, thought of labouring in a similar way, though it might be on a much smaller scale; not, to imitate Franke, but in reliance upon the Lord. May God make it plain! November 21. Today I have had it very much impressed on my heart, no longer merely to think about the establishment of an Orphan-House, but actually to set about it, and I have been very much in prayer respecting it, in order to ascertain the Lord's mind ... November 23. Today I had £10 sent from Ireland for our Institution. Thus the Lord, in answer to prayer, has given me, in a few days, about £50. I had asked for only £40. This has been a great encouragement to me, and has still more stirred me up to think and pray about the establishment of an Orphan-House ... November 25. I have been again much in prayer yesterday and today about the Orphan-House, and am more and more convinced that it is of God. May He in mercy guide me!

Müller spent many hours during the next fortnight praying about his proposed orphanage. Repeatedly he examined his motives for the undertaking. He asked himself whether the whole idea did not originate in a desire to win glory for himself. He called on Henry Craik so that his friend could have the opportunity of probing his heart. Craik duly probed; but found nothing to which he could take exception. Indeed his verdict was encouraging.

Müller's concern for the plight of orphans in nineteenth-century England began rather more than a year before Dickens popularised the situation in *Oliver Twist*. There can be no doubt either about the tragic proportions of the problem or that Müller's anxiety was genuine. When he first arrived in Bristol he had been deeply moved by the common sight of children begging in the streets; and when they knocked on his own door he longed to do something positive to help. In October 1834, too, he had recorded in his journal his distress on hearing an 'account of a poor little orphan boy, who for some time attended one of our schools, and who seems there, as far as we can judge, to have been brought to a real concern about his soul ... and who some time ago was taken to the poorhouse some miles out of Bristol'. The entry concludes, 'May this, if it be the Lord's will, lead me to do something also for the supply of the *temporal* wants of poor children, the pressure of which has occasioned this poor boy to be taken away from our school!'

But there was another equally important reason why Müller contemplated founding an orphanage: he wanted to demonstrate to the world that there is reality in the things of God. As he visited the members of his two congregations in Bristol he discovered repeatedly that people needed to have their faith strengthened. On one occasion he visited a man who was in the habit of working at his trade for nearly sixteen hours every day. His health was suffering and his Christian faith meant little to him. Müller suggested that if he worked less, his health would improve and he would have more time to read his Bible and pray; his spiritual condition would then improve. The reply was sceptical:

'But if I work less, I do not earn enough for the support of my family. Even now, whilst I work so much, I have scarcely enough. The wages are so low, that I must work hard in order to obtain what I need.'

Müller thought, 'This is not trust in God. This is not belief in the words of Christ, "Seek ye first the Kingdom of God, and His righteousness: and all these things shall be added unto you." ' He replied:

'My dear brother, it is not your work which supports your family, but the Lord; and He who has fed you and your family when you could not work at all, on account of illness, would surely provide for you and yours, if, for the sake of obtaining food for your inner man, you were to work only for so many hours a day, as would allow you proper time for retirement. And is it not the case now, that you begin the work of the day after having had only a few hurried moments for prayer; and when you leave off your work in the evening, and mean then to read a little of the word of God, are you not too much worn out in body and mind, to enjoy it, and do you not often fall asleep whilst reading the Scriptures, or whilst on your knees in prayer?'

As he waited for the reply, Müller looked at his friend's expression. It was clear that the man agreed that the advice was sound; but yet there was doubt. He was not fully prepared to take God at his word.

'How . . . how should I get on? How should I get on if I carried out your advice?'

Müller was not annoyed. He was sad. He thought, 'How I long that I had something to which I could point this brother! Something that would act as a visible proof that our God and Father is the same faithful God as ever he was; as willing as ever to prove Himself to be the Living God, in our day as formerly, to all who put their trust in Him.'

Sometimes Müller met businessmen who professed to be Christians yet who were conducting their affairs in a way which was less than honest. In consequence they suffered, amongst other things, from guilty consciences. Some excused their actions by reference to the fierceness of competition or the depression of trade, and maintained that if they carried on their business according to the Bible, it would not do well. Only rarely was a stand made for God; only rarely was there a determination to trust Him for everything. In these cases, too, Müller longed to demonstrate that God had not changed: that He would reward those who did not 'regard iniquity in their hearts'. Müller had proved God in his own life; he was anxious that others should enjoy the same experience. He wrote, 'I judged myself bound to be the servant of the Church of Christ, in the particular point on which I had obtained mercy: namely, in being able to take God by His word and to rely upon it.' He felt that God had used his encounters with Christians who lacked assurance and conviction in their lives 'to awaken in my heart the desire of setting before the church at large, and before the world, a proof that He had not in the least changed; and this seemed to me best done, by the establishing of an Orphan-House. It needed to be something which could be seen, even by the natural eye.'

Müller had decided to embark upon an adventure, far more daring, far more exciting even than the construction by Brunel of his mighty bridge at Clifton. He put the challenge that faced him like this.

Now, if I, a poor man, simply by prayer and faith, obtained, *without asking any individual*, [Müller's italics] the means for establishing and carrying on an Orphan-House: there would be something which, with the Lord's blessing, might be instrumental in strengthening the faith of the children of God, besides being a testimony to the consciences of the unconverted, of the reality of the things of God.

Was the most important consideration which led Müller to found an Orphan-House a desire to ease the orphan's plight, or an attempt to demonstrate God's reality? Let Müller answer:

I certainly did from my heart desire to be used by God to benefit the bodies of poor children, bereaved of both parents, and seek, in other respects, with the help of God, to do them good for this life—I also particularly longed to be used by God in getting the dear orphans trained up in the fear of God—but still, the first and primary object of the work was that God might be magnified by the fact, that the orphans under my care are provided, with all they need, only by *prayer and faith*, without anyone being asked by me or my fellow-labourers, whereby it may be seen, that God is FAITHFUL STILL, and HEARS PRAYER STILL.

One evening that December (1835), Müller was struck by the words in Psalm 81 : 10, 'Open thy mouth wide, and I will fill it'. Until that evening, although he had prayed much about the pros and cons of establishing an orphanage, he had not prayed specifically that God would provide the means to do so. But on reading this psalm he decided to apply the Scripture to the needs of the Orphan-House. He asked God to provide the premises, £1,000 and suitable people to look after the children.

Müller had learnt to rely on God alone for the needs of his own family. Now he looked to Him to house, feed and clothe an altogether larger and needier family; he dared to ask God to give further proof of his reality and love.

CHAPTER SEVEN

'Whose is the Gold and the Silver'

'December 7. Today I received the first shilling for the Orphan-House. Afterwards I received another shilling from a German brother. December 9. This afternoon the first piece of furniture was given—a large wardrobe.'

On the evening of the 9th Müller addressed a meeting at which he outlined his proposals for the orphanage. He made it clear that the home would only be established if God provided the means and suitable people to run it. But, he said, '. . . I have been led more and more to think that the matter may be of Him. Now, if so, he can influence His people in any part of the world, (for I do not look to Bristol, nor even to England, but to the living God, whose is the gold and the silver), to entrust me and brother Corser, whom the Lord has made willing to help me in this work, with the means.' (John Corser was a Church of England clergyman, who had resigned his living to work as a City missionary in Bristol and to help Müller.) Under no circumstances would any individual ever be asked for money or materials. There would be no charge for admission and no restriction of entry on grounds of class or creed.

All who would be engaged as masters, matrons, and assistants would have to be both true believers and appropriately qualified for the work. Only children bereaved of both parents would be received. Girls would be brought up for service, boys for a trade; they would be employed 'according to their ability and bodily strength, in useful occupations, and thus help to maintain themselves'. The Institution would be for truly destitute chil-

dren and any orphans whose relatives were able and willing to pay for their maintenance would be ineligible. They
would receive a 'plain education'; and, in conclusion,
Müller said that 'the chief and especial end of the
Institution will be to seek, with God's blessing, to bring
them to the knowledge of Jesus Christ, by instructing
them in the Scriptures'.

When Müller had finished speaking there was purposely no collection; however, he was given ten shillings.
A woman offered to help in the work and Müller recorded
that he 'went home happy in the Lord, and full of confidence that the matter will come to pass, though but ten
shillings has been given'.

The following day it began to look as if this confidence
would be rewarded. Müller received a letter from a husband and wife who said: 'We propose ourselves for the
service of the intended Orphan-House, if you think us
qualified for it; also to give up all the furniture, etc.,
which the Lord has given us, for its use; and to do this
without receiving any salary whatever; believing, that if it
be the will of the Lord to employ us, He will supply all
our need, etc.' In the evening 'a brother brought from
several individuals three dishes, twenty-eight plates, three
basins, one jug, four mugs, three salt stands, one grater,
four knives, and five forks'.

Next day, Müller prayed that God would give further
evidence of His favour towards the Orphan-House. While
he was on his knees three dishes, twelve plates, one basin,
and one blanket were delivered. Müller thanked God and
asked for another encouragement the same day. Not long
after, he was duly given £50 from an unexpected source;
he felt led by God to pray for even more that same day.
In the evening, twenty-nine yards of material were sent
and a woman offered herself for the work.

And so it went on. 'December 13. A brother was influenced this day to give four shillings per week, or £10

8s yearly, as long as the Lord gives the means; eight shillings was given by him as two weeks' subscriptions. Today a brother and sister offered themselves, with all their furniture, and all the provisions which they have in the house, if they can be usefully employed in the concerns of the Orphan-House.

December 14. Today a sister offered her services for the work. In the evening another sister offered herself for the Institution. December 15. A sister brought from several friends, ten basins, eight mugs, one plate, five dessert spoons, six tea spoons, one skimmer, one toasting fork, one flour dredge, three knives and forks, one sheet, one pillow case, one table cloth; also £1. In the afternoon were sent fifty-five yards of sheeting, and twelve yards of calico.

December 16. I took out of the box in my room one shilling. December 17. I was rather cast down last evening and this morning about the matter, questioning whether I ought to be engaged in this way, and was led to ask the Lord to give me some further encouragement. Soon after we were sent by a brother two pieces of print, the one seven and the other twenty-three and three-quarter yards, six and three-quarter yards of calico, four pieces of lining, about four yards altogether, a sheet, and a yard measure. This evening another brother brought a clothes horse, three frocks, four pinafores, six handkerchiefs, three counterpanes, one blanket, two pewter salt cellars, six tin cups, and six metal tea spoons; he also brought 3s 6d given to him by three different individuals. At the same time he told me that it had been put into the heart of an individual to send tomorrow £100.

December 18. This afternoon the same brother brought from a sister, a counterpane, a flat iron stand, eight cups and saucers, a sugar basin, a milk jug, a tea cup, sixteen thimbles, five knives and forks, six dessert spoons, twelve tea spoons, four combs, and two little graters; from another friend a flat iron and a cup and saucer. At the same time he brought the £100 above referred to.

When he discovered who had sent the £100, Müller was reluctant to accept it. He knew that the donor was a woman who earned about 3s 6d a week by needlework and decided to visit her to find out whether the money had been given in a moment without thought of the cost. He discovered that the woman had been left £480 on the death of her father; on receipt of the money she had parted with a large sum to pay off some outstanding family debts, and had given her mother £100. She had then sent the £100 towards the Orphan-House. Müller spoke to her at great length hoping to persuade her to reconsider. Her reply was brief:

'The Lord Jesus has given His last drop of blood for me, and should I not give all the money I have? Rather than the Orphan-House should not be established, I will give all the money I have.'

Müller left the house not only with the £100, but another £5 for the poorer members of Gideon and Bethesda which she insisted he took. Müller commented, 'during her life-time, I suppose, not six brethren and sisters among us knew that she had ever possessed £480, or that she had given £100 towards the Orphan-House'.

Gifts for the orphanage had, by the end of the year, become so encouraging that Müller was able to talk in terms of opening a small home at the beginning of the following April. At first, he would confine admission to girls between the ages of seven and twelve and allow them to stay until they were ready to go into domestic service. Children would be accepted from any part of the United Kingdom.

Gifts continued to arrive in the new year. On the evening of January 5th there was a ring at the Müllers' house

bell. The door was opened, not to a visitor but to—a kitchen fender and dish, left, no doubt, by a donor with
strong views on anonymous giving. In the opening weeks
of 1836 there were numerous such small gifts in money
and in kind and some more substantial gifts including
another of £100 in early February.

Müller prayed about every detail of his plans and requirements for the proposed home; but until this time he
had never asked God to send children. He had taken it
for granted that there would be plenty of applications.
However, by the beginning of February, although he had
publicised his willingness to receive applications, not one
had been received. He therefore spent a whole evening
praying for applications; next day the first was received.

A large terraced house, No. 6 Wilson Street, close to
Gideon Chapel, had been brought to his attention as
available at a low rental. It was three storeys high and
solidly built. After prayer and careful inspection Müller
decided to rent the property for at least a year. He then
began to furnish it for thirty children. Gifts continued to
arrive and to be eminently suited to the needs of the
moment: 'April 2 . . . six blankets, two counterpanes, four
sheets, eight bonnets, five frocks, six pinafores . . . April
6. One dozen washing basins and one jug . . . a set of fire
irons, a tea kettle, a coal box, a tin saucepan, a tripod, a
tea pot, three cups and saucers, a wash-hand basin, three
small basins, and two plates . . . 22 Hymn Books.' By
early April, furnishing and fitting of No. 6 had been
completed.

April 11th 1836, was the day when the first children
arrived, looking pale and nervous. One of them was
named Harriet—Harriet Culliford. Some of their temporary guardians, who might have expected Mr Müller
to be elderly and bearded, were surprised to find a young
man—he was still only thirty; the children, although they
could detect a 'no-nonsense' look about their new father,
responded to the air of kindness and calm in his expres-

sion. Müller introduced them to the smiling matron and
governess whom he had engaged: no one could ever give
these little girls back their parents, but here were folk
who were determined to do everything possible to make
up the loss.

It is unlikely that they had any illusions about the
immensity of the task which lay ahead. Although they
might not have used the language of modern psychology,
they were well aware of the emotional difficulties which
faced children who had lost both their parents. And,
financially, they knew that every day, three times a day,
for seven days every week there would be thirty hungry
children to feed, besides the staff. Thirty pairs of feet
would wear out thirty pairs of shoes; clothes would grow
too worn or too small and need replacement. Müller knew
that if ever the children went hungry or badly clothed, his
God would be discredited. But he was not alarmed; instead, he would repeat to his family and helpers Christ's
words in Matthew 6:31 and 33: 'Therefore take no
thought, saying, What shall we eat? or, What shall we
drink? or, Wherewithal shall we be clothed? But seek ye
first the Kingdom of God, and his righteousness; and all
these things shall be added unto you.'

By early May there were nearly thirty girls in No. 6,
and money and provisions were still arriving steadily,
'twenty pounds of bacon and ten pounds of cheese . . . six
straw bonnets . . . six night caps and two petticoats . . . a
basket of apples, and three pounds of sugar'. The friends
from Teignmouth had evidently not forgotten their
former pastor, for in June, Müller recorded the arrival
from Teignmouth of a considerable sum of money, 'together with a gown, a boy's pinafore, a pair of socks,
coloured cotton for three children's frocks, two babies'
bed gowns, and five babies' night caps'.

At the end of September a Bristol doctor offered to
attend the orphans, and supply them with medicine as
necessary, entirely without charge. Müller gladly

accepted the offer. On October 14th he recorded the arrival of four and a half gallons of beer, but sadly does not
tell us whether the children were allowed to indulge.

While Müller made it a firm rule that neither he nor
his helpers ever asked any individual for anything 'that
the Lord's own hand might be clearly seen', he did not
hesitate on occasions to ask God to 'incline the heart' of
certain individuals to give towards the work. In
December 1835 he had noted in his diary a prayer that a
particular person known to him should give £100. Some
months later the gentleman in question had sent him £50;
and then on Guy Fawkes' Day 1836 he gave a further
£50. Unusually for Müller, it was some days before he
remembered his prayer of the previous December. In his
delight, he called on the donor and showed him the diary
entry for December 12th 1835, so that they could rejoice
together over the precision of this answer to prayer.

Soon after the opening of the home in No. 6 for girls
aged from seven upwards it became obvious to Müller
that there was a need for a home catering for children
under the age of seven. In October (1836) he managed to
obtain the use of No. 1 Wilson Street for an Infant
Orphan-House, together with a piece of land for a play-
ground. After much prayer a suitable matron and governess were engaged; the house was furnished and the first
children—boys and girls—were taken on November 28th.
Some of the eldest girls from No. 6 were employed to
help at No. 1 under the supervision of the matron and
governess, and it was felt that this training in nursery
work would be useful for them when they went into service—Leah Culliford was among the early occupants of
No. 1.

Christmas for Müller's children in Wilson Street in
1836 cannot have been frugal. Towards the festive season
his diary recorded the arrival of a number of ducks and
turkeys—and a hundredweight of treacle. Müller was
pleased, too, that Christmas when a pound arrived

attached to a note recalling the occasion when Jesus took a child in his arms and said, 'Whosoever shall receive one of such children in my name, receiveth me: and whosoever shall receive me, receiveth not me, but him that sent me.' (Mark 9:37).

In the closing minutes of 1836—the year it all began—Müller wrote in his journal, 'We had this evening a prayer-meeting to praise the Lord for His goodness during the past year, and to ask Him for a continuance of His favours during the coming year. We continued together till half-past eleven.'

By April, there were sixty children in the two Orphan-Houses, thirty infants at No. 1 and thirty girls at No. 6. Typhus fever raged in Bristol that spring, but mercifully only two children caught the disease and both recovered.

It was in the early summer of 1837 that Müller planned to publish the first volume of his *Narrative of some of the Lord's dealings with George Müller*. He had finally decided to write this only after many months of consideration, and examination of his motives; he conceded, in fact, that he had not prayed so much over any other step which he had taken in God's service. On the one hand, he was not at all keen to add to the number of religious books on the market; but on the other hand,

> that which weighed more with me than anything was, that I have reason to believe from what I have seen among the children of God, that many of their trials arise, either from want of confidence in the Lord as it regards temporal things, or from carrying on their business in an unscriptural way. On account, therefore, of the remarkable way in which the Lord has dealt with me in temporal things, within the last ten years, I feel that I am a debtor to the Church of Christ, and that I ought . . . to make known, as much as I can, the way in which I have been led.

By May, 1837 the manuscript was nearly ready to be
sent to the publishers. But before he did so, there was one
prayer in particular to which he wanted to record a complete answer: on December 5th 1835, he had asked God
for £1,000 towards the orphan work. Since then he had
repeated the prayer almost every day, and in eighteen
months he had received over £900. On May 21st he 'gave
himself earnestly' to prayer that God would send the outstanding amount, 'for though,' he wrote, 'in my own
mind, the thing is as good as done, so much so, that I
have repeatedly been able to thank God, that He will
surely give me every shilling of that sum, yet to others
this would not be enough'. In May, a lady whom he had
never seen called on him and gave him £40; smaller sums
arrived daily. On June 15th a gift of £5 made up the
whole sum, and Müller was delighted. Every shilling of
this money, and all the articles of clothing and furniture
which he had received, had been given to him as he
recorded:

> without one single individual having been asked by
> me for any thing. The reason why I have refrained alto-
> gether from soliciting anyone for help is, that the hand
> of God evidently might be seen in the matter, that thus
> my fellow-believers might be encouraged more and
> more to trust Him, and that also those who know not
> the Lord, may have a fresh proof that, indeed, it is not
> a vain thing to pray to God.

Writing recently about Mother Teresa of Calcutta,
Malcolm Muggeridge has said that 'in true evangelical
style, she goes to God with her needs and difficulties,
and is always marvelling at the magnificent response in
meeting her every requirement, great and small. Those of
us who cannot participate in such particular requests are
not so much more sophisticated as less gifted with faith.'
And so it was with Müller—although he denied that he

had been granted a special gift of faith. For, as he wrote some years later,

> It is true that the faith, which I am enabled to exercise, is altogether God's own gift; it is true that He alone supports it, and that He alone can increase it; it is true that, moment by moment, I depend upon Him for it, and that, if I were only one moment left to myself, my faith would utterly fail; but it is not true that my faith is that gift of faith which is spoken of in 1 Corinthians 12:9 . . . it is the self-same faith which is found in every believer, and the growth of which I am sensible of to myself . . .

CHAPTER EIGHT

A Change of Air

It had been announced in London that the King's health was breaking, and early in the morning of Tuesday, June 20th 1837, King William IV died at Windsor Castle in the arms of Queen Adelaide. While Bristol and the rest of England slept, London saw a flurry of activity. The Archbishop of Canterbury, who had performed the last rites, took his leave of Queen Adelaide and drove with Lord Conyngham in the darkness through country lanes to Kensington. At five a.m. they arrived at Kensington Palace but found great difficulty in gaining admission. The porter refused to rouse the young princess. Eventually they were allowed in and the Baroness Lehzen was sent for; she reluctantly agreed to inform the new sovereign of their presence. The Archbishop of Canterbury and the Lord Chamberlain stood as the Princess Victoria entered the room, a shawl thrown over her dressing gown, her feet in slippers, and her hair falling down her back. Lord Conyngham then knelt on one knee and saluted her as Queen.

Victoria was eighteen at her accession and her reign was to be the longest in English history. Müller was thirty-one but he would live to preach a lengthy sermon on the occasion of the Queen's diamond jubilee.

Later that day, news of the King's death reached Bristol and flags were lowered to half mast on ships, churches and public buildings. Some shops were closed and bells tolled until late into the night. But Saturday, June 24th, was a day of rejoicing on account of the proclamation of Her Majesty. The flags were raised and the church bells rang peals. At ten o'clock a procession 'for proclaiming her most gracious majesty Queen Victoria in the Borough of Bristol' wended its way from the top of the High Street via Wine Street, Peter's Pump and Bridge Street over the bridge to Temple Cross. From there, the city police led the mayor, the sheriff, the magistrates, clergy and dissenting ministers along Temple Street and Portwall Lane to Thomas Street, over the bridge along the Back through the Mansion House into Queen Square, where the procession passed the statue of the late King, along the Quay to Quay Pipe and finally to the Council House.

The Victorian era had begun; and for Müller and Craik the responsibility of caring for two large congregations at Gideon and Bethesda continued. God's word in the Bible was the final authority to which they looked in their handling of the two churches. A minor crisis in the summer of 1837, together with the events preceding it, illustrates that they combined their supreme respect for the Scriptures with an intelligent flexibility of approach— particularly when they were themselves uncertain what was 'the mind of God'. From the earliest days of their labours in Bristol they were never quite sure whether only those who had been baptised after becoming Christians should be received into the fellowship at Bethesda or whether all who believed in Christ irrespective of baptism should be received. After a lengthy period of controversy within the church and discussions with Robert Chapman, Müller and Craik decided that they ought to 'receive all whom Christ has received' (Romans 15:7) irrespective of their views on baptism. Chapman, well-known in the history of the Brethren and a life-long friend of Müller, had given up a highly promising solicitor's practice in London to serve God in Barnstaple.

In June 1837 Müller decided to open a third home, for about forty boys aged seven years and above, first because the need for one was so obvious in Bristol and secondly because without one he had nowhere to send the infant boys when they reached seven. By September enough money had been provided and suitable staff had offered themselves; all that remained was to find a suitable house. On October 21st Müller was offered another of the houses in Wilson Street—No. 3—which he gladly accepted.

Early in November, Müller's health again began to deteriorate. He woke in the night of the 4th with a feeling of weakness in his head. After some time, he got off to sleep by tying a handkerchief around his head which seemed to ease the weakness. By November 7th he was unable to work, and although the Boys' Orphan-House was about to be opened and there were certain problems at Bethesda, he decided to leave Bristol for rest and quiet. An anonymous letter arrived from Ireland enclosing £5 for his personal expenses, and he took this as a sign that it was right for him to leave.

On the following morning he left his house with no idea where he would go. The first available coach was travelling to Bath—and Müller climbed aboard. He decided he would not stay with Christians, because that would mean he would have to talk which made his head feel worse. He booked into a hotel at Bath but found it so 'worldly' that he was forced to visit a Christian friend he knew in the city. This brother and his aunts persuaded Müller to stay with them which he did for about a week. The symptoms in his head were now so distressing that he feared he was going insane. The effort required to make conversation proved too much and after a week he returned to Bristol. On receiving another £5 for personal expenses, he travelled with Mary, their daughter Lydia and their servant to Weston-Super-Mare where they took lodgings. Many times, at Weston, Müller was afraid that the trouble in his head indicated the approach of insanity. While there, he received the news that one of the small girls at Wilson Street had died—but that she had trusted

Christ before her death. After ten days at Weston the party returned to Bristol where Müller was seen by a doctor who assured him that, although his nerves were disordered, there was no reason to fear insanity.

Still he remained ill; he took comfort in the kindness of his friends who sent him gifts including a pickled tongue, poultry, cakes and grapes. At the end of the month he wrote to his father thinking it might be the last letter he would write. As in London in 1829, Müller was afraid he might soon die. In December, doctors diagnosed the problem as an inactive liver which was weakening his whole system. He now found that going to meetings at Bethesda made him feel worse, and that any sort of mental exertion exhausted him.

The work continued to grow and funds were ample: there were now seventy-five children in the three homes and more were arriving almost daily; they had room for twenty-one more. On December 12th, a hundred pairs of top-quality blankets arrived at Müller's house for distribution to the poor. It was known that Müller was anxious to ease a number of cases of hardship which had come to his notice in the area, and, despite his illness, he was able to arrange for this to be done.

By the end of 1837, eighty-one children and nine full time staff sat down to meals in the three homes. There were enough applications to fill another home with girls aged seven and above, and many more applications for infants than they were able to accommodate. Three hundred and fifty children were taught in the Day Schools run by the Scriptural Knowledge Institution, and there were three hundred and twenty children at the Sunday School.

Continued ill-health and growing responsibilities were getting Müller down. At the end of the month he wrote in his journal, 'This morning I greatly dishonoured the Lord by irritability, manifested towards my dear wife, and that almost immediately after I had been on my knees before God, praising Him for having given me such a wife.'

1838 did not get off to an encouraging start. On the night of January 1st thieves, apparently with an odd sense of humour, broke into Müller's house: they were prevented from access to much of the building by a second strong door and took nothing but some cold meat. They then proceeded to the school room at Gideon Chapel, broke open several boxes but took nothing. Next day some bones, less the meat, were found—some in the boxes at the Gideon school room and one in a tree in Müller's garden.

Müller's doctor now advised a further change of air. Müller was reluctant to leave Bristol; but when £15 'for the express purpose of change of air' arrived from a lady who lived fifty miles from Bristol, and who had no way of knowing the doctor's advice, he took this as an indication of God's will in the matter. He travelled with Mary and Lydia to the home of some Christian friends in Trowbridge, where he settled down to read Philip's *Life of George Whitfield*. He was struck by the prayerfulness of the man and his habit of reading the Bible on his knees—the importance of which he had known for years, but, he now felt, had practised too little. He continued reading Whitfield's life on the Sunday, but, besides spending several hours in prayer, spent two hours on his knees reading and 'praying over' Psalm 63. He wrote in his journal:

God has blessed my soul much today ... My soul is now brought into that state, that I delight myself in the will of God, as it regards my health. Yea, I can now say, from my heart, I would not have this disease removed till God, through it, has bestowed the blessing for which it was sent ... what hinders God, to make of one, so vile as I am, another Whitfield? Surely, God could bestow as much grace upon me, as He did upon

him. O, my Lord, draw me closer and closer to Thyself,
that I may run after Thee!—I desire, if God should
restore me again for the ministry of the Word (and this
I believe He will do soon, judging from the state in
which He has now brought my soul, though I have
been worse in health the last eight days, than for several
weeks previously), that my preaching may be more than
ever the result of earnest prayer and much meditation,
and that I may so walk with God, that 'out of my belly
may flow rivers of living water'.

The following day, the pain and discomfort in his head
being less severe, he spent three hours on his knees praying over Psalms 64 and 65. While meditating on Psalm
65:2, 'O thou that hearest prayer', he noted down eight
specific requests: two personal ones, two general and four
concerning various aspects of the work at Bristol. At the
bottom of the list he wrote, 'I believe He has heard me.'
Three years later he was able to record that five of the
petitions had been answered in full and the other three in
part.

Despite great discomfort, Müller's spirit was revived
as, reading on in his Bible he came across the fifth verse
of Psalm 68 where God is described as 'A Father of the
fatherless'. He wrote:

By the help of God this shall be my argument before
Him, respecting the orphans, in the hour of need. He
is their Father, and therefore has pledged Himself, as it
were, to provide for them, and to care for them; and I
have only to remind Him of the need of these poor
children, in order to have it supplied . . . This word 'a
Father of the fatherless', contains enough encouragement to cast thousands of orphans, with all their need,
upon the loving heart of God.

The Müllers stayed on in Trowbridge for another

fortnight. On the whole, the improvement in George's spirits lasted the stay—although once or twice he felt ashamed after spending time on his knees reading Whitfield's Life instead of his Bible! On February 2nd, although his physical health had not improved, he gave up all his medicine and left for Oxford where he arrived at the home of friends, the following evening.

At Oxford Müller decided on a spell of horse riding. He managed to hire a well-behaved horse with a placid temperament which, he thought, would suit his troubled nerves. For a while this excellent therapy went well, and Müller followed Wesley's footsteps—although it is not known whether, like Wesley, he read his Bible as he rode. But—alas—after three days with Müller on his back, the horse himself was taken ill! Müller returned to his Bible study and prayer until he was told that the horse was well enough to resume his duties. And so to the stables again, but Müller had not been seated long in the saddle when he discovered, to his great dismay, that this formerly good-natured animal had become self-willed and obdurate. He tried desperately to control the beast, but it was no use: the creature would not be tamed. Müller's equestrian diversion was thus abruptly and sadly halted.

A friend strongly advised him to try the waters at Leamington Spa, and offered to pay his expenses if he would stay there. Having consulted his doctor in Bristol and receiving a favourable reply he decided to accept the offer. At the Spa he found excellent lodgings for ten shillings a week and he was able to write up his journal by his own fireside. 'How very kind of the Lord!', he wrote—it was a typical 'Müllerism'—and retired to bed.

Müller found that the Leamington waters seemed to help his condition, but after ten days he was disturbed by inner tensions and temptations, the nature of which we can only guess from an entry in his journal: 'Grace fought against evil suggestions of one kind and another, and prevailed; but it was a very trying season . . . Today I earnestly prayed to God to send my wife to me, as I feel that by being alone, and afflicted as I am in my head, and thus fit for little mental employment, Satan gets an advantage over me.'

Next day, a letter was delivered a day late announcing that Mary was on her way; and shortly afterwards, the good lady arrived in person to Müller's great delight. The couple spent the following days taking long walks in the Warwickshire countryside and Müller's head began to feel better than it had for several months, although he was still far from well.

At this time Müller was toying with the idea of making a short visit to Germany, partly so that he could offer advice and assistance to some contacts in Berlin who were keen to become missionaries, partly to witness to Christ before his father and brother, and partly also because he thought—rather optimistically perhaps—that his native air would do his health good. He wrote to Henry Craik and his doctor seeking their comments on the idea; Craik's reply was to go ahead, but the doctor's orders were to wait for a month or two lest the trip should prove too exhausting. Thus Müller spent March at Leamington with his wife until on April 2nd his doctor, on a brief visit to the area, pronounced him fit enough to make the trip. Next day George and Mary read Psalm 121 together, 'The Lord shall preserve thy going out and thy coming in from this time forth, and even for evermore', before going their separate ways—Mrs Müller back to Bristol and Mr Müller to the land of his childhood.

Müller arrived in Hamburg on April 9th, having suffered badly from sea-sickness on the early part of the voyage. He spent ten days in Berlin meeting a number of brethren who planned to become missionaries, and then travelled to Heimersleben to stay with his father. Herr Müller had aged markedly and apparently did not have long to live; Müller doubted whether he would survive another winter. Relations between father and son were now good and the strain brought about by George's conversion had been forgotten. Müller found that his brother was living in 'open sin' and took the opportunity to speak to both men about his faith in Christ; neither showed any sign of response. When the day of Müller's departure arrived, his father accompanied him some of the way to Magdeburg; as they parted both felt they would never meet again: as it happened, they were wrong.

Early in May, Müller arrived back in London and spent the night with his friends in Chancery Lane; the 7th saw him in Bristol again. The following evening he went to the prayer meeting at Gideon Chapel: since November 6th 1836, he had been unable to take part at any meeting at Gideon and Bethesda. But that evening the familiar voice was heard again reading Psalm 103.

'Bless the Lord, O my soul: and all that is within me, bless his holy name. Bless the Lord, O my soul, and forget not all his benefits: Who forgiveth all thine iniquities; who healeth all thy diseases . . .'

During the following months, as his strength increased, Müller found that, 'I preached, on the whole, with much more enjoyment, and with much more earnestness and prayerfulness, than I did before I was taken ill. I also felt more the solemnity of the work.'

Müller was approaching his thirty-third birthday. In the years immediately following he had two or three bouts of less severe illness, but during his long life was never again so seriously ill as he had been in 1829 and 1837–8. And the man whom the army had rejected, claimed many years later that he felt fitter in his seventies than he had in his thirties.

CHAPTER NINE

'A Bank Which Cannot Break'

From the commencement of Müller's orphan work in April 1836 to the end of June 1838, finances gave no cause for anxiety: there was always an excess of funds. But as the summer of 1838 drew towards its close, so Müller's journal indicated that times were becoming difficult.

August 18, 1838. I have not one penny in hand for the orphans. In a day or two again many pounds will be needed. My eyes are up to the Lord. Evening. Before this day is over, I have received from a sister £5. She had some time since put away her trinkets, to be sold for the benefit of the orphans. This morning, whilst in prayer, it came to her mind, I have this £5, and owe no man any thing, therefore it would be better to give this money at once, as it may be some time, before I can dispose of the trinkets. She therefore brought it, little knowing that there was not a penny in hand, and that I had been able to advance only £4 15s 5d for house-keeping in the Boys' Orphan-House, instead of the usual £10.

Aug. 20. The £5 which I had received on the 18th, had been given for house-keeping, so that today I was again penniless. But my eyes were up to the Lord. I gave myself to prayer this morning, knowing that I should want again this week at least £13, if not above £20. Today I received £12 in answer to prayer, from a lady who is staying at Clifton, whom I had never seen before.

Aug. 23. Today I was again without one single penny,

when £3 was sent from Clapham, with a box of new clothes for the orphans.

Müller was later to look back on the period from September 1838 to the end of 1846 as the time when the greatest trials of faith were experienced in the orphan work. They were not years of continuous difficulty: rather there tended to be a pattern of a few months of trial, followed by some months of comparative plenty. During the whole period, according to Müller, the children knew nothing of the trial. In the midst of one of the darkest periods, he recorded, 'these dear little ones know nothing about it, because their tables are as well supplied as when there was £800 in the bank, and they have lack of nothing'. At another time he wrote, 'the orphans have never lacked anything. Had I had thousands of pounds in hand, they would have fared no better than they have; for they have always had good nourishing food, the necessary articles of clothing, etc.' In other words, the periods of trial were so in the sense that there was no excess of funds: God supplied the need by the day, even by the hour. Enough was sent, but no more than enough.

Müller's journal often hints at, but rarely attempts to analyse, why it was that God allowed this period of 'trial'. The clue to his understanding of the situation is perhaps best expressed in an entry, in the autumn of 1838, commenting on a gift of money which he had received from Teignmouth. 'It is a most seasonable help, to defray the expenses of this day, and a fresh proof, that not in anger, but only for the trial of our faith, our gracious Lord delays as yet, to send larger sums.' Müller saw a purpose in the trial similar to that in the Old Testament story where God tested Abraham by telling him to offer Isaac as a burnt offering on the mountain in Moriah. In one sense the period was a test of Müller's obedience, and a time when his character was moulded—prepared, in fact, for his life's work. In the opinion of the present director of

Müller's Homes, the years of trial were 'designed by the Lord to deepen Mr Müller's faith and to show him that prayer is no vain thing. Many years afterwards he faced his financial trials with scarcely a tremor. He had learned so much and really knew His God.'

In the evening of Thursday, September 6th, Müller listened to Henry Craik preach from Genesis 12. 'All went well for Abraham,' said Craik, 'as long as he acted in faith, and walked according to the will of God; but when Abraham distrusted God, all failed.' As Müller listened, he began to apply this lesson to his own difficult situation. That morning he recalled, the order-books had been brought to him from the Infant Orphan-House, and shortly afterwards the matron had sent him a message asking when she should fetch them. Müller knew full well that her message was a polite way of asking when she could expect the money she would need for the next few days' provisions. He had sent a message saying 'tomorrow', though he had not a single penny in hand. As he listened to Craik, however, he made up his mind that despite the seeming impossibility of the situation, he would never seek his own deliverance, by means of his own ingenuity. For instance, he thought of a sum of about £220 he had in the bank which had been given him for other spheres of Christian work. It would have been easy for him to write to the one who had entrusted him with this and say that in difficult circumstances he had taken say £20 or even £100 for the orphans. For on a number of occasions he remembered the donor saying that if ever he wanted money he was only to let him know. But, Müller thought, 'this would be a deliverance of my own, not God's deliverance. Besides, it would be no small barrier to the exercise of faith, in the next hour of trial.' In the event he was sent just sufficient money to meet the immediate need at the Infant Home, plus a large quantity of salt, onions and crushed oats.

On the Saturday and Sunday no money came in at all,

with the result that by Monday morning, September 10th, Müller—with a rare touch of drama—described the situation as a 'solemn crisis'. He decided upon an unprecedented step. Until that day he had never taken any of his fellow workers into his confidence as to the state of the funds, with the exception of an obviously close assistant, referred to in his journal only as 'brother T . . .' On this occasion, however, he broke with tradition and went to each of the Orphan-Houses in turn. He called the staff of each house together, frankly stated the financial situation and enquired how much money was needed for immediate needs. Having established the exact proportions of the problem, he announced that he still believed that God would help and led his helpers in prayer. He then gave instructions that nothing more was to be purchased than there was the means to pay for, but that the children were not to lack anything in the way of nourishing food and the necessary clothes. He would, he said, rather send the children away than see them lack anything. An investigation was ordered to discover whether they possessed any needless articles which could be sold. At half-past nine that morning, sixpence came in which had been put into the box at Gideon Chapel. Most men would not have found this a cause for great rejoicing, but Müller at least interpreted it as an earnest of greater things to come.

Müller then left the homes, and visited Henry Craik, to whom he unburdened his heart, putting him fully in the picture. The two men knelt together in prayer.

Soon after ten, Müller returned to his home. While he was praying in his room, a lady called and gave Mary two sovereigns (a farm worker's monthly salary) for the children saying that she had felt herself stirred up to come, but had already delayed too long. A few minutes later, Müller entered the room where she was and she promptly gave him two more sovereigns without having any idea of the need of the moment. Very shortly afterwards, a messenger arrived from the Infant Orphan-House to whom

Müller was able to give £2 and through whom he sent £1 os 6d to the Boys' Home and £1 to the Girls'.

That day, Craik left Bristol to stay with a friend in the country. It had been intended that Müller should accompany his friend, but owing to the critical state of affairs at Wilson Street he did not make the trip.

Later that week, after meeting with his staff for prayer, one of them approached him with sixteen shillings saying, 'It would not be upright for me to pray, if I did not give what I had.' Müller accepted the gift. It was not unusual in these years of trial for members of the staff to give money themselves to the work, and even to sell unnecessary personal articles, to help out at difficult periods. Müller denied that this practice represented a failure of the principles on which the homes operated. On the contrary he argued that under no circumstances could prayer for material things be expected to prevail unless there was a willingness to part with money or unnecessary personal belongings. 'Indeed,' he wrote, 'an Institution like the one under my care could not be carried on by any rich believer, on the principles on which we, by grace, are enabled to act, except it be that he were made willing himself to give of his own property, as long as he has anything, whenever the Institution is in real need.'

Early the following Tuesday morning, Müller took stock of the situation at Wilson Street. 'Brother T' had twenty-five shillings in hand, he himself had three shillings. He would, that day as any other day, be responsible for the well-being of about one hundred people, including staff, in the three homes.

The £1 8s enabled them to buy meat and bread which was needed, a little tea for one of the houses, and milk for all three homes. No more was needed for that day and there was bread for two days in hand. But how would God provide for the rest of the week? The funds were exhausted; all members of staff had given as much as they were able. They met as usual for prayer, but as they rose and went about the duties of the day nothing came in. A good lunch was eaten in all three homes; after lunch Müller returned to prayer. Still nothing came in. How could he face the children tomorrow and announce there was no breakfast? Müller became 'tried in spirit'. Seven years later he was to look back on this day as the only occasion when he felt this way. 'For the first time,' he wrote, 'the Lord seemed not to regard our prayer.'

But at about the middle of the afternoon there was a ring at Müller's house bell. A lady introduced herself to Müller as having arrived four or five days earlier from London, and explained that she was staying next door to the Boys' Orphan-House. Her daughter had given her a parcel of money for the work which she now presented to Müller. It contained £3 2s 6d; enough, at that time, to provide comfortably for all the next day's needs. As soon as the woman had left, Müller permitted himself a rare exclamation of excitement.

> I burst out into loud praises and thanks the first moment I was alone, after I had received the money. I met with my fellow-labourers again this evening for prayer and praise; their hearts were not a little cheered. That the money had been so near the Orphan-Houses for several days without being given, is a plain proof that it was from the beginning in the heart of God to help us; but, because He delights in the prayers of His children, He had allowed us to pray so long; also to try our faith, and to make the answer so much the sweeter.

As autumn gave way to winter in 1838, the needs continued to be met almost by the day. On November 21st, after a good lunch had been taken in all three homes, it was established that there were no funds left in any of the three homes. By sharing the supplies of bread between the three homes, however, it looked as if they would get through another day. But there were no means to take in any further bread. Müller left Wilson Street following prayer at one o'clock, telling the staff that they must wait for help, and see how the Lord would deliver them this time. As he climbed the hill towards Kingsdown, he began to feel bitterly cold and decided that, needing more exercise for the benefit of his circulation, he would walk home a longer way, via Clarence Place. About twenty yards from his house in Paul Street he met a friend who walked back with him, and after a short talk gave him £20. £10 was to be given to the deacons at Bethesda towards providing the poorer members of the church with coal to help them through the winter, £5 was for the work of the Scriptural Knowledge Institution and £5 was for the children. The gentleman had called at No. 21 twice while Müller was at Wilson Street, and had he been half a minute later he would have missed him again. Müller immediately sent the £5, sufficient for several days, to the three matrons.

A week later, things again looked difficult. At twelve o'clock, November 28th, Müller met with the staff for prayer. The previous evening one shilling had been left at No. 1, and all except two pence had now been spent. Müller heard that someone had cleaned the clock in No. 1 free of charge, and had offered to keep the clocks in all the homes in good repair. This was encouraging but it would not provide tea that day for one hundred people. There was sufficient in hand for lunch in the three homes but the Infant and Boys' Homes had not enough bread or milk for tea. As they prayed, there was a knock at the door and one of the ladies left the room. The rest continued silently in prayer for a while and then rose from their knees.

'God will surely send help,' Müller said as he stood up. As he spoke, he noticed a note on the table which had been brought in while they were praying. It was from Mary, enclosing another letter with £10 for the children. The previous evening, someone had asked Müller whether the balance in hand would be as great this time, when the accounts were made up, as last time. Müller never revealed the state of the funds.

'They will be as great as the Lord pleases,' he had said. This was the man who had sent the £10. £6 10s was wanted for immediate needs and £3 10s was put by towards the rent; the same man also gave another £10 to be divided between Craik and Müller to buy new clothes.

The following day £80 arrived from Suffolk of which £30 was for Craik and Müller's personal expenses. In December another large sum of £100 arrived.

Thursday, February 7th 1839, the funds were again exhausted. At about half-past eleven brother T called on Müller to say that about £1 2s would be needed to buy bread for the three homes and to meet other expenses; but they had only 2s 9d. Brother T was due in Clifton where he would make arrangements for the reception of three children.

'Please be so good as to call on your way back, to see whether the Lord might have sent any money in the meantime,' Müller said, before he left.

There was sufficient in the three homes that day for lunch. After lunch a lady from Thornbury came and bought one of Müller's Narratives and a copy of the latest Annual Report, and left three shillings besides. Five minutes later the baker called at the Boys' Orphan-House; seeing him arrive, the matron of the Girls' Home went immediately with the 6s 6d which she had just received to prevent him being sent away—knowing there was nothing in hand at the Boys' Home. With this money, together with the few shillings in hand, she bought sufficient bread for all three homes. At four o'clock brother T returned to Müller's house from Clifton to find that he had received nothing. One of the assistants gave five shillings of his own money. Müller had been asking God to show him a passage to speak from that evening at

Bethesda and seemed to be directed to Matthew 6:19–34.
Just before he left, another five shillings was brought to
his house.

Perhaps the congregation at Bethesda detected a
specially fervent note in the voice of their young pastor as
that evening he read the chosen portion in his strong
Prussian accent:

'Therefore take no thought, saying, What shall we eat?
or, What shall we drink? or, Wherewithal shall we
clothed? ... for your heavenly Father knoweth that ye
have need of all these things. But seek ye first the
Kingdom of God, and his righteousness; and all these
things shall be added unto you. Take therefore no thought
for the morrow: for the morrow shall take thought for the
things of itself. Sufficient unto the day is the evil thereof.'

After the meeting he went to No. 6 for a time of prayer; on
arrival he found that a box had come from Barnstaple. It
contained £10 of which £8 was for the children and £2 for
the Bible Fund; and a separate amount from the Barnstaple
brethren of nearly £3. Besides this, there was some merino
wool, three pairs of new shoes, two pairs of new socks, six
books intended for sale, a gold pencil-case, two gold rings,
two gold ear-rings, a necklace and a silver pencil-case.

'We have now again to look to the Lord for further
supplies,' Müller said to brother T on the following
Wednesday afternoon, having just given him the last of
the money they had in hand.

That afternoon a lady and gentleman visited the Homes in
Wilson Street. At the Boys' House they met two ladies who
were also on a visit, one of whom turned to matron and said:

'Of course, you cannot carry on these Institutions
without a good stock of funds.'

Turning to the matron, the gentleman then said: 'Have
you a good stock?'

'Our funds are deposited in a bank which cannot break,'
the matron replied, cleverly avoiding breaking the rule

never to reveal the state of the funds. Tears came into the eyes of the enquiring lady.

On leaving, the gentleman left £5 at the Boys' Home.

Until early March, supplies were sufficient to meet comfortably all demands. But on the 5th the funds were reduced to five shillings. Müller knew that several pounds would be needed as, besides daily provisions, coal was running low and the treacle casks in two houses were empty. He gave himself to prayer. Whilst on his knees, he received a cheque for £7 10s; and later that day nearly £2 was received from the sale of articles which had been given for the children.

On March 23rd, Müller received a letter from brother T, who was spending a few days in Devon for the benefit of his health. The letter showed that his visit would not be without profit as far as the children were concerned. He had given an Annual Report to an obviously artful brother, who, having read it, devoted himself wholeheartedly to asking the Lord to lead his Christian sister to donate some of her valuable jewellery to the orphans. It was not long before his prayer was answered, and brother T returned from Devon with a heavy gold chain, a ring set with ten diamonds, a pair of gold bracelets and a sum of £2. Müller took the valuable ring, before parting with it, and neatly scratched the words JEHOVAH JIREH ('the Lord will provide') on a pane of glass in his room. Many times afterwards, until he left Paul Street, his heart was cheered as his eyes caught sight of the words on the glass and he remembered the remarkable way in which he came by the ring.

Throughout the summer and autumn of 1839 supplies came in daily: rarely more than enough for a day or two at a time, but never too little. On October 19th Müller was able to record that they were comparatively rich, having enough money in hand for about eight days. Provisions, too, came in steadily—including on one Saturday in November twenty sacks of potatoes and a small barrel of herrings.

The events of the following Monday illustrated how it so often happened that just enough but no more than enough would arrive. Müller had ten shillings left over from the previous day. On the Monday morning he was given a further £1 10s. Shortly after this, he received a note from Wilson Street to say that £3 would be needed that day. While he was reading the note, he received another note from Devon—enclosing a sovereign.

On November 22nd they were again very poor. After breakfast Müller was told that there was nothing in any of the three houses for lunch, except enough potatoes to last for some weeks. At ten o'clock a large box arrived at Wilson Street from Wolverhampton. It contained £12 for the children (at this time current expenditure on food amounted to roughly £2 10s a day for all the houses) and just over thirty shillings for other purposes. Müller and his helpers then laid out the contents of the box before them: four yards of flannel, nine yards of calico, twelve yards of cotton print, four and a half yards of coloured cotton, four yards of stuff, two pairs of stockings and three and a quarter yards of brown holland. Also, the following articles had been sent for sale: two decanters and stands, four glass salt cellars, three scent bottles, a set of cruets and stand, five beer glasses, seven chimney ornaments, three tortoise-shell combs, three fans, two silver vinaigrettes, two silver shoe-buckles, two waist buckles, two silver salt cellars, one pair of knives and forks, with silver handles, a small silver toasting fork, nine silver coins, three gold rings, four pairs of ear-rings, three brooches, a cornelian heart, a silver seal, one pair of silver studs, one gold watch key, one silver pencil-case, five pairs of bracelets, five necklaces and one urn rug!

'The Lord knew that the orphans had no dinner and, therefore, did He now send help,' said Müller, smiling broadly.

And as if this was not enough, that same morning, a

brother sent to No. 6 to ask whether the treacle cask was empty, and if so, to send it to him by the messenger, that it might be filled.

Public meetings to speak about God's provision for the orphans during the previous year had now been fixed for December 10th to 12th 1839. The helpers now began to pray that when the time of the meetings arrived, they would be able to report that ample funds were in hand. They always tried to avoid giving the impression at the public meetings—the only time when the state of the funds was mentioned—that they were simply an opportunity to beg for money. On December 4th God answered their prayer; £100 arrived for the children from the East Indies. Müller rejoiced that at the meetings he would be able to tell of God's rich supply after a time of trial.

At the end of 1839, Müller recorded that his health and mental powers were better than they had been for years. 'I ascribe this to God's blessing, through the instrumentality of early rising, and plunging my head into cold water when I rise.'

The usual end-of-year prayer meeting was held on December 31st. It lasted from seven p.m. until half-past twelve. At about one o'clock in the morning, after the meeting, Müller received a sealed envelope enclosing some money for the children. He remembered that the individual who gave it was in debt, and that she had been repeatedly asked by her creditors for payment. He therefore resolved to return the envelope unopened, being firm in the belief that no one has a right to give while in debt. He did this knowing that there was not enough in hand to meet the expenses of New Year's Day. However, at eight in the morning he received £5, followed by over £5 10s a few hours later.

Throughout January 1840, substantial sums were received at the Homes and, at the beginning of February, Müller was able to leave Bristol for a long awaited trip to Germany. He spent ten days in Berlin before travelling to his father's home at Heimersleben on February 21st. He found his father very weak, and coughing greatly. Throughout the visit, Herr Müller was very affectionate to his son, and Müller noticed that he read prayers and the Bible; but he could not say that he was a true Christian. He left Heimersleben at the end of February, and said farewell to his father for the last time. He died the following month.

Early in March Müller boarded at Hamburg one of the earliest channel steamers bound for London. On deck, he got into conversation with two Russian Jews, who listened with great interest to all that he said, although he did not tell them plainly that he believed Jesus to be the Messiah. After he left them, Müller watched the two men talking to each other and judged from their faces that they took him to be a baptised Jew or a missionary to the Jews. After a while one of them came up to Müller and asked him what he thought of 'that Jesus'. Müller replied that he believed Jesus to be the Messiah, Lord and God, at which the Jew began to blaspheme. From that time, the two men kept well away from Müller.

At dinner that evening, at the captain's table, one of the passengers, who had seen Müller's long conversation, asked him about the two Jews. Müller decided that this would be an opportunity to discover whether there was another Christian at the table and deliberately threw out the remark:

'How remarkable it is that the Jews, in all parts of the world, can be recognised as such; and are not mixed with other nations . . .'

'This can only be explained by the Scriptures, and shows the Bible to be true,' replied the captain.

Müller agreed with the captain and for the rest of the voyage had long and interesting conversations with this 'true brother in the Lord'.

On his return to Bristol on March 9th Mary told her husband that during his absence they had been well supplied and that a moderate sum was actually in hand.

CHAPTER TEN

Looking to his Riches

When Müller and Craik had arrived in Bristol in 1832, they found less than seventy regular attenders at Gideon Chapel; they had taken over Bethesda as an empty building. During 1840 they gave up Gideon Chapel, and those in fellowship at Bethesda now numbered five hundred and twenty-five souls. Of these, over a hundred were added during 1840 of whom nearly fifty were converted under their preaching. In the next thirty years the numbers would again double so that by the 1870s there were over one thousand members. On May 10th 1840, five orphans were baptised and received into the fellowship at Bethesda. This brought the number of older children from Wilson Street in fellowship to fourteen.

It was in 1840 that Mrs Anne Evans arrived in Bristol from London where she had attended a fashionable Baptist church. On arrival at Bristol she went to Bethesda with a friend to hear a sermon on the second coming. She has left us a memorable picture of Bethesda at that time and of the atmosphere at Wilson Street in the early 1840s:

His [Henry Craik's] exposition of Scripture was quite a new feature of worship to me, and it was indeed 'marrow and fatness'. The meaning of the passage was brought out as I never heard it before, and I found myself truly in green pastures. Dr Maclaren of Manchester is the only man I know to compare with Mr Craik. His knowledge of the the original language was beyond that of most men of learning, and his in-

sight into the meaning of Scripture also. It was a great
privilege to hear such a man. 'I shall come again,' I
said, and I did go again and again, and never went
anywhere else while in Bristol. To me it was like a new
conversion. Now I heard a clear gospel that I could
understand. The Bible became a new book to me. The
brotherly love shown was such as I had never seen
before. The godly and simple lives of even wealthy
people, who had moved in the highest society, was such
as to carry one back to the days of the Apostles, and I
felt this was indeed Christianity of a high type . . .
    The day after I was twenty-one I took up my abode in
No. 6 [Wilson St] Orphan-House. Then followed five
years of happy service among the orphans, during
which time, I was behind the scenes and saw much of
the private life of the Brethren, and can therefore testify
to the truly spiritual lives they led; their devotion to
service to the Lord, and the unworldliness of their daily
private surroundings. Here I saw men and women
giving up all and following Jesus in one capacity or
another.

Dr A. T. Pierson later described Bethesda as one of
two truly apostolic churches he knew.

Towards the end of June 1840 Mr and Mrs Müller left
Bristol for Liverpool with eight men and women who
proposed to sail for the mission field from Liverpool. On
July 2nd Müller accompanied the missionaries to the ship,
and before they went on board one of the brethren gave
Müller £6 10s for the orphans.
    'The money which we have in the common stock,' he
said, as he handed Müller the money, 'is enough for us.
[They had about £20 between the eight of them.] For
some months, while we are on board, we need no money
at all, whilst you may lay it out; and when we need more,
the Lord will again supply our need. The other brethren

and sisters have no money of their own, and I desire likewise to have none. The Lord has laid the orphans particularly on my heart, and therefore you must not refuse
to accept it.'

On Saturday, August 15th 1840 there was the possibility of a crisis in Wilson Street. All the stores were low,
and the income during the past week had been small. On
Saturday, too, needs were nearly double those of other
days in order to buy in sufficient for the Sunday. At least
£3 was needed to see the homes through the day; but
there was nothing in hand.

At about half-past twelve two sisters called on Müller
with £2 7s 6d. Müller took this to the Boys' Orphan-
House at one o'clock and found the children sitting down
to lunch. Brother B handed Müller a note which he was
just about to send:

Dear Brother, With potatoes from the children's
garden, and with apples from the tree in the play-
ground (which apples were used for apple dumplings),
and 4s 6d the price of some articles given by one of the
labourers, we have a dinner. There is much needed.
But the Lord has provided and will provide.

Also that day there came in from the sale of Reports,
one shilling; from the box in No. 6, one shilling; from
children's needlework, 6s 6d; from a donation of one of
the sisters in the Orphan-House, six shillings.

In December the usual public meetings were again held
to review God's dealing with the work during 1840.
Müller felt that the first meeting went well; he was particularly glad that he felt happy that evening, so that no
one present could have detected from the expression on
his face that he had nothing at all in hand towards the
supply of the following day's needs. After the meeting

two and a half pence was left at his house.

Next morning, although the funds totalled precisely two and a half pence, Müller looked to the living God. At no time had there ever been less bread in the Orphan-House than that morning, and after breakfast all the bread in the Boys' and Infant-House had been cut up for use. Mercifully, at about eleven in the morning, Müller received from Barnstaple a £5 note and half a sovereign; the second public meeting was held that evening.

Müller reflected at this time on the first five years of the Homes' existence.

The chief end for which the Institution was established [he recalled] is that the Church of Christ at large might be benefited by seeing manifestly the hand of God stretched out on our behalf in the hour of need, in answer to prayer. Our desire, therefore, is not that we may be without trials of faith, but that the Lord graciously would be pleased to support us in the trial, that we may not dishonour Him by distrust.

This way of living brings the Lord remarkably near. He is, as it were, morning by morning inspecting our stores, that accordingly He may send help. Greater and more manifest nearness of the Lord's presence I have never had, than when after breakfast there were no means for dinner, and then the Lord provided the dinner for more than one hundred persons; or when after dinner, there were no means for the tea, and yet the Lord provided the tea; all this without one single human being having been informed about our need . . .

It has been more than once observed, that such a way of living must lead the mind continually to think whence food, clothes, etc., are to come, and so unfit for spiritual exercises. Now, in the first place, I answer that our minds are very little tried about the necessaries of life, just because the care respecting them is laid upon our Father, who, because we are His children, not only allows us to do so, but will have us to do so. Secondly, it must be remembered, that, even if our minds were much tried about the supplies for the children, and the means for the other work, yet, because we look to the Lord alone for these things, we should only be brought by our sense of need, into the presence of our Father, for the supply of it; and that is a blessing and no injury to the soul. Thirdly, our souls realise that for the glory of God and for the benefit of the church at large, it is that we have these trials of faith, and that leads again to God, to ask Him for fresh supplies of grace, to be enabled to be faithful in this service.

During 1840, apart from the children's work, Müller's Scriptural Knowledge Institution entirely supported six Day Schools catering for over three hundred poor children. Also the rent for the school room of a seventh school run by a lady known to Müller was paid by the SKI; and two other such schools, not in Bristol, were assisted with Bibles and Testaments.

Müller decided, at this time, to establish an evening class for adults who could neither read nor write. The class was held twice a week and concluded with a short session when the Bible was read and commented upon.

Since the establishment of the Scriptural Knowledge Institution in 1834 over six thousand Bibles had been circulated. From 1840 it was decided to circulate gospel tracts and books and also publications for Christians in addition to the distribution of Bibles. Within two years over twenty-two thousand of such publications were circulated, of which well over nineteen thousand were actually given away. This aspect of the work of the Institution still flourishes today, although most publications are sold not given.

During 1840, too, over £120 was sent abroad to missionaries by the SKI.

★

By the spring of 1841, although not seriously ill, Müller was again in need of a change of air. When on March 19th he was sent £15, of which £5 was for himself, he took this as a sign that he should leave Bristol for a while. He therefore travelled to Nailsworth in Gloucestershire the following day, and stayed with friends until May 7th.

It was at Nailsworth that spring that he began a practice that he never abandoned during the remainder of his life. Up until this time he had made a habit, after having dressed in the morning, of getting straight down to prayer. But while at Nailsworth it came to him that the most important thing was to concentrate first on reading the Bible, meditating on the chosen portion:

> that thus my heart might be comforted, encouraged, warned, reproved, instructed; and that thus, by means of the Word of God, whilst meditating upon it, my heart might be brought into experimental communion with the Lord ... The first thing I did (early in the morning), after having asked in a few words the Lord's blessing upon His precious Word, was, to begin to meditate on the Word of God, searching, as it were, into every verse, to get blessing out of it; not for the sake of preaching on what I had meditated upon; but for the sake of obtaining food for my soul. The result I have found to be almost invariably this, that after a very few minutes my soul has been led to confession, or to thanksgiving, or to intercession, or to supplication; so that, though I did not, as it were, give myself to prayer, but to meditation, yet it turned almost immediately more or less into prayer ... With this mode I have likewise combined the being out in the open air for an hour, an hour and a half, or two hours before breakfast, walking about in the fields, and in the summer sitting for a little on the stiles, if I find it too much to walk all

the time. I find it very beneficial to my health to walk
thus for meditation before breakfast, and am now so in
the habit of using up the time for that purpose, that
when I get in the open air, I generally take out a New
Testament of good-sized type, which I carry with me
for that purpose, besides my Bible: and I find that I
can profitably spend my time in the open air, which
formerly was not the case for want of habit ... The
difference, then, between my former practice and my
present one is this. Formerly, when I rose, I began to
pray as soon as possible, and generally spent all my
time till breakfast in prayer, or almost all the time ...
But what was the result? I often spent a quarter of an
hour, or half an hour, or even an hour on my knees,
before being conscious to myself of having derived
comfort, encouragement, humbling of soul, etc.; and
often, after having suffered much from wandering of
mind for the first ten minutes, or a quarter of an hour,
or even half an hour, I only then began really to pray. I
scarcely ever suffer now in this way. For my heart being
nourished by the truth, being brought into experi-
mental fellowship with God, I speak to my Father, and
to my Friend (vile though I am, and unworthy of it!)
about the things that He has brought before me in His
precious Word. It often now astonishes me that I did
not sooner see this point ... In addition to this [Müller
wrote some years later] I generally read after family
prayer large portions of the word of God, when I still
pursue my practice of reading onward in the Holy
Scriptures, sometimes in the New Testament and
sometimes in the Old, and for more than thirty-nine
years I have proved the blessedness of it. I take also
either then or at other parts of the day, time more
especially for prayer.

The summer months in 1841 were for the homes a
period of continuous prosperity, or as Müller described

it: 'one continual even running of the river of God's bounty'. At no period for more than three years had there been so much wealth at Wilson Street. But it did not last. For six months from September 1841, Müller reported, 'it pleased the Lord ... to try our faith more severely than during any time since the work first commenced'. A long, hard winter lay ahead.

> Indeed, so sharp were the trials of our faith for more than six months after [September, 1841]; so long the seasons when, day after day, only daily supplies were granted to us, and when even from meal to meal we had to look up to the Lord; so long had we to continue in prayer, and yet help seemed to fail; that it can be only ascribed to the especial mercy of God, that the faith of those who were engaged in this work did not altogether fail, and that they did not entirely grow weary of this way of carrying on the Lord's work, and go, in despair of help from God, back again to the habits and maxims of this evil world ... In the midst of the trial I was fully assured that the Lord would lighten His hand in His own good time, and that, whilst it lasted, it was only in order that in a small measure, for the benefit of the Church of Christ generally, that word might be fulfilled in us—'Whether we be afflicted it is for your consolation.'

After the period of comparative plenty which ended in September, the situation did not suddenly deteriorate; it is true that by the morning of October 1st Müller had again to record that he had not a penny in hand. But help was on the way. In the middle of the morning, ten shillings arrived with a note which read: 'Your Heavenly Father knoweth that you have need of these things. Trust in the Lord'. About five minutes later Müller received £10 from an Irish sister, through her banker in London. At the same time he heard from Tetbury that three boxes,

containing articles to be disposed of for the children, were
on the way. Two hours later, fourteen small donations,
amounting to nearly thirty shillings, were given to him.

A month later, however, it was rare for donations as
large as £10 to arrive:

November 23. Yesterday came in five shillings for
stockings, which provided today the means for the
breakfast in the Boys' Orphan-House. A sister sent also
a gammon and some peas. Now we are very poor
indeed. One of the labourers [meaning a member of
staff] was able to provide a dinner in the Girls' Orphan-
House out of his own means. In this our great need
came in 17s 6d by sale of Reports, which money had
been expected for some months past, but which the
Lord sent just now most seasonably. Besides this, 2s
6d was also received for the children's needlework.
Thus we are provided for this day also. In the afternoon
the Lord gave us a still further proof of the continuance
of His loving care over us, now that we are so poor;
for a box arrived from Plymouth containing clothes,
trinkets etc.

Early next morning one of the articles in the box from
Plymouth was sold for £2 2s. This was sufficient to see
them through the day, as there was a certain amount in
stock in each of the houses. Prayer-meetings were now
held daily at Wilson Street, as a result of the urgency of
the situation. When Müller arrived at this particular
morning's prayer-meeting, he heard that as the infants
had taken a walk with their teacher that morning, a poor
woman had approached her with two pence.

'It is but a trifle,' she said, 'but I must give it to you.'

By the time Müller arrived at the prayer-meeting one
of these two pence had already been needed to make up
the sum which was required for the bread. In the afternoon, another nine pence was received and some more of

the articles from Plymouth were sold for twelve shillings.

December was the usual month when the public meetings were held to give an account of the work. But at the end of 1841, times being so unusually difficult, it was decided to delay the meetings for a while, in case there should be criticism that they had been arranged in order to expose the need; the publication of the Annual Report was delayed for similar reasons. Müller wrote,

> What better proof, therefore, could we give of our depending on the living God alone, and not upon public meetings or printed Reports, than that, in the midst of our deepest poverty, instead of being glad for the time to have come when we could make known our circumstances, we still went quietly on for some time longer, without saying anything ... The Lord was saying by this poverty, 'I will now see whether you truly lean upon me, and whether you truly look to me.'

This courageous step of faith was not instantly rewarded. On the contrary, Müller wrote a few years later that,

> Of all the seasons that I had ever passed through since I had been living in this way, up to that time, I never knew any period in which my faith was tried so sharply as during the four months from December 12th 1841 to April 12th 1842.

Throughout this period it remained true that the children neither knew of the difficulties nor lacked good food, clothes or warmth. But there were some narrow scrapes. At midday on Tuesday, February 8th 1842, there was enough food in all the houses for that day's meals, but no money to buy the usual stock of bread (for future use) or milk for the following morning; two Houses needed coal.

In Müller's view they had never been in greater poverty and he noted that if God sent nothing before nine next day, 'His name would be dishonoured'. Late in the afternoon nine plum cakes arrived, baked by order of a kindly sister. Encouraging—and, no doubt, tasty—as these were, the situation was still grim as Müller retired to bed that night. He finished that day's journal entry with the words: 'Truly, we are poorer than ever; but, through grace, my eyes look not at the empty stores and the empty purse, but to the riches of the Lord only.'

Next morning, Müller walked early to Wilson Street to discover how God would meet the need, only to find on arrival between seven and eight that it had already been met. A Christian businessman had walked about half a mile to his place of work when the thought occurred to him that Müller's children might be in need. He decided, however, not to retrace his steps then, but to take something to the Homes that evening. But, as he later told Müller, 'I could not go any further and felt constrained to go back.' He delivered three sovereigns to the Boys' Home. This donation, together with some other smaller sums, met the needs for two days.

About a month later things were again pretty desperate. Müller left his house soon after seven in the morning to see whether there was enough money at the Homes to buy in milk for the day. As he walked, he prayed: 'Lord pity us, even as a Father pitieth his children. Lay upon us no more than we are able to bear; refresh our hearts by sending us help. Lord, you know what would happen if we had to give up the work for want of means . . .'

Two minutes from Wilson Street his prayer was interrupted when he met a friend on his way to work. They chatted briefly and then parted—but not for long. Müller was soon overtaken by a breathless pursuer who gave him a £1 note for the work. (For many, at that time, £1 equalled a fortnight's wages.)

'It is worth being poor,' Müller thought, 'and greatly tried in faith for the sake of having day by day such precious proofs of the loving interest which our kind Father takes in everything that concerns us.'

By April 1842 Müller and his helpers had lived through six months of severe testing when week after week, with only short periods of relief, the funds had been no more than sufficient. Again and again money or supplies had arrived with only minutes to spare before the children sat down at table. Müller never wavered in his determination that neither he nor any member of his staff should ever appeal for funds. But his faith had at no time been more tried. How much longer would it last?

On Tuesday, April 12th the need had never been greater: since the previous Saturday less than fourteen shillings had been received at Wilson Street. Early in the morning, Müller knelt in prayer:

'Lord pity us! You know that we desperately need some oatmeal, some new pairs of shoes, money for the repair of old shoes and to replenish our stores, and some money for new clothes for the children as well as a little money which is needed for some of the lady helpers. Please send us some larger sums.'

Later that morning an envelope arrived from the East Indies: it contained £100. Müller wrote, 'It is impossible to describe the real joy in God it gave me . . . I was not in the least surprised or excited when this donation came, for I took it as that which came in answer to prayer, and had been long looked for.'

By May, Müller thought it right to publish another Report of the activities of the Scriptural Knowledge Institution including, of course, the Homes. The report had been delayed for five months on account of the period of trial, lest they should appear to be appealing for funds. At this time, however, there was no danger of such an accusation being made.

During the previous seventeen months SKI had financed, besides one hundred children in the Homes, a whole number of other important activities including: (a) two Sunday Schools; (b) two Adult Schools, one for men and one for women at which on four evenings in the week nearly three hundred and fifty people were taught reading and writing, their books and writing materials being supplied free of charge. The opportunity was of couse taken to 'point out the way of salvation' at some classes; (c) six Day Schools, three for boys and three for girls. Müller's aim was that the poorest citizens of Bristol should be able to send their children to school entirely free or on payment of one fifth or one sixth of the expenses. They were also intended to enable Christian parents of modest means to send their children to schools where the teachers were all believers. From March 1834 to May 1842 well over two and a half thousand children were taught at these schools. All these adult and children's schools were entirely financed by Müller's Institution.

In addition, from its foundation in 1834 SKI had circulated nearly seven thousand Bibles. In the seventeen months ending May 1842 nearly £130 had been sent to missionaries in Jamaica, Australia, Canada and the East Indies. In the same period well over twenty-two thousand short Christian books or pamphlets had been distributed, the greater part free of charge.

During those seventeen months there had been very little sickness in Wilson Street and not one child had died. Total expenditure at the homes had been just over £1,337 and total income just over £1,339. Mr Micawber's happiness would have been complete.

CHAPTER ELEVEN

A Just Complaint

Müller spent six months in Stuttgart, with Mary, from August 1843 to February 1844, attempting to sort out some doctrinal wrangles which had arisen in a small Baptist church. At no time during this period was there the slightest financial difficulty at Wilson Street. Apart from the large sum which he had been able to leave behind in Bristol, £450 in cash was received together with a large quantity of valuable gifts in kind. A fourth home was now open in Wilson Street.

Through most of the summer of 1844, too, there was little difficulty but as summer gave way to autumn so the funds grew lower.

On the morning of Wednesday, September 4th the funds at Wilson Street totalled one farthing; there were now nearly one hundred and forty people—children and staff—to be provided for. But as Müller set about his early morning activities, he was not worried: he often said, 'Our need is my comfort.' Today, as on so many other days, he would be fascinated to see how God would send help. A little after nine he received at Paul Street a sovereign from an anonymous donor. Between ten and eleven a note arrived from Wilson Street to say that £1 2s would be required for the day. As Müller finished reading the note a fly stopped outside the house and a gentleman from Manchester was announced. He introduced himself as a believer who had come to Bristol on business; he had heard about the Homes and had been surprised that without any regular system of collection, and without personal application to anyone, Müller received more than £2,000 a year for the work. He gave Müller £2. Also that morning ten shillings came in, being profit from the sale of ladies' bags. Before the evening was out twenty-five shillings was also received, besides a box of valuable articles.

As winter approached Müller began to pray hard that God would supply the means for him to buy a large quantity of new clothes which were needed for the children. He also reminded the Lord that the Boys' Home needed painting and that the staff could do with a little extra money to spend on themselves. On the first evening in October his prayer was answered: he received a bank order for £70. The donor had asked Müller to let him know 'if anything particular should be connected with this donation'. But Müller wrote in his journal 'though the donation comes in so seasonably, I cannot write to the kind donor thus, lest he should be induced to give more, by my exposing our circumstances, and lest also the hand of God should not be so manifest, in providing me with means for the work as otherwise it would'. The Boys' Home was, however, duly painted—inside and out—and the staff received their bonus.

Everyone at Wilson Street enjoyed a prosperous Christmas in 1844: Müller described it as a 'season of rich abundance'. It was a bitterly cold winter, and the children's appetites increased to fight the cold. Whenever possible food was ordered in large quantities, for instance, on a Saturday in February eight hundredweight of rice and eight bushels of peas were bought. February 12th was the coldest morning of the whole winter: on his morning walk for prayer and meditation Müller thought how well he was supplied with coal, good food and warm clothing, and how many 'of the dear children of God' might be in need. He prayed that God would send him more means for himself so that he could be of greater help to those in need; three hours later he received £10 for his own needs. There can be no doubt what he did with this gift, although, of course, his journal is silent. It is known that during his life he gave away over £80,000 out of money given for his own use. Apart from this, many donors were aware of Müller's concern for the poor in general and sometimes earmarked portions of their gifts for this purpose.

Lydia was now twelve, and receiving what Müller described as a 'very good education' at a private school. After she had attended the school for six months, Müller asked for the account, only to be told that the headmistress 'had a pleasure in educating her gratuitously'. He pressed the matter, however, and eventually obtained an account, which he paid, but later the exact sum was returned to him anonymously by the headmistress (as he later discovered). Lydia remained at the school until she was eighteen, but despite several attempts Müller was never again successful in procuring an account. 'I was able,' he recorded, 'and well able, to pay for her education, and most willing to do so; but the Lord gave it gratuitously; thus also showing how ready He is, abundantly to help me and to supply my wants.'

On Thursday morning, October 30th 1845, Müller received what he described as a 'polite and friendly' letter from an inhabitant of Wilson Street. The writer said that he and his neighbours were 'in various ways inconvenienced by the Orphan-Houses being in Wilson Street'. The letter left it to Müller to decide what action to take.

It was not until the following Monday that Müller found time to set aside some hours to pray and think about this new problem. Having asked God to guide him to a right decision he wrote down the reasons for and against moving the children from Wilson Street.

In the first place he accepted that the neighbour's complaint was 'neither without foundation, nor unjust'. It was true that—particularly during play-time—the children were noisy 'even though the noise be only of that kind, that one could not at all find fault with the dear children on account of it'. Müller thought, 'I should myself feel it trying to my head to live next door to the Orphan-Houses . . . I therefore ought to do to others, as I should wish to be done by.' Secondly, with between one hundred and forty and one hundred and fifty persons living in the four Homes in Wilson Street, there had been occasions when the drains had been unable to cope and had even affected the water supply.

There were other reasons for moving, too. The single play-ground at Wilson Street was only large enough for the children of one House at a time; Müller wanted the children to have more room to play. Also he wanted to be within easy reach of land which could be turned into gardens where the older boys could work. Another advantage of larger premises in the country would be that all the laundry could be done at the Homes.

Müller was also concerned that the air at Wilson Street was not as bracing as it might have been and, bearing in mind that many of the children were unhealthy on arrival at the Homes, he was anxious that they should be situated in an as invigorating a position as possible. The teachers and staff, too, he thought, would be glad of somewhere where they could relax in a garden or walk in the fields after hours.

For some years Müller had been looking for property in Bristol which offered these advantages but had found none. Ordinary large houses, built for private families were, he felt, generally unsuitable for use as Homes, being inadequately ventilated.

The more Müller thought and prayed about the matter, the more he began to feel that it was God's will for him to embark on his boldest ever venture of faith: to build a brand new purpose-built Home.

I began to see that the Lord would lead me to build, and that His intentions were not only the benefit of the Orphans, and the better ordering of the whole work, but also the bearing still further testimony that He could and would provide large sums for those who need them and trust in Him for them; and besides, that He would enlarge the work so, that, if I once did build a house, it might be large enough to accommodate three hundred Orphans, with their teachers and other overseers and servants needful for the work.

During no period since the commencement of the work in 1836 had there been so many applications for admission—particularly boys—and Müller found it painful having to refuse so many children a home.

The following Thursday he asked his fellow-workers at Bethesda their opinion and all eight judged that he ought to leave Wilson Street and could see no objection to building. Next day George and Mary began to meet every morning to pray over the matter, and, as soon as they were sure that it was God's will, they started to ask Him for the necessary funds. These would be considerable: Müller estimated at least £10,000.

In November Robert Chapman arrived to work for a while in Bristol. Müller was glad of the opportunity to consult his friend about the building project; Chapman, who was very much in favour of the idea, also said 'You must ask help from God to show you the plan, so that all may be according to the mind of God.'

The last seven years had not been easy: for long periods there had been no excess of funds. Most men would have been content to continue the substantial and worthwhile work at Wilson Street, judging that expansion was neither feasible nor essential. Müller, however, was not content merely to consolidate the work; he was now quite sure that it was God's will for him to expand and build. His God, he often said, was a rich God and there were no limits to his resources: 'The silver and the gold are His, the cattle upon a thousand hills.'

On December 10th 1845, Müller received the first

donation towards the new building: it was a gift of
£1,000—the largest single donation they had ever
received. Müller recorded, 'When I received it I was as
calm, as quiet, as if I had only received one shilling. For
my heart was looking out for answers to my prayers.'

Three days later, Mary's sister returned from a visit to
London with the news that she had met a Christian architect who had recently read Müller's Narrative with great
interest and was keen to hear more about the work. On
hearing the plans to build a new Home, he offered to
draw up plans and superintend the building free of
charge. Müller was delighted and saw this offer plus the
£1,000 as an earnest of great things to come.

He was looking out for a piece of land of at least six or
seven acres somewhere on the outskirts of Bristol. Just at
that time there was a great deal of speculative building
development over the whole area and all suitable land
was fetching high prices. An appropriate site would
probably cost between £2,000 and £3,000; the building
would cost from £6,000 to £8,000; and the cost of furnishing a house for three to four hundred inmates (including
staff) would be £1,500 at least.

Müller deliberately issued no circular giving details of
his plans 'in order that the hand of God may be the more
manifest'. He spoke however to some people about his
plans if conversation led to the subject. At the end of
December he received on the 29th a further £50 towards
the new building, and the following evening another
donation of £1,000. Thrilled as he was by this second
large gift, he was no less pleased to be able to make the
following entries in his journal early in the new
year:

Jan. 3. One of the Orphans gave sixpence.
Jan. 10. One of the Orphans having received half a
crown from a cousin, gave 1s 6d of it towards building
the Orphan-House; a sister in the Lord also gave me

three shillings, a ring, a pair of gold ear-rings, and a gold brooch.

During January Müller looked into the possibilities of a number of sites, but none proved entirely suitable or cheap enough. Next month, however, the following entries appeared in his journal:

Feb. 2. Today I heard of suitable and cheap land on Ashley Down.
Feb. 3. Saw the land. It is the most desirable of all I have seen.

Ashley Down certainly offered enormous possibilities: high up in a bracing position on the north side of Bristol with long views eastwards towards Stapleton and north to Horfield. And yet it was within easy reach of the centre of Bristol and not too far from Bethesda.

The following evening Müller called at the home of the owner of the land only to be told that he was at his place of business. On arrival there, he was told that the gentleman had just left, but that he would be at his house at about eight. Müller, however, decided that it was not God's will for them to meet that evening and returned to Kingsdown.

Next morning Müller once again rang the front door bell of the fine house where the owner of the Ashley Down site lived. This time he was informed that the owner was at home and anxious that Mr Müller should be shown to his room as soon as possible. After the briefest introductory formalities the gentleman said to Müller:

'This morning I awoke at three o'clock and could not sleep again until five. While I was lying awake I could think of nothing else but my land on Ashley Down and your enquiry which had been passed on to me about the possibility of acquiring it for building an Orphan House.

At length I made up my mind that if you applied for it, I would sell it to you at £120 an acre instead of £200 which I was previously asking!'

'How good is the Lord!' thought Müller. That morning he signed an agreement to buy nearly seven acres at £120 an acre.

A week later, Müller received a reply to a letter he had written to the London architect about his offer to help with the plans of the building. It read:

My dear Sir,
   It will afford me gratification, beyond what I can communicate by letter, to lend you a helping hand in the labour of love you are engaged in, and I shall esteem it a very great privilege being allowed to exercise my abilities as an architect and surveyor in the erection of the building you propose to erect for the orphans. I really do mean what I say, and, if all is well, by the blessing of God, I will gratuitously furnish you with plans, elevations, and sections; with specification of the work, so that the cost may be accurately estimated. I will also make you an estimate and superintend the works for you gratuitously . . .'

The following week the architect travelled to Bristol from London, and Müller and he visited Ashley Down together. 'This site is most suitable,' the expert assured Müller, 'on grounds of situation, drainage and water supply.' Müller was delighted.

Money for the building fund was now coming in steadily, and in mid-February Müller received a promise that, on March 25th, £500 would be paid to him. It was in fact paid before the end of February.

By the end of April, the plans for the building were completed: it would accommodate three hundred children, one hundred and forty girls and eighty boys from eight upwards, and eighty infant boys and girls aged up to seven, as well as having proper quarters for all staff and teachers. Work, however, would not commence until all necessary funds had been received. It was planned to invest the land and building in the hands of about ten trustees.

On July 6th 1846, Müller received the largest donation he had so far received for his work: £2,050 of which £2,000 was intended for the building fund. He wrote:

> It is impossible to describe my joy in God when I received this donation. I was neither excited nor surprised; for I look out for answers to my prayers. I believe that God hears me. Yet my heart was so full of joy, that I could only sit before God, and admire him, like David in 2 Samuel 7. At last I cast myself flat down upon my face, and burst forth in thanksgiving to God, and in surrendering my heart afresh to Him for His blessed service.

On November 19th Müller rose at five to pray. There were a number of matters on his mind. For one thing publicity had recently been given to the fact that a number of the inhabitants of Wilson Street were complaining of the inconvenience of the Orphan-Homes there, and Müller was even more anxious to receive enough money to begin the building. For another thing, applications for admission were now well in excess of places in the Homes and Müller hated turning children away. After a period of prayer about all this Müller opened his Bible to Mark 11 and came to verse 24, 'What things soever ye desire, when ye pray, believe that ye receive them, and ye shall have them.' He began to pray again:

'Lord I believe that Thou wilt give me all I need for the work. I am sure that I shall have all, because I believe that I receive in answer to prayer.'

After breakfast he had a time of prayer again and about five minutes after he had risen from his knees a registered letter was handed to him. It contained a cheque for £300 of which £280 was for the building fund, £10 for his own expenses and £10 for Henry Craik. This brought the building fund to over £6,000.

In December he received another gift of £1,000 and on January 25th 1847, another donation of £2,000 bringing the total up to well over £9,000.

The winter of 1846–7 had not been an easy time for meeting the day-to-day needs in Wilson Street. The year 1846 was a year of catastrophic crop failure both of wheat and potatoes. The American cotton crop, too, was well below expectation, sending prices soaring. The British economy suffered a crisis of confidence with the soundness of the many railway companies being called into question, leading to widespread financial panic. In May 1847 Müller recorded: 'Never were provisions nearly so dear since the commencement of the work, as they are now. The bread is almost twice as much as eighteen months ago, the oatmeal nearly three times as much as formerly, the rice more than double the usual price, and no potatoes can be used, on account of their exceeding high price.' But, he continued, '. . . the children have lacked nothing . . . my heart is in peace, in great peace.'

In June he received another £1,000 for the building fund which 'again encouraged my heart abundantly to trust in Him for all that which I shall yet need'. It was now estimated that, including fittings and furniture the whole project would cost not less than £14,500. However these extra expenses—mainly for heating, gas fittings, furnishing, three large play-grounds and a small road—would not be required until sometime after the commencement of the building work. Müller therefore decided to go ahead, and the first workmen arrived on

Ashley Down on July 5th. On August 19th the foundation
stone of the new building was laid.

A gift of £100 in February 1848 enabled Müller to buy
a new suit of clothes for every boy in Wilson Street,
something for which he had been praying for some
weeks.

Throughout the winter, when the weather was fair,
work proceeded on the new home and by May much of
the building was already at roof level. But before the first
children moved up to Ashley Down, Müller had to deal
with the final explosion of a sad affair within the Brethren
movement which had been simmering for some years, and
would have tragic and far-reaching consequences.

CHAPTER TWELVE

Stronger Through Turmoil

To understand the sad events of 1848 requires a few words about one of the most influential figures among the early Brethren: John Nelson Darby. Godson of the famous Admiral from whom he received his second name, Darby was educated at Westminster School and Trinity College, Dublin, where he graduated as a Classical Gold Medallist.

Darby's was a complex personality. On the one hand, when engaged in the many bitter controversies of his life, he could be obstinate, harsh and rude. On the other, he would show himself to be deeply sympathetic and warm-hearted. When travelling, he often preferred to stay with poor families rather than the affluent, and there are many anecdotes which illustrate that he was especially fond of children—and in turn adored by them.

His natural ability was matched by enormous energy: by his death he had founded and guided some fifteen hundred churches in many countries. His writings fill over forty volumes including commentaries on most books in the Bible. He translated the Bible into three languages and wrote many profound and sometimes beautiful hymns.

Darby said that what led him out of the established church was 'the unity of the body: where it was not owned and acted on I could not go'. And his early years in the new movement were characterised by impeccable non-sectarian principles. 'This is the true secret of a church well ordered,' he wrote, 'perfect largeness of heart, as large as Christ's . . . keep infinitely far from sectarianism . . . You are nothing, nobody, but Christians.'

In October 1832, Darby had preached at Bethesda and

Gideon Chapels in Bristol and commented on the 'marked work' which 'dear brothers Müller and Craik' were doing; he added however, 'I should wish a little more principle of largeness of communion.' This was a rather odd comment, considering that Craik frequently preached for nonconformist ministers and, as Rowdon has pointed out, maintained friendly relations with ministers and scholars of the established church, such as Dean Alford, Archbishop Trench and Dean Ellicott. Furthermore, Müller and Craik 'invited well-known divines, among them Bonar of Collace, to preach at Bethesda' (Rowdon).

As early as 1835, however, there is evidence that Darby's early largeness of heart was being eroded by another and fatal principle. In that year, Anthony Norris Groves, having returned from India, visited Plymouth and detected signs that the Brethren there were becoming exclusive and sectarian: as his widow later put it, he found, 'that their original bond of union in the truth as it is in Jesus, had been changed for a united testimony against all who differed from them'.

Before leaving England for the second time, therefore, Groves wrote a long letter to Darby (dated March 1836), in view of the latter's paramount influence not only at Plymouth but at so many other new assemblies. He referred to Darby's 'enlarged and generous purposes that once so won and riveted' him (Groves), but frankly told Darby 'you have departed from those principles . . . and are in principle returning to the city from whence you departed'.

By the middle 1830s the early Brethren movement already embraced divergent tendencies within it. On the one hand, those like Groves, Müller, Craik and Chapman strove to maintain the original non-sectarian principle of receiving all 'whom Christ has received'; on the other, Darby and the growing number of churches under his influence envisaged the establishment of a corporate worldwide witness to the unity of the body of Christ and emphasised separation from evil as God's principle of unity.

Other tensions emerged. In 1839, after a fortnight's retreat to consider certain matters of church order which had arisen at Bethesda, Müller and Craik had adopted the firm view that there was a need for a recognised eldership and for ordered government within the church. Darby, on the other hand, disapproved of any formal recognition of the gifts of preaching and teaching, fearing that this might lead to the emergence of a select group of ministers. He regarded the recognition of elders as a restriction upon the free movement of the Holy Spirit, drawing what many now regard as a false distinction between the arranged and formal (which was 'of man') and the spontaneous and informal (which was 'of the Spirit').

In the early 1840s, another figure enters the story. Benjamin Wills Newton had taken a 'first' at Oxford and had become a fellow of Exeter College. He became, for a while, extremely influential at one of the first Brethren assemblies in England—Ebrington Street, Plymouth—the assembly which gave the movement its popular, though misleading title. Between one thousand two hundred and one thousand four hundred people used regularly to attend from different churches in the area to hear him preach.

Newton began to raise the alarm against what he considered to be Darby's 'strange system of dispensational doctrines', at the heart of which was a sharp distinction between the 'earthly' hopes of the Jewish Church, and the 'heavenly' hopes of the Christian Church. The faithful Jews of the Old Testament were not comprised in the Church, and the dispensations of Old and New Testaments were totally distinct.

Darby had developed much of his dispensationalism in order to defend a new doctrine of the second coming which emerged after the Albury Prophetic Conferences in 1830, and which is associated with the name of Edward Irving. The doctrine, known as the 'Secret Rapture', was a refinement of pre-millennialism, which Müller himself had adopted in 1829. According to the Secret Rapture teaching (which Müller never accepted), the second coming of Christ will take place in two stages: first there will be the 'rapture of the saints' when Christ will return to take all true Christians from the earth. Only then will the Antichrist arise and usher in the period of 'tribulation'. The rule of the Antichrist will be brought to an end by the second stage of the coming—the public 'appearing' of Christ in glory. Newton, however—and he was not alone —objected. If the Church was to be removed before the tribulation began, he asked, who were the faithful ones who, according to the Book of Revelation, would suffer during that period? To Newton, the Church comprised all who were redeemed by Christ; the suffering 'faithful remnant' therefore must have been redeemed by an act of God other than Christ's redemption. Newton regarded the theory as conflicting with a central doctrine of the faith.

Darby asserted that considerable sections of the New Testament applied not to the Church but only to a future dispensation of the restored Jewish remnant. Newton told him that, in making that distinction, Darby was virtually giving up Christianty.

However, the influence of Darby's personality—backed by his more lucid disciple William Kelly (whom some of Darby's opponents mischievously referred to as 'his interpreter') meant that this view of the second coming 'at any moment' gained a wide acceptance not only within the Brethren movement. Over the years it has been adopted by many evangelical Anglicans, large numbers of fundamentalists in all Protestant churches, and amongst free-lance Bible teachers and evangelists; the process was forwarded by the adoption of the theory by Scofield in his popular reference Bible.

Newton was not alone among the early Brethren, however, in rejecting the new view as an innovation. Notably Müller, Craik, Chapman, James Wright and S. P. Tregelles firmly held to the view that certain events must take place before Christ's return; and amongst Anglicans,

Archbishop Trench, Dean Alford, Bishops Ellicott and Ryle, as well as Bonar and Guinness were among those unholding what they considered to be the ancient faith. Their rejection of the new view did not however alter the fact that for them as Müller put it, 'the Coming of Christ, and not death, is the great Hope of the Church, and, if in a right state of heart, we (as the Thessalonian believers did) shall "serve the living and true God, and wait for His Son from Heaven" '.

Sadly these emerging tensions between the early Brethren and particularly between Darby and Newton destroyed the tranquillity of the Ebrington Street meeting. Soon after Darby returned from a lengthy visit to the Continent in 1845, a disastrous strife between him and Newton, who then became rivals, broke the peace of the assembly and almost stopped the progress of the work.

We have already noticed Darby's preference for the companionship of those less well-educated than himself, his affection for the poor and love of children. It is hard to escape the conclusion that the converse of this was that he could not tolerate a rival. On his return to Plymouth, in March 1845, he commenced his own teaching sessions and began to attack not only Newton's doctrines but also, it seems, Newton himself: he accused him of acting 'very badly towards many beloved brethren and in the sight of God'.

Darby thought that he now detected 'evil' at work in Plymouth. On October 26th 1845, he announced at Ebrington Street that he was withdrawing from their communion. (Eight years later, Darby confessed that in so dividing the assembly he had acted precipitately, and did not have the endorsement of the Lord.)

In 1847, the emphasis of the conflict switched to a new point of doctrine, concerning the person and sufferings of Christ. Darby condemned some views Newton had published in a tract as 'blasphemous doctrines' and Müller commented that they seemed to imply 'that Christ himself needed a Saviour'. Craik suspected that Newton's errors were 'only those of a rash speculative intellectualist, who is yet sound at heart and seeking to honour Christ'. In the recent judgment of Professor F. F. Bruce, Newton's views were not heretical, but based on mistaken principles of Old Testament exegesis. 'It is an instance of the irony of history that J. N. Darby, who led the attack against Newton, ran into trouble himself twelve years later because of papers on *The Sufferings of Christ* ... While this thesis was not identical with Newton's, both were based on mistaken exegesis, and some of Darby's most faithful followers saw little to choose between the two, since both implied that Christ endured divine wrath otherwise than vicariously and by the way of atonement.' (F. F. Bruce, *The Humanity of Jesus Christ, Christian Brethren Research Fellowship Journal*, 1974.)

According to F. F. Bruce, both Newton and Darby were genuinely concerned to learn and teach the truth but unfortunately each 'identified their respective interpretations of revealed truth with revealed truth itself, and since their interpretations did not agree, each believed he was defending truth against error'.

Later in the year, realising the error of his thinking, Newton published his *Statement and Acknowledgment respecting certain Doctrinal Errors*. He now readily admitted that he had erred in what he had said in his tract. He concluded his statement with admirable humility:

I would not wish it to be supposed that what I have now said is intended to extenuate the error which I have confessed, I desire to acknowledge it fully, and to acknowledge it as sin; it is my desire thus to confess it before God and His Church; and I desire that this may be considered as an expression of my deep and unfeigned grief and sorrow, especially by those who may have been grieved or injured by the false statement, or by any consequences thence resulting. I trust that the Lord will not only pardon, but will graciously counteract any evil effects which may have arisen to any therefrom.

It is a tragedy that the dispute did not end at this point.

Darby, however, attempted to show that Newton had not renounced his errors despite Newton's sincere profession to have done so. The result was that the church at Ebrington Street virtually disintegrated, and Newton's connection with the Brethren ceased. He lived until 1899, 'retreating into a little circle of two or three churches of his own, and leaving a devoted following, mainly among strict Baptists'. Müller was not satisfied with Newton's doctrinal position in 1847. However, he formed the highest regard for his later writings and wrote (many years later): 'I consider Mr Newton's writings to be most sound and scriptural, and my wife and I are in the habit of reading them, not only with deepest interest, but with great profit to our souls. His books are certainly most valuable, for they exalt the person and work of our blessed Lord Jesus Christ to the very utmost . . . I regard Mr Newton as the most accurate writer on religious themes of the nineteenth century.'

At the end of April 1848 Darby visited Bristol and called on Müller as was his usual custom. Müller asked him to preach the following Sunday at Bethesda, but he declined on the grounds of a previous engagement.

In May two members of Ebrington Street—a Captain Woodfall and his brother—came to Bristol and applied for communion at Bethesda. Captain Woodfall had been on the Continent during the Plymouth troubles and was therefore admitted but his brother's application was held for consideration. Some of Darby's supporters within Bethesda raised objections to the gentleman's reception, and Craik then suggested that the three brethren most opposed to the Woodfalls' reception should visit them. This they did and pronounced the two men clear of Newton's alleged heresy.

At a meeting at Exeter, Darby then publicly announced

that he could never go again to Bethesda because the church had received 'Newton's followers'. He then confirmed this in a letter to Müller; and later alleged that Newton's followers had circulated his writings within Bethesda. Darby's disciples at Bethesda now began to press for a formal investigation by the church into Newton's teachings (which had, of course, already been condemned by their author). In June one of Darby's followers, George Alexander, withdrew from Bethesda; and the elders were forced to summon a church meeting for June 29th 1848. At this meeting a statement (which came to be known as the *Letter of the Ten*) signed by ten of the elders, including, of course, Müller and Craik, was read (with explanations) and sanctioned by the majority of the church. Darby's sympathisers, however, promptly withdrew from fellowship.

The statement made it clear that the truths,

> relative to the person of our blessed Lord . . . the divinity of His person—the sinlessness of His nature—and the perfection of His sacrifice, which have been taught [at Bethesda] are, through the grace of God, those which we still maintain . . . we utterly disclaim the assertion that the blessed Son of God was involved in the guilt of the first Adam; or that He was born under the curse of the broken law, because of His connection with Israel . . . We utterly reject the thought of His ever having had the experiences of an unconverted person; but maintain that while He suffered outwardly the trials connected with His being a man and an Israelite—still in His feelings and experiences, as well as in His external character, He was entirely 'separate from sinners'.

The statement, however, gave nine reasons why 'we have felt a difficulty in complying with the request of our brother, Mr Alexander, that we should formerly investigate and give judgment on certain errors which have been taught among Christians meeting at Plymouth'. Briefly, the ten elders did not feel that because errors were taught at Plymouth or elsewhere they as a body were bound to investigate them. The statement pointed out that the tracts in question (Newton's) were written in such an ambiguous style that the elders would shrink from giving formal judgment on the matter: responsible brethren had come to different conclusions about how much error was contained in the tracts.

> Those who felt desirous to satisfy their own minds, would naturally be led to wish to peruse the writings for themselves. For this, many of us have no leisure time; many would not be able to understand what the tracts contained, because of the mode of expression employed; and the result, there is much reason to fear, would be such perverse disputations and strifes of words, as minister questions rather than godly edifying.

The statement contained a timely reminder that, in any case, those meeting at Ebrington Street had issued a statement disclaiming the errors charged against the tracts. Furthermore, the 'requirements that we should investigate and judge Mr Newton's tracts, appeared to some of us like the introduction of a fresh test of communion'. The final, and ninth, reason introduced a welcome and presumably intentional element of humour into the whole sad business: 'We felt that the compliance with Mr Alexander's request would be the introduction of an evil precedent. If a brother has a right to demand our examining a work of fifty pages, he may require our investigating error said to be contained in one of much larger dimensions; so that all our time might be wasted in the examination of other people's errors, instead of more important service.'

Darby now, on a visit to Yorkshire, found that churches there were sympathising with Bethesda. Thus on August 26th he issued from Leeds a circular excommunicating

Bethesda 'en bloc'. 'Members of Ebrington Street, active and unceasing agents of Mr Newton, holding and justifying his views, are received at Bethesda ... Woe be to (Brethren) if they love the Brethren Müller and Craik or their own ease more than the souls of saints dear to Christ!' Churches sympathetic to Darby were now urged to 'judge the Bethesda question'.

Müller was not a man to panic easily and took no immediate action. In October, G. V. Wigram, now a Darby supporter, attacked Henry Craik's *Pastoral Letters* (published 1835) on the grounds that they contained 'blasphemous and heretical' statements concerning the humanity of Christ. However, it appears that Darby well recognised that the able and experienced Craik was nothing if not orthodox and is reported as saying later 'that Mr Wigram sent him his tracts, and that he [Darby] put them at the back of the fire'.

On October 31st Müller at last decided to act. He publicly announced his personal condemnation of Newton's teachings. During November and December seven church meetings were held at Bethesda and it was made clear that no one defending, maintaining or upholding Newton's views should be received into communion. Several of Newton's sympathisers including the Woodfalls left the meeting as a result.

Henceforth those churches who refused to apply Darby's decree against Bethesda came to be known as 'Open Brethren' and those who followed Darby became known as 'Exclusive Brethren'. A. N. Groves' son, Henry, maintained that more was done in Bethesda to judge and repudiate Newton's views, than by any assembly acting under the Darby discipline.

Bethesda, and the 'open meetings' which sided with her, steadfastly maintained the independence of each local church in deciding whom it received into fellowship; whereas the exclusives argued that this was not 'practical unity of the body'. E. H. Broadbent, in his *Pilgrim Church* noted that, by untiring propaganda, a large number of churches were induced to accept as a necessary test of fellowship the condemnation of the church at Bethesda on account of a doctrine never held by it. By dint of constant repetition this circle of churches came to believe in all sincerity, that Bethesda had been cut off for holding Newton's error, an error which he himself had repudiated, and which the church at Bethesda had never entertained. So consistently was this system carried out that Negro brethren in the West Indies had to judge the Bethesda question, and Swiss peasants in their Alpine villages were obliged to examine the errors attributed to Newton and condemn them. Such a system could not fail to lead to further divisions. Even in Darby's lifetime, several such took place, the parties taking different sides excluding each other as vigorously as they had unitedly excluded Groves and Müller.

Sadly, few exclusives ever saw Newton's acknowledgment of his error. One who joined them in 1858, maintained sixty years later the old bitter hostility to Newton but had never seen the *Acknowledgment*, nor knew of its contents. It was enough for him that 'JND had rejected it!' Writing recently, F. F. Bruce has said that in his view 'the root error of Exclusivism is the embracing of the proposition that separation from evil is God's principle of unity. Biblical unity is based on something much more positive: the common life in the body of Christ—and separation from evil is a corollary.'

Despite the absurdity of Darby's action against Bethesda and the bitterness of some of his attacks on Newton's supporters or sympathisers he continued to display at times a strange—almost incredible—respect not only for Newton himself but also for certain 'Bethesda Brethren'. It is said that on one occasion he heard some of his supporters criticising Robert Chapman, and broke in abruptly: 'Leave Robert Chapman alone:

we talk about heavenly places, but he lives in them.'

Mrs Anne Evans continued to be a member of Bethesda throughout this sad and turbulent period. She described it as a 'time of agony of intense sorrow, and upheaval'. Bethesda was, she wrote,

> for a time shattered from end to end. Friendships were broken up; families were divided—husband from wife, children from parents, business relations were dissolved, health and even reason wrecked. We [at Bethesda] sadly needed humbling. We had begun to think too much of ourselves. We had increased rapidly in numbers and even in worldly standing, for many had joined us from the upper classes. Our leading brethren, too, were without any check . . . All this was more than flesh and blood could stand, so Satan was permitted to come down on us and humble our pride in the dust.

But all was not lost. Mrs Evans continued:

> At this time of sorrow Mr George Müller was a grand stay to us; he did not lose his head; he held the reins with a steady hand; and when at last Bethesda emerged from the turmoil she was stronger, freer than ever before. We had increased in numbers. [By the middle 1850s they were nearly seven hundred in fellowship.] The orphan work, which was to have come to nought, was the 'wonder of the world' . . .
> When the great Revival commenced the Open Brethren threw themselves with heart and soul into it. It was the reading of George Müller's book by two young men that led to it.

But that is the story for a later chapter.

CHAPTER THIRTEEN

Müller's Secret Treasure

By the time Darby's circular excommunicating Bethesda was issued, the new Orphan-House had been entirely roofed in, and part of the interior plastering had been done. Over £11,000 had been given, and rather more than £3,000 were still needed in order to complete the work and fittings. Money was still coming in steadily and by early November (1848) Müller was able to arrange with the clerk of works to buy over thirty grates for the small rooms, two copper furnaces for the wash-house and two iron furnaces for the scullery. A further £1,500 was received in two sizeable gifts that same month.

In February Müller spent long hours making final preparations before he could receive the first children; this work made him realise how much money was still required before all would be ready. He gave himself to prayer that the total cost could soon be covered. In the morning of February 11th, Müller was told that a visitor had called to see him. After a brief conversation, the gentleman explained that he had intended to leave Müller some money in his will but had now decided to give the money during his life time. He was particularly anxious that his name should be concealed and for that reason had not written out a cheque so that even his bank should not know of his donation. He therefore handed Müller the amount in notes: no less than two thousand pounds' worth. 'It is impossible to describe the real joy I had in God, when I received this sum. I was calm, not in the least excited, able to go on immediately with other work that came upon me . . .; but inexpressible was the delight which I had in

God, who had thus given me the full answer to my thousands of prayers, during these eleven hundred and ninety-five days.' This gift gave Müller the means to meet all the expenses for the new home plus some £60 to spare. Altogether he received nearly £16,000 including nearly £70 from the sale of grass and turf from the field on which the home was built, and £750 interest: Müller took the view that, 'as a steward of large sums, which were entrusted to me, I ought to invest the money, till it was actually needed'.

Monday, June 18th 1849—great excitement at Wilson Street: the first children were to be moved up to Ashley Down. How the first sight of this large new building took their breath away! How they enjoyed the sound of the birds singing, the sight of cows grazing in the fields, and the view across the valley towards Stapleton! Once inside even the fresh paint and newly-polished woodwork smelt good, and the whole place was light and well ventilated. Every day for four days, some more children arrived until on Thursday everyone, including the teachers and staff, had moved in: one hundred and forty people under one roof. By Saturday Müller was able to report that 'there is already such a measure of order established in the house, by the help of God, as that things can be done by the minute hands of the time-pieces'.

As if to assure Müller that He would never fail him as the numbers began now to grow towards three hundred children plus staff, God was 'exceedingly kind' during that first week. Müller was showing a gentleman through the new home who said:

'These children must consume a great deal of provisions.'

As he said this he took from his pocket a roll of bank notes amounting to £100. On the same evening a large cask of treacle arrived at the home, with six loaves of sugar. Also a cooper made two large new casks for treacle, free of charge. Next day ten hundredweight of rice arrived. 'After all the many and long-continued seasons of great trial of faith,' said Müller, 'within these thirteen years and two months, during which the orphans were in Wilson Street, the Lord dismisses us from thence in comparative abundance. His holy name be praised for it!'

One day next month, an unexpected visitor arrived at the 'New Orphan-House', as it was now known. Soon after noon, Müller was told that none other than John Nelson Darby was waiting to see him in a room in the house. What actually occurred during the encounter which followed has since been hotly disputed: the following is based on Müller's account. At ten to one Müller entered the room where Darby was and shook him by the hand. Darby said:

'As you have now judged Newton's tracts, the reason why we should not be united no longer exists.' Müller replied:

'I have only ten minutes now free, having an engagement at one o'clock, and therefore I cannot now enter upon this subject; for you have acted so wickedly in this whole affair, that many things have to be looked into before we could be really united again.'

At this Darby rose and left. The two men never saw each other again. Darby later denied that Müller's account of the interview was correct but there is apparently no record of Darby's version of the event. Professor Bruce has commented that 'a more gracious answer [by Müller] might have redeemed that never-to-be-repeated opportunity. Like Müller, Darby had the qualities of his nationality, and his Irish impulsiveness might well have warmed to a less severe response.'

Every week Müller now took in five to eight new children, and by May 1850, over three hundred people sat down every day to meals at the house. This included a staff of over thirty people. Every Wednesday afternoon parties of visitors were shown round the New Orphan-House, and saw for themselves how healthy these previously sickly children looked, how smartly they were dressed and how they were fed. Visitors could judge for themselves the validity of Müller's assertion that the children never had reason to know when times were difficult.

One visitor to the New Orphan-House described his experience like this:

We met at the door, a little after two o'clock, a pretty numerous party of all ranks in life, waiting for admission. When the doors were opened, we found ourselves in a very small hall, from whence a stone staircase leads up into a spacious room in the central buildings, where the visitors wait for their guide. This room is a perfect square, with the four angles taken off by the width of the windows, which we found looked into large pitched play-courts, with covered sheds for the children's use in wet weather. One court we saw was appropriated to infants of both sexes, a number of whom were toddling about under the charge of two or three older girls; another to girls; the third to boys; while the fourth window overlooks the part of the garden through which the visitors approach.

Our guide entered, and took charge of the forty or fifty who had by this time assembled . . . We proceeded into the Infants' Day Room, where we found a tribe of little things, under the care of a nurse. Ranged round one side of this room are a number of little basket beds, for the use of the youngsters when tired of play.

We found in one room about half a dozen boys, under the care of a female, quietly and busily engaged in the very necessary employment of darning stockings, which attracted the sympathy of the female part of the company most wonderfully. One lady, advanced in life, was quite carried away by her enthusiasm—'One thread up

and one thread down, is the very perfection of darning.'
Some, perhaps, of these boys may at a future time be
in the navy, others may chance to be emigrants; and we
can hardly estimate the value of this humble but necessary art in such circumstances. Even in the very
common experience of apprentices in this country, it
will often prove of very great advantage to them. In
any case we admire the practical wisdom that insists,
even in mending stockings, on teaching the best way.

In the younger department are pigeon-holed cupboards
for putting away their toys, when out of use. They were
well-furnished with nearly every description that a
general shop could supply.

The washing-places, we observed, are furnished with
baths, and on the walls is hung each child's little bag,
numbered, with comb and hair-brush. The most scru-
pulous care is evidently bestowed to ensure thorough
cleanliness of both persons and linen, as well as to guard
against the communication of any infectious juvenile
complaints from personal contact.

In going through this most interesting establishment
we were most forcibly impressed with the entire
absence of a pauperised look in the dress and appearance of the children. The hair of the girls is
kept beautifully neat, such as we could fancy a
mother's love had attended to; and there was a
cheerful looking-up at the visitors, and a heart-smile
on the young faces, which prove indisputably that
both in Principal and Assistants the spring of action
is Love, and that the presiding and pervading spirit
which rules the entire establishment is the Law of
Kindness. In fact, it is impossible to help being thor-
oughly convinced that the best of practical management exists in every department, and that everyone
engaged in the work is admirably fitted for his duties,
and has a hearty unselfish love of the work for its
own sake.

Although Müller was now caring for three hundred children, he had a long and quickly growing waiting list of children seeking admission: in December 1850 the list ran to seventy-eight names (by 1856 it had grown to nearly eight hundred and fifty names). He found it distressing to turn even one child away. There was still no other home in the United Kingdom with such a radical admissions policy. Müller was well aware of this. He wrote (in December 1850):

> The constitution of most other charitable Institutions for orphans makes the admission of a really destitute orphan, i.e. a child bereaved of both parents, and without an influential friend, very difficult, if not hopeless; for admission by means of the votes of donors precludes really poor persons from having, in most instances, the benefit of these Institutions, as they cannot give the time nor expend the money necessary for obtaining such votes. I have myself seen that certain candidates had several thousand votes . . . In our case nothing is needed but application to me; and the very poorest person, without influence, without friends, without any expense, no matter where he lives, or of whatever religious denomination, who applies for children born in lawful wedlock, bereaved of both parents, and in destitute circumstances may procure admission.

Neither national nor local government made proper provision for orphans: Müller recorded, also in 1850, that, 'about five years ago, a brother in the Lord told me he had seen in an official Report, that there were at that time six thousand young orphans in the prisons of England'. 'By God's help,' he wrote, 'I will do what I can to keep poor orphans from prison.' Müller therefore began to consider the possibility of building another home large enough to accommodate seven hundred children so that he could care for one thousand altogether.

He was particularly depressed by what he heard about the moral state of the workhouses. 'I have heard it again and again, from good authority, that children, placed in the Unions, are corrupted, on account of the children of vagrants, and other very bad young people who are in such places; so that many poor relatives of orphans, though unable to provide for them, cannot bear the idea of their going there, lest they should be corrupted.'

At the beginning of the new year (1851) Müller received the biggest donation for his work that had so far been received: three thousand pounds. 'This donation is . . . like a voice from heaven, speaking to me concerning a most deeply important matter respecting which I am seeking guidance from the Lord, the building of another Orphan-House.' For five more months, however, Müller continued to think and pray about the matter. He wrote down eight reasons against enlarging the work, plus an answer to each objection and then eight reasons for building a new home for seven hundred children.

In April he received a donation to which a vicar, an archdeacon and one of the Queen's chaplains had contributed.

In May 1851 he finally decided to go ahead with his plans for expansion, and began to pray that God would provide him with the necessary means, which would not, he reckoned, be less than about £35,000. 'The greatness of the sum required affords me a kind of secret joy; for the greater the difficulty to be overcome, the more will it be seen to the glory of God, how much can be done by prayer and faith.'

At the end of May, Müller announced his intention to expand the work. The children themselves began to give and Müller recorded:

June 3. From one of the orphans in the New Orphan-House sixpence, and from another sixpence.
June 4. From another orphan in the New Orphan-

House, sixpence. I received also 8s o½d, which the orphans in the Girls' School of the New Orphan-House gave between them for the Building Fund.

June 5. Through one of the boxes at the New Orphan-House twopence and likewise one half-penny. These two small donations are very sweet to me. I take them as further earnest, out of the hands of my heavenly Father, that He, in His own time, will give the whole sum requisite.

In August Müller received a cheque for £500 but in the early months of the new venture he received few large sums. In October Müller recorded that:

It has now been for several months reported that I have already £30,000 in hand for the Building fund, though this day it is actually only £1,139 19s 2½d ... But none of these things discourage me. God knows that I have not £30,000 in hand. God can influence the minds of His dear children towards this intended Orphan-House, whatever their thoughts may have been hitherto on the subject.

He knelt down and prayed:

Lord, thou knowest how small an amount as yet Thy servant has, in comparison with what is needed; but Thou also knowest that Thy servant did not act rashly and under excitement in this matter, but waited upon Thee for six months in secret, before he spoke about this his intention. Now, Lord, in Thy mercy, sustain Thy servant's faith and patience, and, if it please Thee, speedily refresh his heart by sending large sums, for which he is looking, and which he confidently expects.

There was no immediate answer to this prayer and for some months it seemed that the persistent rumour (Müller, of course, refused on principle to deny it) that he had £30,000 in hand was affecting donations. By March 1852, funds were running so low in the day-to-day expenses account that on the 16th there was actually no money in hand except the balance in the Building Fund. Müller was at his home in Paul Street expecting one of his staff to arrive from Ashley Down for more money. He prayed that he would not have to dip into the Building Fund. Just before the caller arrived he received 'from a noble lady' £15 which he was able to pass on towards immediate urgent needs.

Next day the situation all round was eased when Müller received a donation of £999 13s 5d of which he took £200 for current expenses, £600 for the Building Fund and the remainder for school, Bible, tract and missionary purposes.

This was one of the worst periods in the whole history of the Homes for sickness. Over a period of nearly four months, more than one hundred children in the new Home became seriously ill mainly with scarlet fever and at one time over fifty children were confined to their beds: five children died.

It was not uncommon now for donations to arrive from far away. One donation from Australia came from a shepherd who had read Müller's Narrative while tending his flock, and one from New Zealand came from sales of eggs laid by a hen which a little girl had 'set apart for the orphans'. Others came from the East and West Indies, the United States, Nova Scotia, Tahiti, Canada, India, Ceylon, Africa, China, the Cape of Good Hope, Turkey, France, Switzerland, Germany and Italy. The following letter from India is typical of many received:

> Madras,
> July 9th 1852

Dear brother,

Some time in the year 1842 or 1843 I met with 'The Lord's dealings with George Müller', and, after reading it, was moved to send you something; but at that time I had no means. In fact, I had lent, what little money I had, to a person who was unable to repay me, and I was nearly destitute. The good hand of God has been on me since that time, and I have often wondered whether George Müller was still in the flesh; but never had the resolution to enquire. Last December I met in a friend's house the Twelfth Report, and, after reading it, resolved to cast a mite into the Lord's treasury towards building the Orphan-House for seven hundred children; and may the God of Jacob, that has fed me all my life long, unto this day, accept of it, as acknowledgment of the thousandth part of the mercies I have received at His hands. I therefore enclose a bill of exchange to the value of seventy pounds sterling. I have often mentioned you by name in my appeals to the throne of grace; and if I meet you not on earth, I hope I shall in those regions where we shall see the Lamb on His throne and in His Father's Kingdom, and where there is no more sin or sorrow.

My dear brother,
Ever Yours,

Towards the end of 1852 Müller prayed especially hard that God would send him some larger sums for the work. At last, on January 4th 1853, he received a promise that as the joint donation of several Christians, he was to receive £8,100. 'Day by day, for nineteen months,' he wrote, 'I had been looking out for more abundant help than I had had. I was fully assured that God would help with larger sums; yet the delay was long. See how precious it is to wait on God! See how those who do so are not confounded! ... Have I then been boasting in God in vain? Is it not manifest that it is most precious, in every way, to depend upon God?' The money was paid in four instalments from January to April.

★

By Monday, June 13th the current account was reduced to about £12. Various provisions were needed including: flour—at that time about ten sacks were bought a week, three hundred stones of oatmeal, four hundredweight of soap; and there were a number of fairly minor repairs going on in the house employing a number of workmen, besides the regular current expenses of about £70 a week. On top of this, the previous Saturday Müller had discovered a fault in the heating system which would cost about £25 to repair. Thus about £100 extra was needed plus means for the current expenses.

That morning as Müller climbed the hill from Paul Street to Ashley Down he prayed as he walked. He pointed out to the Lord that although it was a Monday when generally little came in, He could send much if it was His will. On arrival in his room at the New Orphan-House he found a cheque for £301.

> The joy which I had cannot be described. I walked up and down in my room for a long time, tears of joy and gratitude to the Lord running plentifully over my cheeks, praising and magnifying the Lord for His goodness, and surrendering myself afresh, with all my heart, to Him for His blessed service. I scarcely ever felt more the kindness of the Lord in helping me.

Müller still received a variety of gifts in kind as well as in money. Among the more unusual were three autographs of King William IV, one of Sir Robert Peel and two of Lord Melbourne which were sold to aid the work of the Scriptural Knowledge Institution in December.

Early in January (1854) Müller received the promise of a further large donation, this time of £5,207 of which £3,000 was eventually put towards the Building Fund. It was a year before another large sum was received, but in January 1855 Müller again received from a number of Christian friends the promise of £5,700 of which £3,400 was put to the Building Fund. This brought the time much nearer when work on the second building could commence. At the beginning of February Müller applied to purchase two fields immediately adjoining the land on which the first home was built; he discovered however that according to the will of the late owner of the land the fields could not be sold at that time. He said to himself: 'The Lord has something better to give me, instead of these two fields.'

For some time Müller had been thinking that instead of putting up one enormous building for seven hundred children it might be better to build two houses for four hundred in one and three hundred in the other. He therefore measured out the ground on each side of 'No. 1' and judged that the idea seemed feasible. He called in architects to survey the ground and make a rough plan for two Houses and this confirmed that the project was possible.

Thus Müller decided to make an immediate start on building a second House to the south of No. 1 to accommodate four hundred girls. On May 29th (1855) four wells were sunk on the site and work commenced. With an application list now numbering over six hundred names Müller was most anxious to expand his work.

There was now ample evidence of the spiritual as well as social value of Müller's work. The following is typical of many letters Müller received from children formerly under his care:

March 28th 1855

Dear Sir,

Will you graciously accept this mite [ten shillings] from one who thinks of you and yours with gratitude. It is indeed a very small sum. I regret that I have no more to bestow on such a noble work. It will perhaps put a cornerstone in the wall of the intended Orphan-

House. I think I would like to labour for the Lord in that blessed House, if it is His own will, and be the means in the Lord's hand of bringing many of the dear orphans to know the truth as it is in Jesus. It was in the Orphan-House in Wilson Street, 1846, that first the light of life dawned upon my benighted soul. It was there, that I first learned to call God my Father. I have need therefore to love the Orphan-House, not only as concerning temporal things, but especially as its being my spiritual birth-place. May the Lord reward you, dear Sir, for all you have done for me. I am sure He will.

I am, dear Sir, yours most respectfully,

It is not difficult to imagine what a thrill it must have been to Müller to receive this and so many similar letters.

In February 1856, Müller received another large donation of £3,000 of which he put £1,700 into the Building Fund. In March a further £4,000 arrived of which £2,000 went towards the building work.

All sorts of ingenious explanations were offered to account for the remarkable success which Müller achieved in raising these very substantial sums of money without ever appealing for funds. Some said it was because he was a foreigner; others put it down to the novelty of the whole thing. Yet others decided that Müller must have access to some secret treasure; but the most popular explanation was that it was all the result of the Annual Reports which were produced. Müller replied to these objections with admirable brevity and wit:

My being a foreigner, looked at naturally, would be much more likely to hinder my being entrusted with such large sums, than to induce donors to give. As to novelty procuring the money, the time is long gone by for novelty procuring the money, for this is June 1856, and the work commenced in March 1834. As to the secret treasure to which I have access, there is more in the supposition than the objectors are aware of; for surely God's treasury is inexhaustible, and I have that (though that alone) to go to, and have indeed drawn out of it, simply by prayer and faith, more than £113,000 since the beginning of the work.

As to the objection that the Reports were the means by which all the money was raised, Müller replied as follows:

There is nothing unusual in writing Reports. This is done by public Institutions generally, but the constant complaint is, that Reports are not read. Our Reports are not extraordinary as to the power of language, or as to striking appeals to feelings. They are simple statements of facts. These Reports are not accompanied by personal application for means; but they are simply sent to the donors, or to any individuals who wish to have or purchase them. If they produce results, which Reports generally do not, I can only ascribe it to the Lord.

... we doubt not that the Lord has again and again used the Reports as instruments in leading persons to help us with their means. For as we continually stand in need of considerable sums; and as even hundreds of pounds go but a very little way, I entreat the Lord day by day, and generally several times every day, to supply me with means, to speak to the hearts of His dear children, and to constrain them by the love of Christ to help me out of the means, with which he has entrusted them; and so it comes to pass, I doubt not, that the Lord again and again works by His Spirit in the hearts of those who have read or heard the Reports. But whether we are supplied with means through the Reports or irrespective of them; in either case it is God, who is working for us ...

In October, Müller received the following letter:

October 11th 1856

Dear Sir,

In admiration of the services which you have rendered to poor orphans and mankind in general, I think it right that some provision should be made for yourself. I think it right to send you £100 as a beginning (which I hope many good Christians will add to), to form a fund for the maintenance of you and your family, and I hope you will lay out this as a beginning accordingly. May God bless you and your labours, as He has hitherto done everything connected with your institutions.

I am, dear Sir,

Müller saw this letter as a temptation, permitted by God, to put his trust in something other than God Himself, and without a moment's hesitation replied as follows:

21 Paul Street
Kingsdown
Bristol
October 12th 1856

My dear Sir,

I hasten to thank you for your kind communication, and to inform you that your cheque for £100 has safely come to hand.

I have no property whatever, nor has my dear wife; nor have I had one single shilling regular salary as Minister of the Gospel for the last twenty-six years, nor as the director of the Orphan-House and the other objects of the Scriptural Knowledge Institution for Home and Abroad. When I am in need of anything, I fall on my knees, and ask God that He would be pleased to give me what I need; and He puts it in the heart of someone or other to help me. Thus all my wants have been amply supplied during the last twenty-six years, and I can say, to the praise of God, I have lacked nothing. My dear wife and my only child, a daughter twenty-four years old, are of the same mind. Of this blessed way of living none of us is tired, but we become day by day more convinced of its blessedness.

I have never thought it right to make provision for myself, or my dear wife and daughter, except in this way, that when I have seen a case of need, such as an aged widow, a sick person, or a helpless infant, I have used the means freely which God has given me, fully believing, that if either myself, or my dear wife or daughter, at some time or other, should be in need of anything, that God would richly repay what was given to the poor, considering it as lent to Himself.

Under these circumstances, I am unable to accept your kind gift of £100 towards making a provision for myself and family; for so I understand your letter. Anything given to me, unasked for, by those who have it in their heart to help to supply my personal and family expenses, I thankfully accept; or any donation for the work of God in which I am engaged, I also thankfully accept, as a steward for the orphans, etc.; but your kind gift seems to me especially given to make a provision for myself; which I think would be displeasing to my Heavenly Father, who has so bountifully given me my daily bread hitherto. But should I have misunderstood the meaning of your letter, be pleased to let me know it. I hold the cheque till I hear again from you.

In the meantime, my dear Sir, whatever your letter meant, I am deeply sensible of your kindness, and daily pray that God would be pleased richly to recompense you, both temporally and spiritually.

I am, dear Sir,

Yours very gratefully,

George Müller

Two days later Müller received a reply, in which the donor asked him to use the £100 for the support of the orphans, and a few days later received a further £200 for the orphans from the same donor all of which was gratefully received.

By November 1857 Müller was able to open Home 'No. 2' (as it became known) on Ashley Down: it lay immediately south of No. 1 and at right angles to it. It had room for four hundred girls—two hundred infants and two hundred girls from eight upwards, and the first excited children arrived from November 12th onwards.

There were not a few sceptics who doubted whether Müller would be able to provide for seven hundred children, and the large staff which was now needed to look after them. These doubts were confounded: and in the years which lay ahead Müller would startle the world by trebling the size of his work.

CHAPTER FOURTEEN

When the South Wind Blew

Both New Orphan-Houses were fully centrally heated. Towards the end of November 1857, Müller was informed that the boiler which fed the radiators in No. 1 had a serious leak with which it would be impossible to go through the winter. The boiler was entirely surrounded by brickwork and the location of the leak could not be identified without taking down the brickwork, an operation which would probably cause further damage to the boiler. For eight winters there had been no problems and the present fault was quite unexpected. Müller was firmly of the opinion that to have done nothing and to have said, 'I will trust God regarding it', would have been careless presumption, and not faith in God. 'It would,' he said, 'be the counterfeit of faith.' Something, therefore, had to be done, and done quickly.

Müller was concerned that the children—especially the youngest—should not suffer from lack of warmth. He considered the possibilities: a new boiler would take many weeks to install. It was not certain whether the boiler could be repaired but, in any case, it would take several days to dismantle the brickwork to identify the problem. The introduction of temporary gas stoves was another possibility but on investigation it was found that there was not enough gas to spare from the lighting system to heat the large number of stoves which would be required. 'Arnott's' stoves, too, would have been unsuitable as they needed long chimneys to remove fumes. Finance, however, was not the problem: Müller would have gladly laid out hundreds of pounds to prevent the children suffering

from the cold. The problem was to know just what to do
and how to spend the money.

At last [Müller later recorded] I determined on falling
entirely into the hands of God, who is very merciful
and of tender compassion, and I decided on having the
brick-chamber opened, to see the extent of the damage,
and whether the boiler might be repaired, so as to carry
us through the winter.
The day was fixed, when the workmen were to come,
and all the necessary arrangements were made. The
fire, of course, had to be let out while the repairs were
going on. But now see. After the day was fixed for the
repairs, a bleak north wind set in. It began to blow
either on Thursday or Friday before the Wednesday
afternoon, when the fire was to be let out. Now came
the first really cold weather, which we had in the beginning of that winter, during the first days of
December. What was to be done? The repairs could
not be put off. I now asked the Lord for two things,
viz., that He would be pleased to change the north wind
into a south wind, and that He would give to the workmen 'a mind to work'; for I remembered how much
Nehemiah accomplished in fifty-two days, whilst
building the walls of Jerusalem, because 'the people
had a mind to work'.
Well, the memorable day came. The evening before,
the bleak north wind blew still; but, on the Wednesday,
the south wind blew: exactly as I had prayed. The weather was so mild that no fire was needed. The brickwork is removed, the leak is found out very soon, the
boiler makers begin to repair in good earnest.
About half-past eight in the evening, when I was going
home, I was informed at the lodge, that the acting
principal of the firm, whence the boiler makers came,
had arrived to see how the work was going on, and
whether he could in any way speed the matter. I went

immediately, therefore, into the cellar, to see him with the men, to seek to expedite the business. In speaking to the principal of this, he said in their hearing:

'The men will work late this evening, and come very early again tomorrow.'

'We would rather, sir,' said the leader, 'work all night.' Then I remembered the second part of my prayer, that God would give the men 'a mind to work'. Thus it was: by the morning the repair was accomplished, the leak was stopped, though with great difficulty, and within about thirty hours the brickwork was up again and the fire in the boiler; and all the time the south wind blew so mildly, that there was not the least need of a fire.

In July (1858) Müller received what he considered to be a 'deeply important' letter from a manufacturer. It read:

I enclose a Post Office Order for £5, which by the blessing of Almighty God I am enabled to send you this year. You will, no doubt, remember that the first sum I sent you was five shillings, I think now four years ago; and indeed at that time it was a large sum for me to send, I might say considerably larger than the present. For some years previous to the time I sent you the first amount, I was at times much perplexed on the subject of giving; and the end of my reasoning was always, that a person so straitened in circumstances as I was then, was not called upon to give. I kept this opinion, until one of your Reports fell into my hands, and, from the accounts contained therein, was encouraged to send you the first amount of five shillings. Soon after I thought my circumstances got something easier. I then began to seek out cases of distress, and relieved them to the best of my ability; and, to the astonishment of many, who did not know the secret, who

wondered how I could give, I have proved, that, just as
I give, the Lord gives in return; for during the time,
since I first made up my mind to give, what with weakness of faith, and false reasonings of friends, I sometimes withheld when I ought not, and just as I withheld, the Lord in His infinite mercy withheld also.
During the panic, which has scarcely passed over us, I
dealt out to all who came within my reach, according
as I considered the circumstances required; and the
result is, that, although many in the same trade have
been almost ruined, it has been the most prosperous
year I have had since I commenced business. It would
fill your heart with joy, if time and space would permit,
for me to relate how, in many instances, I was directed
to go to such a house and enquire how they were getting
on, and to find that I had arrived just in time. But,
above all, I have to thank God that my spiritual condition is much improved since I began to give. Etc.

Müller commented on this that,

It is impossible to use for God the much or the little
with which He may entrust us, without being blessed
in our souls; for we walk, in this particular, according
to His mind. In this way also life has a most blessed
object. If we are willing to give back to Him the means
with which He entrusts us, then occupation in our
earthly calling becomes food for the inner man; for we
work, because He would have us to work; and in order
that our occupation of body or mind may be used for
God. Laying up treasure on earth, and living for this,
not only decreases spiritual enjoyment in the children
of God, but weakens them more and more spiritually;
whilst laying up treasure in heaven not only increases
spiritual enjoyment, but develops and strengthens the
spiritual faculties and powers; we are thus 'laying hold
on eternal life' 1 Timothy 6:17-19.

Donations for the third home were still arriving: in the early months of 1858, one gift of £3,000 was sent and two others of £800 and £700. These and similar gifts meant that Müller now had enough funds to begin work on No. 3. In September Müller bought eleven and a half acres of land on the other side of the road from Nos. 1 and 2. He decided, the site being a large one, to build No. 3 spacious enough to accommodate four hundred and fifty children instead of the three hundred originally planned. This would mean that he would be caring for one thousand one hundred and fifty children instead of one thousand. Several thousand extra pounds would now be needed. In December he was told that a glass manufacturer would supply freely all the glass for No. 3's three hundred and fifty large windows. Early in January, 1859, he received a gift of £7,000 of which he took £4,000 for the Building Fund.

During 1859 and 1860 gifts came in steadily and included numbers of very substantial donations towards the building. Even while No. 3 was being built and well before it was opened, Müller's thoughts turned towards a further dramatic enlargement of his work. After a long period of daily prayer and self-examination, he decided to build two more large Homes on Ashley Down for eight hundred and fifty children so that he would eventually care for over two thousand children. What were Müller's reasons for such a daring expansion and was it really necessary?

As to the need, the number of applications for admission was, in the early 1860s, increasing all the time. Fresh applications arrived almost daily, sometimes three or four new ones a day. Moreover, Müller had until this time concentrated more on providing a home for girls than for boys. 'Girls,' he said, 'are the weaker sex; and are still more exposed than boys to utter ruin if neglected; and we can easily keep them till they are eighteen or nineteen years of age.' Thus there had been a policy of taking in rather more girls than boys. 'But now,' Müller continued, '. . . I was led to consider whether something more might be done for boys also, to prevent if possible, the necessity of refusing the boys of a family, when the girls could be received.'

Accommodation in other orphan establishments in the United Kingdom was still inadequate; and their admissions policy highly selective. Müller said that:

> Even if there were room in them, which is not the case, still, the existing rules of admission by votes, which are in use in most of them, make it difficult if not impossible, for the poorest and most destitute persons, to avail themselves of them . . . Some time since I had an application for some orphans, whose mother, a widow, in attempting to obtain votes for one of her fatherless children, was actually so worn out, that one day she came home, over-fatigued by canvassing for votes, sat down and died.

The only other alternative for these poor children continued to be the workhouses where, Müller still insisted, 'vice abounds'.

Many of the children received by Müller since the beginning of his work had been quite unable to read when they arrived at the Homes. This was true even of children of thirteen years and upwards. Müller reported that they had 'had the joy of educating hundreds, who otherwise might have had no mental cultivation; besides teaching them a great variety of other things which are profitable for this life, in order to make them useful members of society'. But, he continued, 'all physical and mental improvement regarding them could never satisfy us. All would be exceedingly little in our estimation, if they were not spiritually benefited . . . And this blessing has been granted to us, not concerning twenty or fifty of the orphans, but concerning hundreds.'

Looking back on nearly thirty years of the work, there was ample incentive for Müller to expand the Institution's activities. Increased administrative work would present little problem: by the early 1860s Müller already employed three full-time personal assistants who relieved him of much of the correspondence, accounting, etc. His staff could be expanded as necessary. But the expense of looking after two thousand children plus staff would be enormous. Two new Homes with the necessary land (a large field for cultivation by the boys would be required) would cost about £50,000. 'And how,' people said, 'will you be able to keep up the work, provided you are able to accomplish the building, as then the regular current expenses will amount to about £35,000 a year?'

I feel the force of all this [Müller replied] looking at it naturally. I am not a fanatic or enthusiast, but, as all who know me are well aware, a calm, cool, quiet, calculating businessman; and therefore I should be utterly overwhelmed, looking at it naturally; but as the whole of this work was commenced, and ever has been gone on with in faith, trusting in the Living God alone for everything, so it is also regarding this intended enlargement. I look to the Lord alone for helpers, land, means, and everything else needed. I have pondered the difficulties for months, and have looked steadily at every one of them; but faith in God has put every one of them aside.

Indeed, it was to demonstrate what can be wrought by faith that Müller originally began his work.

My chief object was the glory of God, by giving a practical demonstration as to what could be accomplished simply through the instrumentality of prayer and faith, in order thus to benefit the Church of Christ at large, and to lead a careless world to see the reality of the

things of God, by showing them, in this work, that the
Living God is still, as four thousand years ago, the
Living God. This my aim has been abundantly
honoured. Multitudes of sinners have been thus converted, multitudes of the children of God in all parts of
the world have been benefited by this work, even as I
had anticipated. But the larger the work has grown, the
greater has been the blessing, bestowed in the very way
in which I looked for blessing; for the attention of hundreds of thousands has been drawn to the work and
many tens of thousands have come to see it. All this
leads me to desire further and further to labour on in
this way, in order to bring yet greater glory to the name
of the Lord ... That it may be seen how much one
poor man, simply by trusting in God, can bring about
by prayer; and that thus other children of God may be
led to carry on the work of God in dependence upon
Him, and that children of God may be led increasingly
to trust in Him in their individual positions and circumstances, therefore I am led to this further enlargement.

Thus it was that at the end of May 1861 Müller announced his intention of enlarging his work to cater for
two thousand children. By the end of the year not quite
£1,000 had been received towards the £50,000 which
would be needed to build houses Nos. 4 and 5. Müller
wrote that, 'after this rate, it would take about twenty-
five years before all that is needed for the Building Fund
would come in. However, I am not discouraged. I believe
in God.'

January 11th 1862: before retiring to bed Müller was
able to write the following in his journal:

I had again had my long season for prayer this evening
for all the various objects of the Institution, and a variety of subjects in connection with them, as also for

individuals for whom I daily pray, and, amidst other things, also asked the Lord again for means for the Building Fund, when, about half an hour afterwards, I found at my house a crossed cheque for £2,000, with the following lines: 'I enclose a cheque, value £2,000, which accept with my best love and the expression of my heartfelt thankfulness to God for the privilege of being fellow-helper in the work of caring for orphans. I would like it to be applied towards the building you propose (DV) erecting. I shall consider as though I had £1,000 in each building; but you are at liberty to use the whole for the first, if you wish. Inasmuch as it is done to the Lord, I know it is well spent.'

Three days later he received another £2,000 and a fortnight later a further £2,500. The twenty-five-year wait before Nos. 4 and 5 were built began to look less likely!

It was in the early summer of 1861 that the Townsend family moved to Bristol. A close friendship developed between Müller and John Townsend who greatly assisted Müller in his Sunday School work. Townsend's daughter Abigail was not yet three when the family arrived in Bristol but she soon grew very fond of Müller and was often with him on Ashley Down and at his home in Paul Street. She was filled with wonder at what she saw and at what she heard her parents say about the way God provided for Müller and his children. She often said that she wanted 'to be like George Müller'.

On one occasion at Paul Street she said: 'I wish God would answer my prayers like He does yours, George Müller.'

'He will.'

Then, taking Abigail on his knee he repeated God's promise, 'What things soever ye desire when ye pray, believe that ye receive them and ye shall have them,' and explained the meaning of the words to her.

'Now, Abbie,' he asked, 'what is it you want to ask God for?'

'Some wool.'

Clasping her hands in an attitude of prayer, Müller said, 'Now, you repeat what I say: Please God, send Abbie some wool.'

'Please Dod send Abbie some wool.'

Jumping down Abigail ran out into the garden to play, perfectly sure that the wool would come. Then suddenly the thought came to her that God did not know what kind of wool she wanted, so she ran back to Müller.

'I want to pray again.'

'Not now, dear, I am busy.'

'But I forgot to tell Dod the colour I want.'

Taking her up on his knee again, Müller said, 'That's right, be definite, my child, now tell God what you want.'

'Please Dod, send it wa-re-gated,' said Abigail who possessed a wide vocabulary but could not pronounce her 'v's. (Later that day she asked her mother the meaning of the word 'definite' and Caroline Townsend obliged with an explanation.) Next morning her joy knew no bounds when a parcel arrived addressed to Abigail containing a quantity of variegated wool. Her Sunday School teacher, remembering that her birthday was close although uncertain of the date, and remembering too that she was a keen knitter, had purchased some wool and sent it—not on her birthday—but on the right day to demonstrate to the child that God hears and answers prayer.

On one occasion Caroline Townsend had tactfully to suggest to her daughter that it might be better if she ended her prayers 'for Jesus' sake' instead of 'like you do George Müller's' as she had been in the habit of doing.

One of the best loved 'Müller anecdotes' also concerns Abigail Townsend. The story is not recorded in Müller's journal but is included in a short biographical sketch entitled, 'The Adventures of Sister Abigail' and is quoted by Nancy Garton in her biography of Müller.

Early one morning Abigail was playing in Müller's garden on Ashley Down when he took her by the hand.

'Come, see what our Father will do.'

He led her into a long dining-room. 'The plates and cups or bowls were on the table. There was nothing on the table but empty dishes. There was no food in the larder, and no money to supply the need.' The children were standing waiting for breakfast.

'Children, you know we must be in time for school,' said Müller. Then lifting his hand he prayed, 'Dear Father, we thank Thee for what Thou art going to give us to eat.'

According to the account, a knock was then heard at the door. The baker stood there.

'Mr Müller, I couldn't sleep last night. Somehow I felt you didn't have bread for breakfast, and the Lord wanted me to send you some. So I got up at two o'clock and baked some fresh bread, and have brought it.'

Müller thanked the baker and praised God for His care.

'Children,' he said, 'we not only have bread, but the rare treat of fresh bread.'

Almost immediately there came a second knock at the door. This time it was the milkman who announced that his milk cart had broken down outside the orphanage, and that he would like to give the children his cans of fresh milk, so that he could empty his waggon and repair it.

During the summer of 1861 one of the contractors building the third Orphan-House had found it difficult to get hold of sufficient men to carry on the work and this had led to serious delays. Another contractor also experienced other difficulties and the building was not opened until March 2nd 1862. (This meant that well over £10,000 was in hand on the opening day to meet current expenses.) No. 3 was the largest of the buildings erected by Müller on Ashley Down. Its position was also the most

prominent and it became (as it remains) a familiar landmark in Bristol. A man living in Horfield, in sight of
Ashley Down, said that, 'whenever he felt doubts about
the Living God creeping into his mind he used to get up
and look through the night at the many windows lit up
on Ashley Down, gleaming out through the darkness as
stars in the sky'.

But with a waiting list now of nearly a thousand children, Müller was anxious that still more stars should
shine on Ashley Down. In October 1864 a donation of
£5,000 brought the Building Fund to over £27,000 and
Müller felt justified in taking steps to buy land on which
to build the fourth Orphan-House. For some years he
had had his eye on a beautiful site on the same side of
Ashley Down Road as Nos. 1 and 2, opposite No. 3. The
site was about eighteen acres and had a small house and
out-houses built at one end, close to the point where
Sefton Park Road (then a narrow track) meets Ashley
Down Road. Müller had prayed hundreds of times that he
would be enabled to erect two large houses on this site.

Now that enough money was in hand to build the
fourth Home, Müller saw the agent who acted for the
owner of the land and asked him whether the land was
for sale. He replied that it was but that it was let until
March 25th 1867. Müller was not discouraged; he
expected, through prayer, to come to an arrangement with
the tenant whereby he would leave early in return for fair
compensation. Two other difficulties, however, now
arose. First, the owner asked £7,000 for the land which
Müller judged to be considerably more than its value.
Secondly, he read that the Bristol Water Works Company
intended to build an additional reservoir on the site, and
to get an Act of Parliament passed to that effect.

Several times a day Müller now gave himself to special
prayer about these three problems. He then went to see
the committee of directors of the Bristol Water Works
Company about their reservoir. They told him that only

a small area of the land would be required, not enough to interfere with his plans; and that if possible they would try not to take even this land. Müller then visited the tenant and told him of his plans, explaining that he hoped they could settle the matter in a pleasant and friendly manner. The tenant asked for a few days to think things over. While he thought, Müller prayed. After a week, he paid a second visit to the tenant who said that he did not wish to stand in the way of the land being used for such a worthwhile purpose; however, as he had spent a good deal of money on the house he expected fair compensation for leaving early. Müller was quite prepared and happy to do this.

He now had to tackle the last and most difficult problem: that of the price wanted for the land. Typically, he combined ardent prayer with shrewd business sense: here we see Müller the tough negotiator.

I knew well [he wrote] how much the land was worth to the Orphan Institution; but its value to the Institution was not the market value. I gave myself, therefore, day by day, to prayer, that the Lord would constrain the owner to accept a considerably lower sum than he had asked; I also pointed out to him why it was not worth as much as he asked. At last he consented to take £5,500 instead of £7,000, and I accepted the offer; for I knew that by the level character of the land we should save a considerable sum for the two houses, and that by the new sewer, which only a few months before had been completed, running along under the turnpike road near the field, we should be considerably benefited. In addition to these two points I had to take into account that we can have gas from Bristol, as in the three houses already in operation. And, lastly, the most important point of all, the nearness of this piece of land to the other three houses, so that all could be under the same direction and superintendence. In fact, no other piece of land, near or far off, would present so much advantage to us, as this spot, which the Lord thus so very kindly had given to us.

A missionary, who, despite his youth, greatly impressed Müller, paid a visit to Ashley Down in August 1865: James Hudson Taylor. From the commencement of his Christian life, Hudson Taylor had been profoundly influenced and inspired by Müller's example; and now that— at the age of thirty-three—he was himself being led out along similar lines, he valued more than ever Müller's prayers, his judgment and advice.

On August 22nd he arrived at Ashley Down with a party of outgoing missionaries and that evening recorded in his diary:

Had an hour with Mr Müller. He spoke most preciously on the call and spirit of the missionary; on the consecutive reading of the Scriptures; on prayer and faith in God; on obstacles and thorn hedges.

Next day Taylor recorded:

Mr Müller spoke on communion with God being work for God; on the need of not acting uncertainly; on mixing freely with the people, and restraining the speaking of English among ourselves (in the presence of Chinese who could not understand); and finally promised to pray for the party.

As this little band of missionaries was shown around the three houses, and saw those hundreds of children, laughing, healthy, and well-clothed, they could not help but reflect on the value of that promise to pray. And for the next twenty years, Müller's practical support of the China Inland Mission was to be crucial to its development. But that, too, is a story for another chapter.

CHAPTER FIFTEEN

Indescribable Happiness

'I was going up Ashley Hill the other morning when I met Mr Müller walking towards the city. Had I not known him, I should have said he was a gentleman of leisure and without a care, so quietly did he walk and so peaceful and stately was his demeanour! The twenty-third Psalm seemed written on his face.' Such was a west-country farmer's testimony to the man who had the care of so many.

Müller was now (in 1865) in his sixtieth year; and still very much in his prime. His health was, indeed, far better than it had been in his twenties and early thirties. Arthur Tappan Pierson, who knew Müller well, wrote:

His form was tall and slim, always neatly attired, and very erect, and his step firm and strong. His countenance, in repose, might have been thought stern, but for the smile which so habitually lit up his eyes and played over his features that it left its impress on the lines of his face. His manner was one of simple courtesy and unstudied dignity: no one would in his presence, have felt like vain trifling, and there was about him a certain indescribable air of authority and majesty that reminded one of a born prince; and yet there was mingled with all this a simplicity so childlike that even children felt themselves at home with him. In his speech, he never quite lost that peculiar foreign quality known as accent, and he always spoke with slow and measured articulation, as though a double watch were set at the door of his lips . . .

Those who knew but little of him and saw him only in his serious moods might have thought him lacking in that peculiarly human quality, humour. But neither was he an ascetic nor devoid of that element of innocent appreciation of the ludicrous and that keen enjoyment of a good story which seem essential to a complete man. His habit was sobriety, but he relished a joke that was free of all taint of uncleanness and that had about it no sting for others. To those whom he best knew and loved he showed his true self, in his playful moods—as when at Ilfracombe, climbing with his wife and others the heights that overlook the sea, he walked on a little in advance, seated himself till the rest came up with him, and then, when they were barely seated, rose and quietly said, 'Well now, we have had a good rest, let us go on.'

Müller was very fond of Ilfracombe: he loved to wander around the harbour, protected from the sea winds by Capstone hill, or to explore the old town built on the cliffs above. Then, if the weather were fair he would take his family with him to climb the wooded heights which form a semi-circle around the town.

In September 1865 he made one of his visits to Ilfracombe 'for a change of air'. On the morning of the 4th he climbed the Capstone hill with Mary and Lydia. While returning from the top, two men approached them.

'Please excuse me,' one of them said, 'are you not Mr Müller?'

'I am.'

'I have to give to you some money for the orphans.'

Müller asked the stranger to sit with him for a while on a nearby bench, so that they could talk further.

'I live in the neighbourhood of M. I am a businessman, and, what would be called, a hard-working businessman. Sometime since one of your Reports fell into my hands, but, I honestly confess it, I could not believe that you did obtain your funds simply in answer to prayer; I questioned the truth of it. However, the thing came up into my mind again and again. While I was thus considering whether God was really with you, and whether you really obtained simply by faith and in answer to prayer these large sums of money, I heard of a certain property to be sold, which I thought I should like to buy, if it were disposed of reasonably. I looked it over, and had it valued by a competent businessman, who told me it was worth so much. I then said to myself, in a kind of sceptical way, I will now see whether God is with Mr Müller or not. If I get this property for so much (fixing a low price on it), I will give Mr Müller £100. I then instructed a person to bid for me at the auction, where this property was sold at a distant place; but so great was my curiosity to see, whether God really would appear for you in this matter, that by the next train I set off to the place where the auction was, that I might obtain as early as possible information, how the matter would end; and I found, to my great surprise that I had actually obtained this valuable property, at the exact low price which I had fixed. I was astonished. But I began now to reflect more on the principles on which you act, and I wondered, that, as a Christian, I or anyone else could call in question what you say about answers to prayer; and the more I consider the matter, and the more I read your Report, the more I see how right and proper it is, to come to God for all we need, and to trust in Him for everything. The conveyance having been made, and all being now settled about the sale, I felt it right to pursue my promise; so my friend, whom you saw just now with me, and I set out on a tour of Devonshire, and then, on our way home, called the day before yesterday at your house; but found you were from home. We stopped yesterday in Bristol, and having there learnt your address, we came on here to Ilfracombe today, for I wished to know you personally.'

'Well,' said Müller, 'I am not at all surprised at God's working thus for me, since day by day I seek His help, and thus, in answer to prayer, obtain from the most unlikely persons, and entire strangers, donations for the work. For instance, I had a letter from a lawyer at M. where you come from, not long since, asking me to send him a proper form of a legacy to be left to the orphans, as one of his clients wished to leave a legacy of a £1,000 for the orphans. Now, as far as I know, I am not personally acquainted with a single person at M., nor do I know the name of the individual who purposes to leave this £1,000.'

'About this legacy,' replied the stranger, 'I can tell you something. After I had got this property, and saw how wrong I had been in looking in such a sceptical way on your work, as if there were no reality in prayer, I decided on helping you further. I thought to myself, though I am a man in health, and of middle age, yet it might be well to make my will, and to leave you a £1,000 for the orphans.'

Thus Müller discovered that this was the individual on whose behalf the lawyer had written to him. An hour later, this one time sceptic called at Müller's lodgings with a cheque for £100.

In 1859 Müller's friend and fellow-worker Henry Craik had been told by his doctor that he had a weakness in his heart. From the summer of 1865 it was clear that Craik, who, like Müller, was also sixty, was desperately ill. By January 1866 it was obvious that the man who had twice refused an honorary doctorate from St Andrews University (they offered him an LL.D. or D.D., whichever he preferred) in recognition of his theological writings was going to die. Among letters Craik received that January was an affectionate one from Darby calling him his 'dear brother' and regretting their 'ecclesiastical separation'.

Müller was often at his friend's bedside and after one visit wrote:

After I had kissed him, when I purposed to go, he, being too weak to converse any more, said, 'Sit down,' and also asked Mrs Craik to sit down, that he might look on us, though he could not converse. I sat thus silently still a while, and then left. This was our last interview. The next day I took cold, and was for several days kept at home, during which time my dear friend fell asleep ... Both of us had then known the Lord a little above forty years; and both of us were then a little above sixty years of age. My beloved brother and friend now had finished his course; I was privileged and honoured, further to labour for the Lord, and to do now this without him, with whom I had often taken counsel.

The immense crowds which gathered at Bethesda for Craik's funeral were a fitting testimony to the loss which was felt by the Christian community.

In May 1866 building work began on the fourth Orphan-House; and in January 1867, a further £7,000 having been received, work began on No. 5. The contracts for both houses amounted to over £41,000. All the glass for the seven hundred large windows in the two buildings was freely given by a large firm of contractors. On Guy Fawkes' day 1868 the fourth House was opened: three days earlier, over seven hundred children's knives and forks, twenty-four carvers and forks, thirty-six table knives and forks and thirty-six dessert knives and forks had arrived in the nick of time from Gloucestershire. On January 6th 1870, the last of Müller's great buildings on Ashley Down, 'New Orphan-House No. 5' was duly opened. For a few weeks, reception into the new building was hindered by a mild form of measles and scarlet fever which was affecting some of the children; but it would not now be long before Müller was caring for some two thousand children.

Thus Müller's vast expansion programme on Ashley

Down was complete. Twenty-five years had elapsed since
he had first announced his plans to build his own Orphan-
House. But there was no sense at all in which Müller
could now sit back on his laurels. Every morning he rose
at half-past six and at a quarter to eight, after his usual
period of Bible study and prayer, he began the task of
going through his correspondence. Then, as *The Times*
recorded some years later, 'at ten o'clock he was waited
on by nine assistants, to whom he gave instructions'.
(Until the 1850s he had conducted a correspondence of
about three thousand letters a year without a secretary.)

Expenses for the children's work now amounted to
nearly £30,000 a year. Müller wrote that:

These two thousand orphans are not only to be fed,
but clothed; their clothes are to be washed and repaired.
The one single article of shoes and boots alone, think
of it, for two thousand, both the supplies of new and
repairs: how many hundred pounds it takes! Hundreds
of fresh orphans are received year by year, and the
newcomers are to be fitted out; hundreds of boys and
girls go out as apprentices and servants, and they are to
be provided with an outfit, at the expense of the
Institution. The considerable number of boys who are
sent out as apprentices, year by year, have a premium
paid for them to their masters, which is about equal to
another year's support.

Then come the heavy expenses connected with keeping
in repair these five large Houses, in which there are
more than seventeen hundred large windows and above
five hundred rooms ... It may therefore easily be
supposed how much the mere painting, white-washing,
colouring, repairs, etc., must cost year by year! Then
consider the many thousands of articles of table linen,
bed linen, towels, etc.; all has to be kept up. The
thousands of articles of furniture ... have to be kept
in repair, or to be replaced by new articles, which

continually become more or less needful.

The children are ill, or one or the other even dies; all the extra expenses are to be met. The children leave as servants or apprentices; the travelling expenses are to be paid. Further . . . the large staff of overseers of one kind or another, such as school inspector, matrons, teachers, medical officers, assistants helping the directors, etc.; all their salaries are to be obtained from the Lord. All the nurses in the infirmaries in each of the five Houses, the nurses for little infants, the laundresses and other servants . . . all this costs much, and for all this we look to the Lord. And there are, over and above, year by year, heavy extra expenses, not here referred to, occasioned by extraordinary circumstances, for all of which we look to the Lord . . . We are able with as much ease, if not greater ease than very rich noblemen, to accomplish this simply by looking in our poverty to the infinitely rich One for everything.

Mary Müller was the ideal wife for the director of five large Orphan-Homes.

'My darling,' Müller would say to her, 'God himself singled you out for me, as the most suitable wife I could possibly wish to have had.'

During the years of trial from 1838 to 1846, when, as Müller recalled, 'hundreds of times the necessities of the orphans could only be met by our means, and when all our own money had to be expended', Mary 'never found fault with me, but heartily joined me in prayer for help from God, and with me looked out for help, and help came; and then we rejoiced together, and often wept for joy together'.

Also, in addition to an excellent general education, she possessed a thorough knowledge of every kind of needlework and of the quality of material for clothes, linen, etc. so useful on Ashley Down where it was her duty to order hundreds of thousands of yards of all kinds of material. She would approve or reject the material which was delivered; Müller said 'it was to get good blanketing or good blankets, that she was busied, thus to serve the Lord Jesus, in caring for these dear bereaved children, who had not a mother or father to care for them'. She regularly examined all the account books every month and checked hundreds of bills for the matrons of the various Houses. It was said that 'should any tradesmen or one of the matrons at any time have made the least mistake, it would be surely found out by her'. Every day, except on Sundays, she would be seen on Ashley Down and would pay particular attention to the sick children.

Müller said of their marriage that:

Every year our happiness increased more and more. I never saw my beloved wife at any time, when I met her unexpectedly anywhere in Bristol, without being delighted so to do. I never met her even in the Orphan-Houses, without my heart being delighted so to do. Day by day, as we met in our dressing room, at the Orphan-Houses, to wash our hands before dinner and tea, I was delighted to meet her, and she was equally pleased to see me. Thousands of times I told her—'My darling, I never saw you at any time, since you became my wife, without my being delighted to see you.'

Further, [Müller continued] day after day, if anyhow it could be done, I spent after dinner twenty minutes or half an hour with her in her room at the Orphan-Houses, seated on her couch, which the love of a Christian brother, together with an easy chair, had sent her in the year 1860, when she was, for about nine months, so ill with rheumatism. I knew that it was good for her, that her dear active mind and hands should have rest, and I knew well that this would not be, except her husband was by her side; moreover, I also needed a little rest after dinner, on account of my weak digestive powers; and therefore I spent these precious moments with my darling wife. There we sat, side by side, her hand in mine, as an habitual thing, having a few words of loving intercourse, or being silent, but most happy in the Lord, and in each other, whether we spoke or were silent. And thus it was many times . . . in the fortieth year of our conjugal life. Our happiness in God, and in each other, was indescribable. We had not some happy days every year, not a month of happiness every year; but we had twelve months of happiness in the year, and thus year after year. Often and often did I say . . . 'My darling, do you think there is a couple in Bristol, or in the world, happier than we are?'

Müller believed that one of the greatest secrets of their marital bliss was that besides their times of private prayer, and family prayer, he and Mary frequently prayed together.

For many years my precious wife and I, had, immediately after family prayer, in the morning, a short time for prayer together, when the most important points for prayer, with regard to the day, were brought before God. Should very heavy trials press on us, or should our need of any kind be particularly great, we prayed again after dinner, when I visited her room . . . and this, at times of extraordinary difficulties or necessities, might be repeated once or twice more in the afternoon . . . Then in the evening, during the last hour of our stay at the Orphan-Houses, though her or my work was never so much, it was an habitually understood thing, that this hour was for prayer. My beloved wife came then to my room, and now our prayer, and supplication, and intercessions mingled with thanksgiving, lasted generally forty minutes, fifty minutes, and sometimes the whole hour. At these seasons we brought perhaps fifty or more different points, or persons, or circumstances before God.

Mary Müller was now (in 1870) seventy-two. For a year or two it had been obvious to Müller that her health was failing: she was growing thinner and tiring quickly. Müller begged her to work less and eat more, but, he said, 'I could neither prevail as to the one nor the other.' Sometimes she would lie awake at night for two hours or more and Müller would express his concern.

'My dear,' she would say, 'I am getting old, and old persons need not so much sleep.'

Two years earlier she had said to him, 'My darling, I think the Lord will allow me to see the New Orphan-Houses No. 4 and No. 5 furnished and opened, and then I may go home; but most of all I wish, that the Lord Jesus would come, and that we might all go together.'

And indeed the Lord had allowed her to see both No. 4 and No. 5 opened; and throughout 1869 she had spent nearly every day at work at the five buildings.

Sadly she had worked too hard.

CHAPTER SIXTEEN

'No Place Ever Seemed So Dear'

'I never knew what it was for my mother to caress me, take me to church or teach me a child's prayer.' Such was the experience of William Ready who had been born in a London workhouse on January 23rd 1860. His father was an alcoholic and unable to support his wife and William's nine brothers and sisters; by 1865 both parents had died and the ten children were left orphans.

Thus William had begun the life of a waif sleeping in dustbins or the dark corners of railway arches.

> Many a time [he later recorded], I have picked up a piece of orange peel as eagerly as if it had been a six-pence and I have even nibbled at cigar ends to allay the pangs of hunger. Sometimes we went into public houses to sing the comic songs we had learned on the streets, which usually paid us well ... On Saturday mornings, at four o'clock, I used to carry the produce at Covent Garden Market, and my feet and hands were often frostbitten.

It was in this state that at the age of twelve, in 1872, William Ready was rescued by James Walk, a London City Missioner, connected with St George's Church in Bloomsbury. Walk eventually arranged for Ready to go to Ashley Down.

Ready recorded:

> I was not happy I can assure you, when I found myself inside the block, with the great iron gates closing

behind me. I did not look upon those as my friends who had interfered with my liberty of the streets. No sooner had the doors closed when I began to feel I was in bondage and a real home-sickness came over me. I yearned for the streets of the Metropolis and the lights of London. I was as a bird in a cage and if anyone had said to me 'You may go back,' I should have said, 'Thank you, Sir! You are my friend.'

William was given a bath and put into his uniform— corduroy trousers, a blue vest, coat, and white collar.

Never shall I forget the day when I was first shown into the dining-hall. The boys gathered around me like flies round a sugar basin and they began to pinch me and pull my hair. The bell rang and we passed to our places. For the first time in my life I was not feeling hungry. Oh! to go back to my old haunts, to the rush of cabs and buses! Two slices of bread and treacle were set before me on a little tin plate but I could not touch them. A boy said to me, 'Don't you want your tea?' I answered, 'No!' The boys on either side of me soon finished my share.

On his first evening on Ashley Down the other boys teased him until his Irish blood rose; while tackling one boy the bully of the place came forward. William pulled off his coat and vest and launched into a spirited attack on young Curly Oliver, as he was known. Just as he was enjoying this encounter, a master entered with his cane and conducted the victor to his dormitory.

'Your bed number is twenty-two,' he said.

Next morning at six [Ready recalled] the bell rang to call us out and at eight we went into breakfast. The tables were laden with basins of porridge and I did not give the boys the chance of asking if I wanted my breakfast, for my appetite had returned . . .

It was at this breakfast that he first heard the Bible read.

The first lesson that morning was reading: William's master discovered that he did not know the letters of the alphabet. In the next few months, however, William Ready was taught to read well. For the first time, too, he learned about God, Christ, and salvation and memorised portions of Scripture. He soon became popular with the other boys, and for a while conducted a clandestine class teaching eager pupils the acrobatics of London streets. Eventually a master discovered that he had been charging those able to pay a penny postage stamp a week for his instruction. As the boys had paid of their own free will and without pressure, nothing more was said.

On one occasion, William led a gang of boys on an invasion of the masters' dining-hall in the dark to demolish the remains of their evening meal. He was caught and after the punishment had been administered 'with the usual amount of preaching', the master who had used the cane, had pity on the lad and gave him some sweets.

'That,' said Ready, 'did more to drive the devil out of me than all the flogging and preaching.' Indeed, towards the end of his stay on Ashley Down, a more understanding treatment produced better results and, 'it was kindness rather than punishment that settled me down to reason and order'.

One morning in 1876 William was called out of school to see Mr French who was in charge of the department which placed boys in apprenticeship.

'How would you like to be a flour miller, Ready?'

'I would, yes, Sir,' answered William not knowing what the job involved in the slightest.

Before long he was measured for and provided, as was usual before a boy left, with three suits of clothes at the expense of the Institution. Then came the final interview with Müller.

'How vividly comes back to my mind that last meeting with the father of the fatherless before leaving his care! He received me kindly when I went into his prayer room at No. 3 orphanage. Ah! what wonderful prayers had been offered there on behalf of the orphans and what remarkable answers he had there received!'

Müller put half a crown into his left hand and a Bible in his right.

'You can hold tighter with your right hand than with your left, can you not?'

'Yes, sir.'

'Well, my lad,' said Müller, 'hold to the teaching of that book and you will always have something for your left hand to hold.'

Müller then asked William to kneel, and putting his hand on his head, he committed him to God's keeping. Helping him then to his feet Müller said, 'Trust in the Lord and do good; so shalt thou dwell in the land and verily shalt thou be fed. Goodbye, my lad, goodbye!'

As he left Ashley Down, Ready recalled that 'my belongings were my Bible, my clothes and half a crown and, what was best of all, the priceless blessing of George Müller's prayers.

'Shall I ever forget my journey that day to Newton Abbot and my meeting with Mr Perryman, the man with a flowing beard and a straw-hat?'

'Are you William Ready?'

'Yes, Sir!'

'Well, I am your master, or your father if you like. Get into the trap, my son!'

During the seventeen-mile drive through the lovely Devon countryside to Perryman's home at Chagford, William's new father won his heart by his friendly and kindly conversation. William Perryman led a saintly life and it was not long before Ready himself was converted during his apprenticeship at Chagford. A few years later, he became a Free Church Minister and, moving to New

Zealand, became one of that country's most popular preachers.

Looking back on his years on Ashley Down he wrote, 'I can see now that it was just the place for me and what a blessing it was that I was sent there. If my own children were left orphans I could wish for nothing better than that they should be trained and cared for at Müller's.'

Nowadays, of course, it is no longer considered proper to house children in such large buildings as those Müller built on Ashley Down. Indeed, the Müller Homes today have long since felt it right to come into line with current official policy which is to house children in small house groups so that life should conform as closely as possible to a normal home atmosphere. However, by nineteenth-century standards, George Müller must be considered both a pioneer and a radical. He, alone, offered modern homes to thousands of children who would otherwise have been either homeless, or sent to a workhouse or debtors' prison, or grudgingly offered a corner in the overcrowded home of a relative. And there were no barriers to entry to Müller's Homes on the grounds of poverty, class or creed. Noting that admittance to other orphanages in the eighteenth and early nineteenth centuries was normally gained, not according to the relative needs of the child, but upon personal recommendation or by a majority of votes at the periodic meetings of subscribers, Kathleen Heasman has credited Müller with leading the way in

> giving priority to the needs of the child ... The fact that subscribers' meetings were not held, and the names and amounts given by particular donors were not made public, meant that children were usually selected according to their need, or all who applied were admitted. Thus the system of voting was rarely found in evangelical children's homes, and this example

[Müller's] gradually led to the abolition of the voting
system altogether.

Müller's large Homes also offered certain advantages
which smaller modern houses cannot. Life may have been
regimented, and the routine predictable, but the shared
fun of so many youngsters living and growing up together
meant that it was often jolly. There was also a stability
and security about them which was absent from smaller
homes. An orphan who began life in a small London home
and only arrived at No. 4 at the age of ten noticed the
difference: in London there had been constant changes in
staff and children. But in Bristol 'a teacher who had done
twenty-five years was just beginning'; some ex-Ashley
Down children actually returned with their grandchildren
to find their old masters still there. Similarly smaller
homes offered the children a more limited choice of
friends, whereas if Ashley Down children quarrelled, they
could always make new friends.

One former orphan wrote of her years on Ashley Down
thus: 'I am glad to see a number of orphans remember
the dear old Home, in which they spent their happiest
days; for truly there have been none happier to me than
those spent in the dear Orphan-House Number 3. How
happy we were in our own little world, brought up in
such a holy atmosphere.'

Another wrote: 'As I look back on my schooldays, just
left behind me, I think they were the jolliest days of my
life.' And yet another recalled: 'I was only a small child
then, and am still a child when I think of Ashley Down.
It was a lovely, lovely spot . . : and no place ever seemed
so dear.'

To impressionable teenagers, the experience of living
under the care of people with a deep personal faith in
Christ, together with the exhilaration produced when
numbers of their own contemporaries came to share this
same faith, was never to be forgotten. The many hundreds

who became Christians in this devout atmosphere felt an enormous debt of gratitude towards Ashley Down. One Christian girl soon after going into domestic service sent this letter:

> Beloved and respected Sir, I cannot feel grateful enough to you for all the kindness I received whilst under your fatherly care in the dear Orphan-House, and the years I spent there I can truly say were the happiest I ever spent in my life; for not only were we cared for temporally, but spiritually also; and I do indeed feel very thankful to the Lord that I was ever received there, and that He so soon brought me to a knowledge of Himself; and it is my heart's sincere desire to know more of Him, to become more like Him for He is truly to me the chiefest among ten thousand, and the altogether lovely ... I must thank you for the very nice situation in which I am placed. My mistress is very kind to me, and I hope to give great satisfaction to her ... May you ever be the orphans' friend and protector; and may the Lord still give you more abundant answers to your many prayers for the conversion of the dear orphans, who still remain unconverted. Will you please remember me very gratefully to dear Mrs Müller, Miss Groves, Mr L, Mr W, Mr H, also Miss D and all the teachers. I remain, dear Sir, yours very gratefully and respectfully.

Mrs Nancy Garton has written of the uniform worn by the children in Müller's day as giving 'the orphans a grace and a dignity, and as it became antiquated, a sentimental appeal, which the modern dress introduced in 1936, with its knee-length skirts and squashed-on hats, entirely lacked'.

According to Mrs Garton,

> The older boys wore a navy-blue Eton jacket, with a

waistcoat buttoning up to the white starched collar, both of heavy serge; brown corduroy trousers; caps with a glazed peak; and in bad weather, short cloaks. Each boy had three suits.

The small boys, up to about eight or nine years old, wore for everyday a garment which seems a strange choice from the practical point of view. It was a plainly-cut smock, with no collar, in white or unbleached cotton. Possibly, being white it could soon be boiled and restored to its original purity, but who, knowing boys, can help suspecting that it spent much of its time being anything but white. Blue serge shorts, socks and strap shoes completed the costume. For best wear, the little boys discarded their smocks, and wore Norfolk suits with broad Eton collars, in which they looked most attractive. Their caps were the same as the older boys.

The girls' outdoor dress in cold weather was a long cloak in green and blue plaid; in mild weather a shepherd's plaid shawl took the place of the cloak; in hot weather, for best wear, the dress was a thin one of dull lilac cotton, over which was worn a small cape or tippet of the same material, a tiny ruff at the· neck. Throughout the year the girls wore bonnets of natural-coloured straw. To each bonnet was attached a long strip of thin material with a green and white checked pattern, which formed a band across the top, crossed at the back and was stitched at the sides, so that the two ends formed the strings by which the bonnet was tied on.

The everyday dresses for girls of all ages were of navy cotton covered with small white dots, to which ́for walking out was added a white tippet when the weather was too warm for cloaks or shawls. Indoors, the girls up to fourteen wore blue-checked gingham pinafores, cut high to the neck and buttoning behind. The girls over fourteen, who had left the schoolroom and were

called 'House Girls', wore aprons with strings to dis-
tinguish them from their juniors. The most senior girls,
those who were due to leave the Homes for situations
within a few months, were known as 'Cap Girls', and
wore caps, aprons to the waist and white collars. Every
girl had five dresses.

The stockings were all hand-knitted by the girls; black
wool for winter, and white cotton for summer. A pair
of these white stockings is to be seen in the Museum at
Müller House. The shoes were mostly of the ankle-
strap style.

With the old uniform, the girls had no waterproofs,
and in doubtful weather there was one cotton umbrella
for every two children. The privilege of carrying the
umbrella was not one that was eagerly competed for.
The walk on wet days was often a quiet squabble, as
the more strong-minded of each pair in the crocodile
pressed the umbrella into her partner's unwilling hand.

Mrs Garton has also given us a fascinating description
of the children's hair-dos:

The girls' hair was managed rather cleverly, considering that hundreds of heads of hair had somehow to be
made presentable every day. The tiny girls had theirs
almost as short as a boy's, but beautifully glossy and
well-brushed. Those from about eight years old up to
eleven had a dutch bob, with centre parting and fringe,
such as they could comb into place themselves without
assistance. The older girls, who were capable of doing
their own hair, were allowed to grow it to shoulder
length or longer, and hold it back with a velvet ribbon
band. The most senior girls put their hair up.

Former Ashley Down children recall that children who
came with their parents to visit the Homes were sometimes
envious of the pretty hairstyles worn by the residents.

The nursery infants [Mrs Garton continues] do not seem to have been always in uniform, so probably the many babies' clothes which must have been sent to the Homes were fully utilized. Some photographs show little groups of toddlers decked out with loving care in frilled and embroidered pinafores which have no suggestion of the pauper about them.

Müller deserves also to be regarded as a pioneer and a radical by virtue of his educational policy. He was actually criticised for educating children 'above their station'; not many years earlier, in his book *An Experiment in Education*, Dr Andrew Bell had written,

It is not proposed that the children of the poor be educated in an expensive manner, or even taught to write and to cypher ... there is a risk of elevating by an indiscriminate education, the minds of those doomed to the drudgery of daily labour, above their condition, and thereby rendering them discontented and unhappy in their lot. It may suffice to teach the generality, on an economical plan, to read their Bibles and understand the doctrines of our holy religion.

Müller did not agree. As well as religious education, he saw to it that his children were taught reading, writing, arithmetic, dictation, grammar, geography, English and world history, composition, singing, needlework and—for the girls—domestic science. Needlework for the girls included instruction in making and mending their own clothes; for the boys it meant learning to knit and darn their socks. The boys also made their own beds, cleaned their shoes, scrubbed their rooms, were sent on errands, and dug, planted and weeded the gardens. The domestic science involved the girls in some work in the kitchens, sculleries, wash-houses and laundries at the five Houses. Lewis Court has claimed that, even in Müller's day, if an aptitude were shown, a higher education for one of the professions was provided, but this seems to have been rare.

Müller employed a school inspector to maintain the educational standards at the school for his own children on Ashley Down and at schools financed and run by the Scriptural Knowledge Institution.

The Annual Examination of the children was held during the months of February and March [the inspector, at that time a Mr Horne, wrote in 1885]. The children were examined and arranged in the Second, Third, Fourth, Fifth and Sixth Standards, in many particulars according to the Government Code. Each child was examined separately in reading. Each child showed his or her copy-book, to determine the mark for writing. Ten questions were put on each of the following subjects, viz, on Scripture, Geography, History and Grammar. The answers were given in writing. Six sums were given in Arithmetic. The answers were given on paper. The average percentage of all the marks the children received during the examination was 91·1.

'To all who are acquainted with such matters,' commented Müller with some pride, 'the last sentence will show, with what success our children are educated.'

Because of the duration of the education he provided, Müller was accused of robbing the factories, mills and mines of labour; he was not deterred. In general girls remained under his care until they were seventeen and sometimes longer. They were then usually recommended to a suitable domestic situation and fitted out at the Homes' expense; some would go on to train as nurses. Generally the boys were apprenticed when they were between fourteen and fifteen years old. But fixed rules were deliberately avoided and a flexible policy was maintained so that the needs of each individual were taken in account.

In theory each boy was allowed to choose the trade he wanted to learn, although in practice the selection process was no doubt often similar to William Ready's case quoted above. The boys were provided with three suits of clothes at the expense of the establishment; and any other expenses connected with an apprenticeship were also met. Some boys left the Homes to become Post-Office and telegraph clerks, or clerks in other offices. Others among the brightest would go on to be teachers, perhaps in the Homes themselves—in which case they would do their training at a school in Purton, Gloucestershire, financed and run by the Scriptural Knowledge Institution.

As to discipline in the Homes, Nancy Garton has aptly summed it up as 'strict, but not harsh'. A group of former Ashley Down children (there not long after Müller's death), told the author, 'if we were punished we deserved it'. There were occasions when it was found necessary to expel a child who had become an unacceptable influence on the other children. But expulsion—that is, returning a child to a relative or guardian—was always a last resort after repeated warnings and attempted reformation; and after an offender had left, he was followed by the prayers of Müller and his staff.

Müller recalled the case of one boy who had arrived on Ashley Down in October 1849.

He was then not quite eight years old; but though so young, it was soon found that he was old in sin, for he was a confirmed liar, thief, etc. He gloried in it among the other boys, and told them that he had belonged to a juvenile gang of thieves, before he had been admitted into the Orphan-House, that he had often stolen from the ships iron, brass, etc. and sold it. We thought at first that he spoke thus merely in the way of boasting, yet it proved but too true, that he was experienced in such matters; for twice he ran away from the Orphan-

House, carrying off things belonging to the other children. Moreover, he could pick locks, etc. We received him back twice, after having run away, hoping that, by bearing with him, and using a variety of other means, he might be reclaimed; but all in vain. At last, having borne with him, and tried him for five years and four months, he was solemnly, with prayer, before the whole establishment, expelled, if by any means this last painful remedy might be blessed to him. Yet we follow even this poor young sinner with our prayers, and hope that the Lord may yet show him his evil ways, and give us even now joy concerning him, as we have had before in a similar instance.

One boy, so the story goes, was about to be dismissed before the whole company for repeated bad behaviour over a long period, when Müller placed his hand on his head and began to pray for him. To show how brazen and unconcerned he was, the boy turned to face Müller with eyes wide open, and saw, to his amazement, tears rolling down the old man's cheeks. There and then, according to the story, the boy was converted and his life dramatically changed. And yet another, later in life described his dismissal by Mr Müller and Mr Müller's final words, with tears, of 'I am sorry! God bless you.'

The Times once reported that:

amongst those who visited his [Müller's] Homes and expressed their admiration of the management, and working, were the late Earl of Derby, Lord Salisbury, Lord Hampton, and many others of all ranks interested in beneficent social movements.

Nancy Garton has described how that Charles Dickens once visited Ashley Down. 'He had heard a rumour of the sort that circulates wherever charitable institutions are concerned; in this case to the effect that the orphans were starved. With his usual thoroughness Dickens set himself to investigate the matter in person. Müller received him with courtesy, and as soon as he understood the purport of Dickens' enquiries, decided to let demonstration rather than argument prove the falsity of the report. He sent for a subordinate, handed him a bunch of keys, and requested that Mr Dickens might be shown over any of the five Orphan-Houses he chose to see. This was done, and Dickens went away entirely reassured.'

Former Ashley Down residents whose memories go back almost to the Müller era, recall having meat regularly on Mondays, Thursdays and Fridays while on Wednesdays and Saturdays they were served a broth with meat in it. On Tuesdays and Sundays (when many of the staff would be at Bethesda for the morning service) a dish of rice and raisins was a common lunch. Frequently the meat was either Australian mutton, known to the children as 'og' or (more popular) corned beef; bread incidentally was often referred to as 'toke' due to the wording of the favourite Ashley Down grace, 'We thank thee Lord for these tokens of thy love!' Bristol's situation as a port meant that it was not unusual for the children to receive fresh fruit, particularly bananas and oranges. Occasionally, at times of surplus, large quantities of free fruit would be delivered to Ashley Down to prevent it rotting. Eggs were a regular feature of the menu, but to some extent also seasonal: on his birthday every child was entitled to two eggs, one for himself and one for his best friend. Milk and water was the usual beverage.

There can be little doubt that the predictability of the menus and the routine of events in general tended to make life on Ashley Down somewhat monotonous, although routine, it should be borne in mind, is not something of which children are quick to complain. There were a number of annual events, however, which interrupted the routine and provided the children with both happy memories and highlights to which they could look forward.

First, there was Mr Müller's birthday on September 27th, at which time a week's holiday from school was always taken and when, as one old girl recalled, 'we used to go out most days, blackberry picking. How we all enjoyed it!' The day itself was always marked by special helpings of cake and an enormous apple dumpling for each child.

The annual summer treat was the outing to Pur Down, when the children set off in the morning each armed with either a pink or blue cotton bag filled with sweets and sweet biscuits to eat on the journey. This was one of the days when, on arrival at the field, the children of the five Houses could mix as they pleased. The picnic lunch (of bread and cheese) and tea (of bread and butter and cake) was transported to Pur Down in large hampers. A group of now elderly former Ashley Down children, who could never remember it raining on Pur Down, proudly showed the author an old oak tree under which they used to play on that great day. The outing concluded with the launching of five fire balloons, one for each House.

But probably the event which the children anticipated with the greatest excitement was Christmas. Well before the time, they began to prepare for the celebrations—learning to sing carols and other songs from the Ashley Down Song Book (often in parts without accompaniment); making the decorations, and memorising poems, sketches and plays to be recited and performed at the parties.

Each December, Müller's journal took on a seasonal tone:

December 16th 1884—From a Bristol wholesale house eight barrels of flour, one barrel of currants, and sixteen quarter boxes of Valencias, for the children's Christmas puddings ... December 23rd 1878—From Clifton we received for the children a number of dolls, some fancy boxes, albums, games, balls, tops and a great variety of other play-things—From Durdham Down, as Christmas presents for the orphans, dressed dolls, boxes and packets of chocolate and sweets, some drums, tops, balls, marbles, whips and guns, boxes of toys, books, fancy cards, paint boxes, transparent slates, pocket-handkerchiefs, wool ties and ruffs, baskets and boxes, pencils, trumpets and other play-things ... From a Bristol wholesale house, fifteen boxes of fruit, ten boxes of oranges, ten boxes of figs, and a sack of nuts for the orphan's Christmas Treat.

One Christmas, one hundred and fifty pheasants were sent to Ashley Down from a donor in Cornwall.

And so a child could recall, 'well do I remember the happy Christmases spent at No. 4; the start of the preparations for the decorations; the arrival of the great, big Christmas tree, nothing on it, but I knew before Christmas it would be loaded with toys and presents; and somewhere amongst the many there would be one for me!' And another, who wrote to the Homes one Christmas, 'I expect the times are just as exciting as when I was there. I imagine the decorations being got ready, and the secrecy of it all, and then learning the lovely carols, and the Christmas Shop! I would love to peep in, to see if it is really like it used to be. I don't think it could possibly be better.' Mrs Garton notes that the Christmas Shops were little sweet shops, opened in each wing of the Houses, managed by members of the school staff who bought the sweets from the large Bristol sweet manufacturers on special terms. In time these shops came to be opened in other seasons as well.

It would be foolish to pretend that every child was happy on Ashley Down: some clearly were not. The experience was especially unhappy for children who had known for a while the love of their own parents and a normal home life; for these children—arriving on Ashley Down perhaps aged eleven, twelve or more—the five great buildings naturally appeared particularly barrack-like and uninviting. And no doubt mistakes were made in the appointment of staff with the result that kindness and understanding were sometimes in short supply. As a pioneer in the field, Müller was forced to learn by his mistakes: and mistakes there were. Almost certainly the children's existence on Ashley Down was too sheltered, too remote from the realities of the outside world. Today, Müller's children attend normal local authority schools and mix freely, with other boys and girls. But in the founder's day, of course, Bristol could not have offered free education for some two thousand children and it is difficult to suggest the alternatives which were open to him.

In the event, however, the children received a sound education which they would have been fortunate to have obtained elsewhere. They received, too, a treasure of immeasurable value: teaching which was able to make them 'wise unto salvation' and which offered to those who would accept it, 'life more abundant'.

CHAPTER SEVENTEEN

Letter to Yangchow

A few months after his visit to Ashley Down (Chapter 14), Hudson Taylor set off on May 26th 1866 for Shanghai. With him in the *Lammermuir* were his wife Maria, six other men and nine women who would join the eight missionaries already in China, to form the new China Inland Mission.

The story of the dramatic events which led to the commencement of Müller's substantial support of the CIM, at a time of crisis and controversy, well illustrates his great interest in the work of nearly two hundred missionaries in many parts of the world.

The ninety-one protestant missionaries of all societies already in China were confined to a few of the ports; beyond, in the country's vast interior, there was hardly a voice to preach the gospel to two hundred million Chinese. Taylor wrote, therefore, that, 'Our great desire and aim are to plant the standard of the Cross in the eleven provinces of China hitherto unoccupied . . .'

Inspired by Müller's example, the founders of the China Inland Mission went forth in faith—trusting in God to supply their needs. When anxious friends expressed concern that with no committee to represent them at home, the missionaries would be forgotten in a distant land, Taylor replied:

I am taking my children with me, and I notice that it is not difficult for me to remember that the little ones need breakfast in the morning, dinner at midday, and something before they go to bed at night. Indeed, I could not forget it. And I find it impossible to suppose that our Heavenly Father is less tender or mindful than I.

It was a great principle of the CIM that the Chinese should never have reason to feel that Christianity was a 'western religion', foreign to their own way of life. Taylor and his companions therefore went into the homes of the people, dressed as they were.

In April 1868 Hudson Taylor (accompanied by Maria and the four children) led a party of missionaries—including six Chinese evangelists—into the interior of China. In June they arrived at Yangchow, where they successfully procured and occupied a suitable house; not long after they had settled in, however, trouble began, stirred up by the 'literati', a section of Chinese society vehemently hostile to foreigners, especially missionaries. These men held a meeting at which they decided to circulate anonymous hand-bills and posters designed to excite popular feeling against the missionaries. According to *The Times* correspondent in Shanghai the circulated material accused Taylor and his colleagues of 'kidnapping children and boiling them up for medicine; of abstracting the heart and liver from dead bodies and eating it; of administering drugs and philters to Chinamen which turned them into foreigners . . .'

By early August, this organised campaign was bringing about a change in the attitude of the people. Mr Reid, another CIM missionary who had come over from Nanking to join the party in Yangchow, wrote home that on Sunday, August 16th (1868),

the people assembled at an early hour, and began knocking and battering upon our door . . . until we thought it best to go out and try to pacify them . . . I think I never felt more the power and value of speaking gently than on that day. Dear Mr Taylor spoke often to those assembled in a very kind manner; and while we watched, those inside the house prayed, and God graciously brought us through, confirming to our hearts the promise, 'Lo, I am with you always.'

Later that week two 'foreigners' came up to visit Yangchow, wearing not the native costume adopted by Taylor's party but undisguised 'foreign dress'. They were seen in various parts of the city before leaving with the impression that all was quiet. This was too good an opportunity for the literati to miss: they began to circulate reports that children were missing in all directions, entrapped by the 'foreign devils'. Revenge was demanded against all foreigners, and the prospect of plunder in Taylor's premises was held out as an incentive. The weather was intensely hot and feelings became easily excited; at last a crowd of 'several thousand people' (according to the account in *The Times*) surrounded the house.

Taylor managed to send a verbal message to the British Consular authorities informing them of the situation. Then, after night had fallen, he and Mr Duncan decided on a desperate attempt to summon aid from the Chinese authorities. Leaving their wives and children and the women missionaries in the care of Messrs Rudland, Reid and Judd, they set off to face the fury of the people. On arrival at the judgment hall, after a terrifying dash through the hostile crowd, Taylor recorded:

We were taken to the room of the chief secretary, and kept waiting three-quarters of an hour before we had an audience with the Prefect, all the time hearing the yells of the mob a mile or more off, destroying for ought we knew, not only the property, but possibly the lives of those so dear to us. And at last when we did get an audience, it was almost more than we could bear with composure to be asked as to what we really did with the babies; whether it was true we had bought them, and how many; what was the cause of all this rioting? etc., etc.

At last I told His Excellency that the real cause of all the trouble was his own neglect in not taking measures when the matter was small and manageable; that I must now request him first to take steps to repress the riot and save any of our friends who might still be alive, and afterwards make such enquiries as he might wish, or I would not answer for the result.

'Ah,' said he, 'very true, very true! First quiet the people, and then enquire. Sit still, and I will go to see what can be done.'

He went out telling us to remain, as the only chance of his effecting anything depended on our keeping out of sight; for by this time the number of rioters amounted to eight or ten thousand. The natives estimated them at twenty thousand.

We were kept in this torture of suspense for two hours, when the Prefect returned with the *Ts'-ao-fu* (governor of the military forces of the city, some three thousand men) and told us that all was quiet; that the *Ts'ao-fu* himself, the *Sheo-pe* (captain of the soldiers who guard the gates), and two local Mandarins had been to the scene of the disturbance; that they had seized several of those who were plundering the premises, and would have them punished. He then sent for chairs, and we were returned home under escort. On the way back we were told that all the foreigners we had left were killed. We had to cry to God to support us, though we hoped this might prove exaggerated or untrue.

When they reached the house it seemed sadly certain that the report was true.

Here, a pile of half-burned reeds showed where one of the attempts to fire the premises had been made; there, debris of a broken-down wall was lying; and strewn about everywhere were the remains of boxes and furniture, scattered papers and letters, broken work-boxes, writing-desks, dressing-cases, and surgical instrument cases, smouldering remains of valuable books, etc.— but no trace of inhabitants within.

Taylor and Duncan were horrified. Where were their wives, their children and their fellow-workers? Were they injured? Or were the reports that they had all been killed true? In great fear and with sickness of heart they began to search for their loved ones.

After Taylor and Duncan had set off to summon help, the women and children had assembled in Maria's room. There they had pleaded for God's protection on themselves and on the two men who were facing the anger of the people. Meanwhile Messrs Rudland and Reid had done their best to keep the crowd from entering the premises. But their attempts had failed. The rioters broke into the house and began to ransack its rooms. The ladies had to throw their children from the verandah roof into the arms of the men below; then Reid stood ready to catch Maria and Emily Blatchley, but as he braced himself he was struck in the eye by a brick-bat: he lost the eye. Maria jumped, and badly injured her leg; Emily followed and came down on her back on the stones. She was fortunate not to break her spine or skull. The rioters then set fire to the lower storey of the building.

Mercifully the terrified missionaries managed to escape in the darkness to a neighbour's house. There, as the danger of discovery increased, they were taken from one room to another until finally they were left without a glimmer of light in the inner part of the house. Reid lay groaning with pain; Maria was almost fainting from loss of blood; Emily's arm was bleeding from a bad cut and was so painful that she could not move it; all of them

were stiff and sore with bruises. The children longed for
sleep but their mothers dared not let them, not knowing
when they might have to flee again.

It was here that Taylor and Duncan found them.

At last, [Maria recalled] after a much shorter time than
it appeared to us, we heard my dear husband's voice
outside the door, which had been barred for greater
safety . . . He told us that the rioters had all been driven
out, and he thought we might venture back to our own
rooms (which had *not* been burned down) . . . for there
would be a guard around the premises. How our hearts
went up to God in thanksgiving that He had spared us
to each other! . . . A short time before we heard my
husband's voice, I had felt encouraged to hope that help
was at hand, by the fact that my own strength was
rapidly ebbing away from loss of blood. I was anxious
not to let any one know how much I was hurt, as I felt
it would alarm them, and it seemed most important
that all should keep calm.

It was after midnight when we returned . . . We found
the floor of my room strewn with clothes, etc., which
had been turned out of boxes in the search for gold and
silver. The leaves of my poor Bible, which I had been
unable to take with me, were scattered about in every
direction. Kind, loving hands collected them for me.
Some, I was told, were found downstairs, and not a
leaf is missing.

There was little sleep that night. Early on the Sunday
morning, when the guard retired, the people began to
come in again to plunder the building. Once more, Taylor
was forced to go to the judgment hall, and, once more,
Maria's room became their sanctuary. Just as it seemed
the crowd would be upstairs, the alarm was given that
the Mandarin had come, and his soldiers dispersed the
people. Taylor managed to send a pencilled note to the

Consular authorities informing them of the night's developments.

That afternoon, Taylor and his group of CIM missionaries in Yangchow, their wives and children, left the city for Chin-Kiang under an escort of soldiers who saw them safely to the Yangstze. The Mandarins had insisted on their leaving for a while, so that the house might be repaired and the people quietened. The foreign residents of Chin-Kiang received them kindly and managed to accommodate all the refugees.

Unfortunately, as Dr and Mrs Howard Taylor have written, 'the troubles at Yangchow were made public in a way Mr Taylor would have least desired. A resident at Chin-Kiang, with the kindest intentions, wrote stirring accounts to the Shanghai papers, and public feeling demanded that action, prompt and decisive, should be taken by the British authorities.'

At home, readers of *The Times* learnt of what followed from the paper's Shanghai correspondent.

On hearing of the affair Mr Medhurst, the British Consul at Shanghai . . . went to Chin-Kiang and, finding how matters stood, ordered up Her Majesty's ship *Rinaldo*, in order that he might be fittingly supported in his representations to the authorities.

Meantime [*The Times* correspondent continued] excitement spread to Chin-Kiang, where a riot was got up among the Tartar soldiery, and threats expressed of destroying the foreign settlement and burning down the Consulate. But the scheme was thought better of next day, when the guns of the *Rinaldo* were seen looking over the town. There is every reason to believe that this riot was got up by the authorities; the people of Chin-Kiang took no part in it . . . To the Viceroy it would be represented as a popular row, and the position of the Yangchow officials would be lightened. They would be able to point to Chin-Kiang to show how deep and widespread was the antipathy to foreigners. This, however, is by the way. Mr Medhurst went into the city with a guard of marines and blue jackets from the *Rinaldo*, and insisted on the punishment of the ringleaders.

On September 8th, still with a guard from the *Rinaldo*, Mr Medhurst went to Yangchow, visited the scene of the riot, and had an interview with the Prefect, from whom he demanded the release of the lessor of the mission-house, and the punishment of the 'literati', who were believed to have instigated the proclamation and the attack. The Prefect, who was white with fear, defended himself anxiously, as best he could, but failed signally, conceded at once the first part of the demand, but professed his utter inability to comply with the latter. Finding it impossible to settle matters satisfactorily on the spot, Mr Medhurst determined to go to Nankin and negotiate with the Viceroy himself, and requested the unhappy Prefect to accompany him. The latter did go as far as Chin-Kiang, and anchored his boat alongside the *Rinaldo*, but slipped out during the night, and went off in a fast row-boat, to try to get the start of Her Britannic Majesty's Consul and to see Tseng-kwo-Fan [the Viceroy who held his court in Nankin] before him. He had miscalculated however the power of steam. The *Rinaldo* passed his boat about half-way next morning, and left him gesticulating wildly to be taken in tow. He arrived after Mr Medhurst's interview with the Viceroy was over. This occurred on the 11th (September), amid all due state and ceremony. His Excellency showed every disposition to concede the different points asked—the punishment of the instigators, the payment of an indemnity of 2,000 taels by the actual rioters, the release of the lessor of the house, and the engraving on stone of a proclamation declaring that foreigners had a right to live at Yangchow unmolested. Everything promised a speedy

settlement of the affair, when suddenly Captain Bush
withdrew the *Rinaldo*, and left Mr Medhurst to finish
his negotiations in a Chinese house-boat. Relieved from
her presence, the Viceroy retracted everything; abandoned politeness for insolence; became obstinate, instead of yielding; refused to punish anybody or to
remove the magistrates; offered 1,000 taels only as
compensation; and though offering to issue the notifi-
cation, declined to give it the required importance by
engraving it on stone. Her Britannic Majesty's Consul
had, of course, no option but to reject these terms,
withdraw to Shanghai, and place the matter in the
hands of Sir Rutherford Alcock [The British Am-
bassador], where it now rests.

It is time to explain that Captain Bush's departure was
occasioned by illness; but his withdrawal of the *Rinaldo*
was utterly unnecessary . . .

The effect of our temporary defeat is every day apparent. A proclamation posted in Chin-Kiang by order of
the Viceroy, declaring that foreign missionaries had a
right to reside in the interior, and that officals must aid
them in obtaining houses, evoked a counter-proclama-
tion signed 'The People of Chin-Kiang', declaring that
they would burn any house so let, and throw the missionaries and the landlord into the flames; that any official
favouring the lease of a house should have his *ya-men*
burnt down, and that he himself should be similarly
treated. A placard has been posted outside the East Gate
of Shanghai violently abusive of Catholic missionaries;
but at the instance of the French Consul General it has
been torn down, and a proclamation by the Taotai sub-
stituted condemning the terms of the original.

. . . it is believed by all who are familiar with the circumstances and with the country that the . . . procla-
mations are issued by the 'literati' with the connivance
of the Mandarins, and that the mob is only collected at
their instigation . . .

The action taken by the British authorities caused grave concern to Hudson Taylor. He was, of course, grateful for Medhurst's desire to help, but would have preferred to have returned quickly to Yangchow at his own risk to live down unfriendliness and opposition by patiently carrying on his work. In fact, by the time *The Times* report was published, on December 1st 1868, the party had already returned to Yangchow. Medhurst's demands had all been conceded, even to the placing of a stone tablet at the entrance to the mission-house, stating that the foreigners were there with the full recognition of the authorities. Quite a function had been arranged by Chinese neighbours to reinstate the party; and on November 18th Taylor had written from Yangchow that 'the result of the case will probably be greatly to facilitate work in the interior'.

Dr and Mrs Howard Taylor wrote that, 'it was the family life and friendly spirit of the missionaries that disarmed suspicion and gradually won its way among the people. They could not but be touched when the children were brought back after all that had taken place, and when it appeared that Mrs Taylor had not hesitated to return under conditions which made peace and quietness specially desirable.' And when Hudson and Maria's fourth son was born, their Chinese neighbours joined in the congratulations.

The action of the Consular authorities, however, gave rise to a storm of protest at home. On the whole, the account of the affair by the Shanghai correspondent of *The Times* had been accurate and fair; but two days later the editor published a leader highly critical of the CIM.

The Gospel of Peace ought not to be made an occasion of war . . . The Apostles and early missionaries certainly did not propagate their faith under the protection of fleets and armies. They did not bring war in their train . . . When we read that imposing displays of force are made, heavy guns pointed against quiet inland cities, all on behalf of men whose mission is to preach and pray, we may be excused if we feel rather shocked.

In general, the British press misrepresented the situation by implying that Taylor had demanded the support of gunboats. In fact, as Maria Taylor pointed out in a letter written on February 11th 1869, 'Mr Medhurst, and through him Sir Rutherford Alcock, took up the matter without application from us.' She suggested however that it would be undesirable to print this fact, as, 'it would be ungenerous and ungrateful were we to render their position still more difficult by throwing all the onus, as it were, on them'. The only contact which Taylor had had with the British authorities during the riot had been the verbal message on the Saturday and the pencilled note the following morning, referred to above, which simply informed the Consul of the situation. Yet Taylor was accused of bringing the country to the verge of war by his irresponsible conduct.

At home, William Berger, the first home director of the CIM, recorded, '*The Times* is very severe, and incorrect in some things. Whether to reply to the false statements I scarcely know . . . At present the Yangchow outrage is the all-absorbing subject.'

On December 31st, in a letter to Taylor, Berger said, 'I am so unable to say how, or how far, you called upon the Consul in the matter, that I greatly question the wisdom of replying [to the accusations in the press and in correspondence] at all. God is a refuge for us, "A very present help in time of trouble".'

In February (1869), Berger spent a week in Bristol. He told Taylor: 'The sympathy expressed for you and those with you in the late trial was great and very sweet; and none spoke more warmly of you than dear Mr Müller.' Berger asked Müller his opinion respecting the 'appeal' to the British Consul; it is not clear whether he was yet in a position to tell Müller precisely what the circumstances and extent of Taylor's contacts with the Consul had been—certainly he cannot at that time have received Maria's letter of February 11th. At all events Berger was able to tell Taylor in his letter,

> you would have rejoiced to have heard him [Müller] repudiate the spirit of judging you, or of fault-finding. He said he would never have spoken to me on the subject, had I not asked him for his judgment: after which he said that, had poor George Müller been in such circumstances, he cannot tell what he might have done; still he thought the more excellent way would have been to trust in God ... That we must not set up what *we* think the more excellent way, as a rule for others, he quite agreed with me ... Finally, Mr Müller only allowed me, upon my request, to refer to his opinion with the understanding that it was that we might help each other in serving the Lord, and not in any spirit of fault-finding or condemning you.

One result of all the bad publicity was a decline in the Mission's income. Taylor would have been faced with a serious shortage of funds in China were it not for the fact that George Müller began to increase his gifts. He had been sending regularly to several members of the Mission since 1865, and now, within a few days of the Yangchow riot, he wrote to Berger asking for the names of others who were satisfactory in their work whom he might add to his Institution's list. Berger sent him six names from which to choose, and Müller's decision was to support them all. 'This was not only a substantial help,' wrote Taylor's biographers 'it was a great encouragement, for it meant added sympathy and prayer on the part of one who knew the way to the Throne.'

In March the Yangchow incident was debated in the House of Lords. The Duke of Somerset asked what right we had to send inland missions to China. He asserted that the nation was propagating Christianity with gunboats, and demanded that the inland missionaries should be recalled. Anxieties were expressed about the effect of the Yangchow and similar incidents on British trade. The Bishop of Peterborough, however, replied that to the least zealous of missionaries, there was something more sacred than the interests of British trade—namely, 'obedience to the command of his Master to go forth and preach the gospel to every living soul'.

The Lords debated the matter at some length and—at times—with considerable animation; but the Duke of Somerset was, of course, quite unsuccessful in his demand for the recall of missionaries from inland China. Indeed, by August (1869) Yangchow and Chin-Kiang had become virtually the headquarters of the CIM, and the growing church at Yangchow and the demands of the printing-press at Chin-Kiang were imposing an enormous workload on Taylor. There were a number of baptisms at Yangchow that summer.

But at the end of 1869, there is no doubt that the Taylors were feeling the shortage of funds and doing all they could to lessen personal expenses, in order to help their fellow-workers. Taylor wrote, 'More than £1,000 less have been contributed during the first half of this (financial) year than last year. I do not keep a cook now. I find it cheaper to get cooked food brought in from outside at a dollar a head per month.' It seems that Chinese take-away food has always been good value. 'Let us pray in faith for funds,' he continued in this letter to a fellow-worker, 'that we may not have to diminish our work.'

The prayer was answered. The CIM did not have to diminish its work; on New Year's Eve, in the words of Taylor's biographers, 'a beautiful thing happened'. A letter arrived from William Berger.

Mr Müller, after due consideration, has requested the

names of *all* the brethren and sisters connected with
the CIM, as he thinks it well to send help as he is able
to each one, unless we know of anything to hinder . . .
Surely the Lord knew our funds were sinking, and thus
put it into the heart of His honoured servant to help.

Müller's cheques to each of the missionaries arrived by
the same post; and with the cheques a letter, 'for all the
dear brethren and sisters connected with the China Inland
Mission', which read:

My chief object is to tell you that I love you in the
Lord; that I feel deeply interested about the Lord's
work in China, and that I pray daily for you. I thought
it might be a little encouragement to you in your difficulties, trials, hardships and disappointments to hear
of one more who felt for you and who remembered you
before the Lord. But were it otherwise, had you even
no one to care for you, or did you at least seem to be in
a position as if no one cared for you, you will always
have the Lord to be with you. Remember Paul's case at
Rome (2 Tim. 4:16–18). On Him then reckon, to Him
look, on Him depend; and be assured, if you walk with
Him and look to Him, and expect help from Him, He
will never fail you. An older brother who has known
the Lord forty-four years, who writes this, says to you
for your encouragement that He has never failed him.
In the greatest difficulties, in the heaviest trials, in the
deepest poverty and necessities, He has never failed me;
but, because I was enabled by His grace to trust in
Him, He has always appeared for my help. I delight in
speaking well of His Name.

The letter was read by each of the missionaries as they
received their cheques. What a comfort it must have been
to them after all they had been through in the last eighteen
months! Many false rumours and half-truths had been

circulating about Taylor and the CIM during 1869, but it is said that Müller did not believe them. In 1870 he sent Taylor £1,940, and for the next few years approximately £2,000 annually. He was now largely assisting twenty-one missionaries, who with twelve wives constituted the entire staff of the Mission—thirty-three, including Mr and Mrs Taylor. (The figures do not include the children.) The CIM itself (now the *Overseas Missionary Fellowship*) has recently commented that this was 'a massive contribution when one considers the value of money then. In practice Müller almost if not completely supported the entire staff of the Mission in its early days.'

CHAPTER EIGHTEEN

Safe to Glory

Not many days after the opening of No. 5 in January 1870, Mary Müller—now in her seventy-third year—caught a heavy cold which left her with a troublesome cough. Müller persuaded her to see their doctor who insisted that she should now drive (rather than walk) to and from Ashley Down and rest after dinner.

At night Müller would feel her pulse and find it feeble and irregular; but Mary would not agree that much was the matter with her. Towards the end of January the cough eased and she was again able to attend the Sunday morning service at Bethesda. On the evening of the 30th, however, she felt a pain across the lower part of her back and her right arm. On Monday the pain grew worse, but as they were unable to contact the doctor, Mary set off for Ashley Down with Lydia and directed affairs at the Homes more or less as usual. At tea-time she drove back to Paul Street with her sister Miss Groves, and Lydia. Müller went off to the prayer meeting at Salem Chapel. When he arrived home he found that their doctor, Josiah Pritchard, had ordered Mary to bed, to remain there, and to have a fire lit in her bedroom. She had rheumatic fever.

Müller expected the worst. But, he said, 'though my heart was nigh to be broken, on account of the depth of my affection, I said to myself, "The Lord is good, and doeth good; all will be according to His own blessed character. Nothing but that, which is good, like Himself, can proceed from Him. If He pleases to take my wife, it will be good, like Himself. What I have to do, as His child, is to be satisfied with what my Father does that I may glorify Him." '

Next day, on the Tuesday evening, Müller sat alone in his wife's room at No. 3. Mary was at home in bed for the first time in nine years. On the wall was a day-to-day calendar called *The Silent Comforter*; Müller looked at the text for the day; it was from Psalm 119, verse 75, 'I know, O Lord, that Thy judgments are right, and that Thou in faithfulness has afflicted me'. Müller read the words again and again.

'Yes, Lord,' he said to himself, 'Thy judgments are right, I am satisfied with them. Thou knowest the depth of the affection of Thy poor child for his beloved wife, yet I am satisfied with Thy judgments; and my inmost soul says, that Thou in faithfulness has afflicted me. All this is according to that love, with which Thou hast loved me in Christ Jesus, and whatever the issue, all will be well.'

Underneath this text, *The Silent Comforter* had the words 'My times are in Thy hand' (Psalm 31, 15).

'Yes, my Father,' thought Müller, 'the times of my darling wife are in Thy hands. Thou wilt do the very best thing for her and for me, whether life or death. If it may be, raise yet up again my precious wife, Thou art able to do it, though she is so ill; but however Thou dealest with me, only help me to continue to be perfectly satisfied with Thy holy will.'

During that week, the words of the hymn 'One there is above all others', kept coming into Müller's mind:

> Best of blessings He'll provide us,
>   Nought but good shall e'er betide us,
> Safe to glory He will guide us,
>   Oh how he loves!

'My heart,' he said, 'continually responded—"Nought but good shall e'er betide us".' On the Wednesday, Mary was in rather less pain, and before he left Paul Street for Ashley Down, Müller sat on her bed and read a verse from Psalm 84, 'The Lord God is a sun and shield: the Lord will give grace and glory: no good thing will be withheld from them that walk uprightly.' Then he said:

'My darling, we have both received grace, and we shall therefore receive glory; and as, by God's grace, we walk uprightly, nothing that is good for us will He withhold from us.'

Later in the day, Mary told their daughter Lydia the verse which Müller had read and how it had comforted her. And as Müller went about his work on Ashley Down he said to himself again and again, 'I walk uprightly, and therefore my Father will withhold nothing from me, that is good for me; if therefore the restoration of my dearest Mary is good for me, it will be surely given; if otherwise I have to seek to glorify God by most perfect submission to His holy will.'

That evening Dr Pritchard gave Müller instructions that every two hours through the night he was to give his wife a small quantity of beef tea, or a teaspoon full of wine in a tablespoon of water. Each time he did so, he prayed for about a minute with her.

On the Friday evening, Dr Pritchard told Müller that he would feel easier if his colleague Dr Black could see Mrs Müller as the situation was very grave. Müller replied that he was perfectly satisfied with Pritchard's treatment but that if he would feel happier then he must make an appointment.

On the Saturday morning, Müller stayed at home with Mary to be with her as long as possible. After lunch he said:

'My darling, I am sorry to have to leave you, but I shall return as soon as I can.'

'You leave me with Jesus,' was the reply.

That night her pains grew worse than ever before. Müller spent nearly the whole night trying to ease her suffering; Mary was now quite unable to move any of her limbs.

At ten in the morning Dr Pritchard called, followed an hour later by Dr Black, who told Müller that all hope of recovery had gone. After the doctors had left, Müller 'felt it now my duty to tell my precious wife, that the Lord Jesus was coming for her'. Her reply was:

'He will come soon!'

Müller took this to indicate that she believed that He would soon return and that they would then be re-united.

At half-past one, Müller gave her her medicine, and a little later a spoonful of wine in water. Mary had difficulty in swallowing, and a few minutes later her speech became indistinct. She tried to make George understand, but he could not. He sat quietly beside her and noticed 'that her dear bright eyes were set'. He called Lydia and Miss Groves and told them that Mary was dying. At once they came into the room and were joined by another of Mary's sisters. For two and a half hours, the four of them sat and watched the last moments of their loved one, until at twenty-past four, Sunday, February 6th 1870, Mary Müller passed away. Müller fell to his knees and thanked God for her release, and for having taken her to Himself, and asked the Lord to help and support them. She had died in the fortieth year of their marriage.

On February 11th 1870 Müller himself 'sustained by the Lord to the utmost' conducted the funeral service at Bethesda and at the cemetery. About one thousand two hundred children followed in the procession; they were joined by the staff from Ashley Down who could be spared, and hundreds of believers from Bethesda. Before he preached his funeral sermon it is said that Müller sat in the vestry repeating again and again, 'Oh Mary, my Mary!' He took as his text, 'Thou art good, and doest good', from Psalm 119:68. He recalled that his wife had become the first member of Bethesda church when it was formed in August 1832; that she had lived to see two thousand seven hundred believers received into communion; and that when she died there were nine hundred and twenty in communion about one thousand five hundred having either died, left Bristol or joined other churches.

After a detailed outline of her life he said: 'Perhaps all Christians who have heard me, will have no difficulty in giving their hearty assent that "the Lord was good, and doing good" in leaving her to me so long; but I ask these dear Christian friends to go further with me, and to say from their hearts, "The Lord was good, and doing good" in the removal of that useful, lovely, excellent wife from her husband, and that at the very time when, humanly speaking, he needed her more than ever. While I am saying this, I feel the void in my heart. That lovely one is no more with me, to share my joys and sorrows. Every day I miss her more and more. Every day I see more and more how great her loss to the orphans. Yet, without an effort, my inmost soul habitually joys in the joy of that loved departed one. Her happiness gives joy to me. My dear daughter and self would not have her back, were it possible to produce it by the turn of the hand. God himself has done it, we are satisfied with Him . . .'

But, despite these brave words at the funeral, in the months that followed Mary's death, Müller felt the loss deeply. He recorded that 'my earthly joy was all but gone'; and about ten days after the bereavement he became, for a while, very unwell. As he recovered from this illness he found that when 'now between eight and nine o'clock in the evenings, I went home from the Orphan-Houses, instead of in company with my beloved Mary, as for so many years past (for she was always with me), I said to myself: "I shall not meet my beloved wife at home, but I shall meet the Lord Jesus, my precious Friend; He will comfort me"; and I thanked God, that he had left my beloved daughter to me, who always watched

for my arrival, to greet me, and did all she could, to soothe
my bereaved heart. But the loss was great, the wound
was deep, and, as weeks and months passed on, while
continuing habitually not only to be satisfied with God,
but also to praise Him, for what He had done in thus
bereaving me, the wound seemed to deepen instead of
being healed, and the bereavement to be felt more and
more . . .'

The loss was felt too by the children and old boys and
girls who had passed through the homes; Müller received
hundreds of letters of sympathy, even months after the
event. One such, from one of the first Wilson Street children, arrived on March 19th:

Dear Mr Müller, Not from ingratitude is it, I have not
written before, but because I knew you had so many
letters; but not a particle do I love dear Mrs Müller
less, than those who have written. I think I loved her
with you as my parents. True I never knew my parents,
to know what it was to love them; but I do know what
it is to love you and her, and from my heart I mourn
her loss. I know you miss her daily. I miss her going by the
House; for I always watched you go by; but now you are
alone. I trust it may please God to spare you, for years to
come, to us all, as well as to your own dear child and
family; for oh! it would be a blank, indeed, were you
removed from us. I remain yours very respectfully,

The writer of this letter was not alone in her anxiety as
to what would happen if Müller were taken.

'What, Mr Müller, will become of the Orphan-Houses,
when you are removed?' people sometimes asked.

'The Orphan-Houses,' Müller would reply, 'and the
land belonging to them, are vested in the hands of eleven
trustees, and therefore the Institution stands on the
same footing, in this particular, as other charitable
Institutions.'

'But where will you find the man, who will carry on the work in the same spirit in which you do, trusting only in God for everything that in any way is needed in connection with the work?'

'When the Lord shall have been pleased to remove me from my post, He will prove, that He was not dependent on me, and that He can easily raise up another servant of His, to act on the same principles, on which I have sought to carry on this work.'

People then told Müller that he ought to pray that God would raise up a successor to carry on the work after him, to which he always replied that he did so regularly.

It was during the period of his illness shortly after Mary's death that Müller sent for James Wright. Since Wright's boyhood, Müller had watched his 'consistent godly deportment', and for nearly twelve years he had been one of Müller's most valuable helpers in all aspects of the work of the Scriptural Knowledge Institution, including, of course, the children's work. For some years, George and Mary had prayed specifically that God would fit him to become the successor.

Now in his illness, Müller opened his heart to James Wright and announced to him that he considered it God's will that he should succeed him. Wright produced a number of reasons why he considered himself unfit for the job, none of which Müller would accept as being valid. Wright's wife felt that her husband would find the task a great burden and tried to persuade him not to accept; after some weeks, however, she changed her mind. After much hesitation Wright decided that it would not be his duty to refuse any longer. If Müller were taken, James Wright would be his successor. Very shortly after this, Wright's wife died, and thus within a few months of each other Müller and Wright sustained a similar bereavement.

It was said of Wright that his 'beautiful face and radiant smile showed, better than any words possibly could, that peace and joy ruled his heart. His dignified yet gracious demeanour at once won the respect of all. Of his faith and love his works bear witness, but it may be added that his humility was equally apparent to an observing mind.'

Wright was very fond of music and for many years his beautiful bass voice led the singing at Bethesda. He loved to join a group gathered around a piano or organ and sing hymns from the *Bristol Tune Book*.

Eighteen months later, in August 1871, Müller recorded in his journal that James Wright 'asked for the hand of my beloved daughter. This request was as unlooked for on my part as anything could have been, while, at the same time, I knew no one, to whom I could so willingly entrust this my choicest earthly treasure.' A little later he recorded:

My beloved daughter had the greatest conflict in her mind for about two weeks, before she accepted this offer, her only and great difficulty being because of having to leave me. It was only on beseeching her, not to let this stand in the way, and pointing out to her, how great my comfort and joy would be in seeing her united to such a husband, that she at last decided to accept the offer.

They were married at Bethesda on November 16th 1871: Wright was forty-five and Lydia thirty-nine. Wright later described their life together as a time of 'unbroken felicity'.

Bethesda was soon to see another wedding.

CHAPTER NINETEEN

Return to the Rigi

Nearly two years after Mary's death, Lydia's engagement, amongst other things, finally led Müller to the decision to marry again—a decision reached, he said, 'in the fear of God, and in the full assurance that I had the sanction and approval of my Heavenly Father'. He recorded that he had known Miss Susannah Grace Sangar for 'more than twenty-five years as a consistent Christian, and regarding whom I had every reason to believe that she would prove a great helper to me in my various services'. They were married on November 30th.

For the next two years or so Susannah Müller learned more and more about the work and sought to relieve her husband of as much as she could. And then, in March 1874, she developed a heavy fever: it was typhoid. At first it seemed that the attack was not unduly serious.

On Thursday, March 26th [Müller recorded], I left my dear wife for the Orphan-Houses better than she had been for several days; more quiet, less under the power of the fever apparently, and having had a better night than several nights before. My dear daughter, Mrs Wright, took my place in the house, in case anything should need direction, during my absence. At half-past one, p.m., my dear daughter came to the Orphan-Houses, to fetch me, as my dear wife had had a haemorrhage. I hastened home and found that she had had the most fearful loss of blood. Dr Williams had been sent for, and soon was on the spot. My dear wife looked as pale as death, and the perspiration of death was on her brow; but by the means used, after a while seemed brought back again to life. But now as to my feelings, when I came home and saw the death-like countenance of my dear wife. There was naturally everything to make one excited to the utmost, yea, to be over-whelmed; because there seemed nothing but death to be expected within a few hours. My soul, however, by the grace of God, was calm and in perfect peace. I was enabled, through my knowledge of God, to take this cup out of the hands of my Heavenly Father, as the best thing for me under the circumstances. I delighted myself in God. I was satisfied with His dealings with me, being assured that much good would come out of this to me.

On Sunday, April 5th, Susannah became delirious; the fever was at its peak. In the evening Dr Williams consul-ted Dr Black whose judgment was that Mrs Müller might recover if she could have some sleep; but for more than thirty hours she had not shut her eyes for a moment. A third nurse was sent for so that one of the other two could get some rest. 'This was the second time, when my dear wife seemed on the very brink of the grave. I did what I could in seeing that all medical directions to the utmost were carried out; but my hope was in God alone. I knew Him, and I knew He would do what would be best for me. My heart was satisfied with Him. I delighted myself in Him.' By that time, Mrs Müller's condition was known in many parts of the world. Thousands of prayers were offered up on her behalf.

That night the crisis came and passed. She slept for five hours and through most of Monday. From that day very slight signs of improvement were seen. But still, Susannah's pulse was about 120 and very weak. On April 17th Müller recorded:

I was told, that one of the most eminent and most experienced London physicians had stated that he had never known a patient to recover after such an haemorrhage as my dear wife had had. [He wrote:] For the third time now my inmost soul sought to be satisfied with God, to delight myself in God, to kiss the hand which smote me; and, by His grace, I did so . . . I know what a lovely, gracious, bountiful Being God is, from the revelation which He has been pleased to make of Himself in His holy Word; I believe this revelation; I also know from my own experience the truth of it; and therefore I was satisfied with God, I delighted myself in God; and so it came, that He gave me the desire of my heart, even the restoration of my dear wife.

By the beginning of May Mrs Müller was well enough to be wheeled in an easy chair out of her bedroom to a sitting-room to be on a sofa, first for two hours a day, then for three or four hours, then six and eight hours until on May 11th she was strong enough to be taken out in a carriage for an hour.

By the end of May the couple were able to travel to Burnham, Somerset, so that Susannah might enjoy the benefit of sea air. And then, in September, they journeyed to Ventnor, on the Isle of Wight, for a stay of two months. There, on the Island, Mrs Müller's health was completely restored.

Since coming to Bristol in 1832 Müller had preached almost exclusively in that city, but it often occurred to him that it might be God's will for him to preach and teach further afield. However his position as pastor of the large church at Bethesda, and as director of the Scriptural Knowledge Institution had tied him to Bristol. But the situation at Bethesda was changing: there were numbers of gifted and experienced brethren who could shoulder the responsibilities. And James Wright had already proved himself to be an able co-director of the work on

Ashley Down and of the Institution generally. Thus after a good deal of prayer and waiting upon God, Müller decided to devote his closing years to a world-wide ministry of preaching and teaching as long as his health and strength permitted.

He was convinced that there were many people who were perfectly genuine in their desire to be right with God, but who lacked peace, because they relied upon their feelings. After more than half a century of daily, systematic and consecutive study of the Bible, Müller would now aim to share with a wider audience the truths that he had discovered, and to encourage Christians to become lovers of the Bible themselves; and to test everything by the word of God.

Another of Müller's aims in embarking on his preaching tours would be (in the true spirit of Groves and the early Brethren) to break down the barriers of denominationalism and to promote, as he put it, 'brotherly love amongst true Christians'.

> Though not agreeing at all, with some of their opinions and practices, I nevertheless preach amongst all, having seen for many years how greatly the heart of the Lord Jesus must be grieved by the dis-union that exists among His own true disciples. On this account, therefore, I have sought (in my feeble measure) to unite all real believers; but, as this cannot be done, by standing aloof from our brethren in Christ, until they see eye to eye with us, in every point, I have gone amongst them, and have united with them, in so far as nothing has been required of me which I could not do with a good conscience.

Susannah Müller loved travel and would make an ideal companion on Müller's tours. Her husband's health was still good and he was an excellent traveller; but it would have been impossible for him to complete the arduous

programme of world-wide engagements which would
occupy the next seventeen years without Susannah at his
side to act as nurse-cum-secretary. She would ensure, too,
that the tours would not be all work and no play: for, no
doubt partly due to her influence, the couple took some
time off from George's numerous engagements to visit
the tourist attractions, and places of historic interest, in
most of the countries they visited.

Their first tour—not leaving English shores—was a
short one in the spring and early summer of 1875. Müller
was in his seventieth year and Susannah about fifty.
Spurgeon asked Müller to preach for him, and, in the
famous Metropolitan Tabernacle, Müller addressed a
large congregation. In June he held eighteen meetings in
Newcastle, before returning to London to speak, at last,
at the Mildmay Park Conference. This was the inter-
denominational, evangelical 'Keswick' of its day (the
Keswick Convention itself had just begun), and the con-
veners had again and again invited Müller to speak but
he had been unable to accept until then. He spoke three
times to about three thousand people.

Gavin Kirkham, himself a gifted evangelist, and first
secretary of the Open-Air mission, wrote at the time:

> Mr Müller's appearance is striking; he is tall and com-
> manding. He is in his seventieth year. He has a strong
> German accent, though he is easily understood by any
> English hearer. In his public ministry, he is em-
> phatically a *teacher*, yet he frequently brings in the way
> of salvation, in a clear, sweet, persuasive manner.
> Preachers may learn from his *method* of preaching. He
> first of all gets a message from the Lord: that is he
> waits upon the Lord, by reading the Scriptures, medi-
> tation and prayer, till he realises that he has the mind
> of the Spirit as to what he shall say. He has sometimes
> been in doubt till almost the last minute, but never
> once has the Lord failed him. He strongly advocates

and practises expository preaching. Instead of a solitary
text detached from its context, he selects a passage, it
may be of several verses, which he goes over con-
secutively, clause by clause. His first care is to give the
meaning of the passage, and then to illustrate it by other
Scriptures, and afterwards apply it.

This is done sentence by sentence, so that it is defini-
tion, illustration, and application all the way through.
Yet there is no uncertainty to his hearers as to when he
is coming to a close, as he intimates at the outset how
many verses he purposes to consider. His illustrations
are occasionally taken from history, biography, or
nature, but chiefly from the Scriptures or his own personal experience.

One of the most striking things about Mr Müller's
preaching is the way in which he induces his hearers to
reconsider what has already been said. He frequently
says: 'Let us ask ourselves, Have I understood this?
How does it apply to *me*? Is this *my* experience?'

The first tour was a relatively short one, with Müller
preaching some seventy times in public; but one thing
was obvious: wherever he went in the years that lay ahead,
he would be assured of eager and attentive audiences.

In August 1875 Moody and Sankey arrived back in
New York after a campaign in Britain which had made
them famous. Moody had described Müller as one of
three men in England he longed to meet; he had duly
visited Bristol, in his biographer's words, 'to imbibe a
heady draught of Müller's faith'.

On the day that Moody and Sankey returned to New
York, Mr and Mrs Müller set off on their second tour of
Britain which would last until July 1876. Müller described his particular aim as being to 'help forward the
work of the devoted brethren, Moody and Sankey . . .
These dear brethren, from having been able to stay on a
comparatively short time in each place, were unable to

lead on the young converts in knowledge and grace; I therefore sought to follow up their labours, and, in my feeble measure, to do what I could to supply this lack of service.' He was particularly anxious to instruct young converts and therefore held fourteen meetings at the Mildmay Park Conference Hall in London: often speaking to three thousand people at once.

They then travelled to Scotland where he preached at a Convention in Glasgow to five thousand people on the power of the Spirit. Even then not all who came could get in to the hall, and Müller accepted an invitation to speak to an overflow meeting of about one thousand two hundred in a neighbouring church. During thirty days in Glasgow he preached thirty-eight times, and every Sunday evening for five weeks addressed three thousand people in the Prince of Wales Theatre.

Then, after spending three weeks in Dublin and preaching twenty-one times including a number of addresses to a packed Merrion Hall, the Müllers travelled to Liverpool. There Müller was invited to preach at the immense Victoria Hall which had been built for Moody and Sankey.

In this vast audience [wrote W. H. Harding] sits a bronzed, weather-beaten man, now the captain of a merchant vessel, who in other days was an inmate of the Orphan-House. How can such a man, still unconverted, sit in peace while this old benefactor, grey and obviously ageing, delivers once again, as in the long ago, the blessed message of eternal life? The scarred captain listens, weeps, apprehends spiritually the motive of Müller's life, and steers straight for the haven of soul rest.

This conversion, of a former Ashley Down boy, on his first evening at Liverpool was an enormous encouragement to Müller. He stayed on to preach over fifty times; on Sundays to between five and six thousand and on week-days to from two thousand to two thousand five hundred. Then the Müllers travelled on to Kendal and Edinburgh (fifty-three meetings), Arbroath, Montrose and Aberdeen where Müller spoke to numbers of ministers and theological students. Susannah recorded that while staying at the village of Crathie 'we became acquainted with a Christian housekeeper living at Balmoral Castle, who kindly conducted us one afternoon through the Queen's residence in Scotland; and, a short time before we left Crathie, Her Majesty arrived at the Castle, whom we saw driving out occasionally, accompanied by the Princess Beatrice'.

The third tour was of Europe, and the Müllers spent the last two weeks of August 1876 in Paris.

In September they arrived in Berne where Müller preached in German for the first time in thirty-one years. On the following Sunday afternoon he preached in a large hall known as the *Festhutte* to an audience of nearly two thousand pastors, young men, Sunday School teachers, country women in Swiss costumes and children. The following afternoon they went to *Die Enge*, a hall on the side of a steep hill outside Berne, where about a hundred and fifty brethren and sisters had been invited by Colonel von Büren to meet them. They were given a hearty welcome to Switzerland, and drank coffee looking across to the distant Alps, whose snow-covered peaks appeared rose coloured in the light of a setting sun.

'*Le bon Dieu l'a fait exprès pour vous donner plaisir,*' said someone, and there was general agreement.

An intensive programme of meetings lay ahead of the Müllers in Switzerland, but before embarking on this they took the opportunity for a few days' relaxation. Boarding a steamer at Lucerne they crossed the lake to Vitznau at the foot of the Rigi. More than half a century had passed since Müller had last seen the mountain. How much had happened since he had climbed to the summit

with Beta and his other student friends in that summer of
1825! Fortunately, in the intervening years, someone had
built a cog-wheel railway, and George and Susannah
travelled to the summit in relative comfort. But the view
across the Bernese Oberland to Geneva in the south and
up to the Black Forest in the north had not changed.

It was bitterly cold and as snow began to fall the couple
were glad to find shelter in a hotel beneath the summit.

At half-past four the next morning [wrote Mrs Müller]
we rose and ascended the Rigi Kulm, whence splendid
ranges of innumerable snowy mountain peaks and distant glaciers could be seen extending far and wide, to
which, illuminated as they were by the bright beams of
the rising sun, a gorgeous prismatic colouring was
imparted; and there we stood for a considerable time,
gazing round upon that grand, wild, solitary, silent
region with an interest that could scarcely be exceeded.

Their next excursion was to the Hospice, at the top of
the St Gothard Pass, nine thousand feet above sea level
and enveloped in a dense fog. Once again the cold was
intense; and the former governess from Clifton and her
husband were 'thankful to accept the very poor accommodation afforded at the Hospice, and, in spite of the
smoke from the cigars of some Italians that filled the only
room with a fire in it which the house contained, were
glad to be allowed to share it with them, and with any
other travellers who happened to come in'.

This pleasant, if chilly, break lasted for almost a week,
but on the 17th Müller was at Zürich to fulfil the engagements he had made there. On the Sunday he preached
twice at the Anna Capelle to large congregations overflowing into the staircases and doorways. For the next
month, meeting followed meeting, until the Müllers
arrived at Constance where they took the opportunity to
visit the Council Chamber in the Merchants' Hall, where

John Huss had been tried and sentenced to be burned at the stake. Then, at Schaffhausen after visiting the Rhine Falls, Müller preached to about three thousand people in the immense Johannes Kirche: he preached four more times in the same church 'with great help from the Lord'. At Basle, he addressed theological students at the university and spoke for an hour and a quarter to missionary students and their lecturers.

Then to Germany for crowded meetings at many towns including Strasburg, Stuttgart, Frankfurt, Bonn (with theological students at the university), Cologne, Düsseldorf and Essen. While at Stuttgart Müller was sent for by the Queen of Württemberg, and at the palace answered a number of questions from Her Majesty about the orphan work in Bristol. At Darmstadt he held a drawing-room meeting at the house of the Court preacher giving (by special request) an account of his life and work. Four drawing-rooms were thrown open, and Princess Karl (mother of Prince Louis. of Hesse, husband of Princess Alice of England), Princess von Battenberg, and several people connected with the court were present. The two Princesses shook the Müllers warmly by the hand and expressed great interest in the work on Ashley Down. At Düsseldorf, the City Missioner approached Müller in some distress. He had six sons, for whose conversion he had been praying for many years. 'Tell me what I should do?' he asked Müller.

'*Continue* to pray for your sons,' Müller replied, 'and *expect* an answer to your prayer, and you will have to praise God.'

By now, spring (1877) had arrived and Mr and Mrs Müller visited the Wartburg Castel near Halle where Luther had been imprisoned in 1521. They saw the sitting-room where the reformer had translated the Bible into German, his bed and other relics. At Halle, too, Müller preached at Francke's Orphanage, the institution which had been such an inspiration to him in the early days at Bristol. Müller was also delighted to find that his old tutor, Professor Tholuck was still alive and now Counsellor of the Upper Consistorium of Prussia. The two men had a joyful reunion and a long conversation.

On the way to Berlin, at Wittenberg, they saw the church on whose door in 1517 Luther had nailed his ninety-five theses against indulgences; and at an old monastery were shown the room where he had lived as an Augustinian monk. They also visited an oak which marks the spot where Luther had burned the papal bulls.

For over three weeks, at Berlin, Müller preached nearly every evening to large congregations. On April 7th, Count Bismarck (a cousin of the famous Prince), came one hundred and twenty-five miles on purpose to see and hear the man whose Narratives, he said, 'had been a great blessing to his soul'.

In May the couple visited an Orphan-House for four hundred and fifty children, seven miles from Nimegen, Holland, which had been established as a direct result of the Ashley Down example, and was carried on according to the same principles. Müller spoke to the children, with translation into Dutch—this being one of the few European languages in which he was not fluent. After conducting meetings in most towns in Holland, Müller ended his European tour having preached over three hundred times. While he was at Amsterdam, a letter had arrived from the United States, signed by the Rev. E. P. Thwing and four other pastors begging him to come to America and preach.

This invitation was the most recent of many which Müller had received over the years to visit the United States. At last, he felt able to accept.

CHAPTER TWENTY

To the White House

After spending a few weeks on Ashley Down, the Müllers set off for the United States in August 1877 aboard the *Sardinian*. They had been allocated the chief officer's deck room, for their cabin, which Mrs Müller found to be 'tolerably comfortable'.

Off Newfoundland the weather turned cold and the ship's progress was seriously retarded by fog. The captain had been on the bridge for twenty-four hours when something happened which was to revolutionise his life. George Müller appeared on the bridge.

'Captain, I have come to tell you I must be in Quebec by Saturday afternoon.'

'It is impossible,' said the captain.

'Very well,' said Müller, 'if your ship cannot take me, God will find some other way—I have never broken an engagement for fifty-two years. Let us go down into the chart-room and pray.'

The captain wondered which lunatic asylum Müller had come from.

'Mr Müller,' he said, 'do you know how dense this fog is?'

'No, my eye is not on the density of the fog, but on the living God, who controls every circumstance of my life.'

Müller then knelt down and prayed simply. When he had finished the captain was about to pray, but Müller put his hand on his shoulder, and told him not to:

'First, you do not believe He will; and second, I believe he has, and there is no need whatever for you to pray about it.'

The captain looked at Müller in amazement.

'Captain,' he continued, 'I have known my Lord for fifty-two years, and there has never been a single day that I have failed to get an audience with the King. Get up, captain, and open the door, and you will find the fog is gone.'

The captain walked across to the door and opened it. The fog had lifted. It was the captain himself, who later told the story of this incident, and who was subsequently described by a well-known evangelist as 'one of the most devoted men I ever knew'.

'Land!' cried some of the passengers, and Belle Island was seen to starboard, only a short distance from the ship. That evening Müller held meetings in the forecastle and chart room.

On the Saturday, as they drew near Quebec, the *Sardinian* fired her guns as a signal of her approach. The voyage had lasted nine days. At the Hotel St Louis, a number of letters were awaiting the Müllers, welcoming them to America, and numerous invitations for George to preach. Before travelling south to New York, they found time to visit Niagara.

The couple were rather disappointed by their first distant view of the Niagara Falls. After driving to a bridge just above the American Falls, they made a partial circuit of Boat Island on foot. Then, climbing a staircase to Luna Island, and standing by a railing close to the edge of the precipice they began to appreciate the size and grandeur of the American Falls.

'This,' they thought, 'surpasses everything; surely this must be the grandest cataract in the world!'

But it was not; a few more steps brought them into full view of the great Horse Shoe Fall, on the Canadian side of the river, gushing (every hour) its one thousand five hundred million cubic feet of water over the cliffs to form a huge, boiling cauldron at the bottom. And then their attention was attracted to the Rapids where the Niagara descends 'over rough ridges of rock, great masses of stone and large boulders', and where, observed Mrs Müller, 'its waters surge and foam, in ten thousand fantastic shapes, and in the wildest turmoil, as though frantically eager to rush over the precipices into the abyss below'.

After spending the night at the Clifton Hotel, they left the following afternoon for New York travelling all night in a Pullman sleeping-car. They were taken to Pierpoint House in Brooklyn where they were to spend the next six weeks. On Sunday morning, September 9th, at Dr Talmage's Tabernacle—said, at that time, to be the largest church in the United States—Müller was introduced to the congregation by Professor Thwing who had been responsible for inviting him over. Pausing in the course of a short speech, he shook hands warmly with Müller and welcomed him to the States. Müller then preached for three-quarters of an hour, and again in the evening. After the evening meeting, one of those who pressed forward to greet the Müllers was a former Ashley Down girl, now married and settled in America.

Müller preached about fifty times in the Brooklyn and New York area, including a number of times in German to the large German population. They then travelled to Boston where Müller's first engagement was at Moody's Tabernacle—an enormous building holding seven thousand people.

On November 4th Müller preached twice at the Old Presbyterian Church Newburyport, founded by George Whitefield. Müller caused a stir by reading from the Bible which had belonged to the great man; the book was not normally used. He occupied the pulpit which stands just above the spot where Whitefield's remains are buried.

At Philadelphia his engagements included addressing five hundred ministers and pastors from various denominations who had assembled to hear him. He spoke for an hour and twenty minutes on fifteen aspects of service for the Lord. After the meeting, a large number of men pressed around Müller, expressing their thanks and inviting him to preach in their churches. Müller considered this occasion 'one of the most precious opportunities of witnessing for Christ ever afforded to him in his whole life'. On December 14th Müller preached on Psalm 103 at a packed All Saints Episcopal Church. Mrs Müller commented that 'no clerical gown was put on, and a *few collects only* were read by the minister at the commencement of the service'.

From Philadelphia to Baltimore where Müller preached night after night to immense audiences: at the large Methodist Episcopal Church every available square inch including the aisles was taken up with people; and at the First Presbyterian Church many had to stand and others were turned away for lack of room.

Outside Washington, at Wayland Seminary, Müller addressed about a hundred coloured missionary students and he and Susannah were thrilled to hear them sing.

'God sent you to America, dear Brother!' a pastor said to Müller after he had preached at Dr Mitchell's Church in Washington. 'That's just the kind of teaching we want; something that will rouse and wake up Christians as well as the unconverted. God sent you to America, Sir; of that I am certain.'

On the morning of January 10th, at half-past nine, the Müllers had a very special appointment. They had been invited to the White House to meet the President and Mrs Hayes. 'They received us with much courtesy,' said Mrs Müller, 'and, after making some enquiries about our work in England, the President entered for half an hour into conversation with Mr Müller. Mrs Hayes afterwards conducted us through the White House, a large old mansion, and showed us the State apartments, with the various objects of interest which this residence contains.'

Müller had a gruelling three weeks in Washington, often preaching twice a day, but they found time to climb the four hundred feet to the top of the dome on the Capitol building, and to admire the view.

From Washington they travelled up to Salem in the Alleghany Mountains, where Müller preached twice at the Lutheran Church to crowded congregations. On the first evening Mrs Müller described the audience as consisting of 'pastors, theological students, ladies, country people, Negroes, children, the visitors from the Duval Hotel—where we were staying—its three proprietors, the servants (one woman only being left at home); and', she continued, 'an elderly Welsh minister from Merthyr Tydfil, for thirty years a resident in the United States, walked seven miles from the country to be present at the meeting'.

By the second evening Müller's fame seems to have spread even further afield.

Hundreds of young men were present, most of them students from Roanoke College and the Theological Seminary, many of whom were standing at the entrance closely packed together; whilst others sat upon the pulpit side by side. The gallery was thronged. At the back of it several young men were standing upon forms, with their heads near the ceiling, and upon the edge of the front seats in the gallery a few boys were perched, with their legs hanging over the pews, in a somewhat dangerous position.

It is perhaps surprising that there were no serious accidents, for Müller spoke for an hour and thirty-five minutes, having been particularly asked to give an account of his life and work.

The next journey took them four hundred miles to Columbia in South Carolina, where they stayed with Chief Justice Willard. Mr Willard took them to the State House and introduced them to the Governor, the Secretary of State for South Carolina and other government officers. Müller was asked to open the day's deliberations at the House of Representatives with prayer, an invitation which he accepted.

After a number of engagements at Columbia, they moved on to Charleston where heavy rain kept congregations small at first. But on the evening of Sunday, February 10th, most of the churches in the town were closed to enable their ministers and congregations to hear Müller preach at the large Citadel Baptist Church. Two days later, at the Centenary Church, 'an immense congregation of Negroes and coloured persons assembled, many of whom stood in the aisles and outside the doors, whilst numbers were unable to get in'.

On next to Savannah, amidst its luxuriant plantations of orange and lemon trees, where the Müllers were lavishly entertained at the mansion of a Christian merchant.

At the end of February the Müllers boarded the river steamer *City of Bridgetown* for a tedious journey down the river Savannah to Jacksonville. Here, at the Polk's Hall a vast audience assembled to hear Müller; it was said to be the largest congregation ever known in Jacksonville.

More meetings followed in Montgomery and New Orleans before, at the end of March, the intrepid pair boarded the *John Scudder* for the long voyage up the Mississippi to Memphis. Although the food provided on board was excellent, they were disturbed to find that no drinking water was available, except the unfiltered water of the Mississippi. This was so full of impurities and muddy sediment, which formed a thick deposit in the bottom of any vessel into which it was poured, that poor Mr and Mrs Müller could not make up their minds whether to drink it cold, or in the form of tea or coffee; it was said, in any case, to be bad for the health. They eventually hit upon the expedient of procuring a jug filled with ice, allowing the ice to melt, and then mixing a little wine with the water to take off the chill, thus making a palatable draught. After just over five days, the *John Scudder* tied up at Memphis after a voyage of about eight hundred miles.

Their next destination was St Louis, Missouri, where Müller began a busy schedule of meetings for ten days. These included an address to at least two thousand five hundred people in the largest church in the city, Centenary Methodist Episcopal Church.

On April 18th the Müllers rose at half-past five, and set off on the long journey to San Francisco, nearly two thousand four hundred miles from St Louis. They travelled in the reserved compartment of a Pullman carriage, which even Mrs Müller conceded was comfortable with excellent sleeping arrangements. The following morning they pulled into Council Bluffs for breakfast, after which they were surrounded by a large number of emigrants to California, amongst whom the Müllers promptly distributed tracts. After Omaha, Nebraska, their journey now took them through the prairies, and for a while Mrs Müller could not understand why the train proceeded at a mere fifteen miles an hour. At last she realised (or perhaps George told her) that they were gradually climbing thousands of feet above sea level: indeed, so long and so steep was the climb that the engine broke down and the passengers were able to get out to view the immense plains surrounding them. The evangelist and his wife grasped this as another opportunity to distribute tracts to their fellow travellers. Once the engine had been partially repaired, the journey continued still upwards—at reduced power and pace—until they could see large patches of snow on the ground. And then, just before Archer, they caught their first glimpse of the Rocky Mountains. On they crawled through Cheyenne and in the night to Sherman the highest railway station in the world, where the cold was intense and the snow deep.

At Ogden, where the Union Pacific ended and the

Central Pacific began, the only private compartment in the next train had been engaged and the couple had to make do with a 'section' of a carriage. On arrival at Wells, they saw groups of Indians wrapped in scarlet blankets and striped woollen mantles dyed with brilliant colours; and (before the day of televised 'westerns'), Mrs Müller was intrigued by their 'curious-looking hats, trimmed with feathers and wide ribbons', and noticed that they 'had their faces painted with patches of vermilion'.

'At some of the stations,' she recorded, 'a few Chinese also were standing about, with their hair plaited in long tails, reaching nearly to the heels. At Bewawe and Battle Mountain there were more Indians, and towards evening we reached Winnemucca, where several copper-coloured men and women gathered round the train.'

As dawn broke on the morning of April 23rd they had their first sight of California; at six o'clock they reached Summit Station, over seven thousand feet above sea level.

Here a magnificent prospect of indescribable grandeur suddenly burst upon our view. Far above the station innumerable mountain peaks were towering towards the sky; the sun, which shone brilliantly, lighted up the snow to a whiteness that was dazzling; deep abysses, chasms and ravines surrounded us; millions of pine and fir-trees were growing up the mountains' sides; and thousands of feet far down below, valleys clothed with the richest verdure, added beauty to the scene.

At eight o'clock the door of the compartment was thrown open.

'Cape Horn!' shouted the conductor.

All the passengers jumped up and looked out of the windows. The train was travelling slowly along the edge of a precipice nearly two thousand five hundred feet high: this was 'Cape Horn'.

Then, through 'Emigrant's Gap' they began to descend further into California. The weather grew warmer and Mrs Müller observed that 'the fields were covered with grass, intermingled with brilliant masses of wild flowers; lupins, eschscholtzias, wild roses, geraniums, etc. were flourishing . . . and millions of Californian poppies of an intense yellow, deepening into orange colour, outshone all the rest'.

'I never saw flowers till I saw them in California,' commented an American.

On they travelled, through Sacramento and San José until they arrived at Oakland station, a suburb of San Francisco. Here two friends were waiting to greet them, and took them on board the *El Capitan* which ferried them across San Francisco Bay to the magnificent city itself. They were then escorted to the Palace Hotel and shown the suite of rooms which, as Mrs Müller—feeling rather guilty perhaps—was quick to point out, their friends had engaged for them. The journey from St Louis had taken six days.

On their first Sunday in California, Müller addressed two thousand people at the Tabernacle Presbyterian Church in Tyler Street.

The following Tuesday a friend called in his carriage and took them on a drive to see the sights. They walked along the beach and felt the Pacific breeze against their faces.

After walking some time upon the sands [Mrs Müller recorded] our friend conducted us to Cliff House, an hotel built upon a high rock overlooking the ocean, where, from a balcony, we had an opportunity of observing the sea-lions, by which the rocks that stand out in the sea are frequented. Hundreds of these curious, amphibious creatures were there, with their pointed heads, and bodies shining with salt water. Some were basking in the sunshine on dry portions of

the cliffs, others were plunging into the sea, several
were climbing up sloping places on the rocks, and
others were barking discordantly. Soon after our arrival
at Cliff House, a young waiter introduced himself as
the brother of Emma Evans, one of the orphans
formerly at Ashley Down. He knew we were in the
United States, and having often heard Mr Müller
preach in Bristol years ago, recognised him with great
delight, and before our departure presented us with a
beautiful bouquet of flowers, as a little token of his
gratitude.

On May Day they visited China Town, Sacramento,
where Mrs Müller noticed that the ground floors of many
of the houses inhabited by Chinese 'contain shops filled
with curious and costly articles, manufactured by the
natives of China and Japan; but most of the Chinese live
down in places like cellars underneath their shops, where
they dwell crowded together, smoking and eating quantities of opium'.

Next Sunday evening Müller preached at the large
Calvary Presbyterian Church. The building including the
galleries was packed; several people sat on the platform
and the steps leading up to it were fully occupied.
Numbers who could not gain admittance went away, and
it was said that Müller's 'appeal to believers, and words
of warning to the unconverted, were of a weighty, solemn
character'. Müller addressed a meeting of Californian
pastors for an hour and twenty minutes, some of whom
had come fifty miles to hear him.

On then to Oakland, where all principal churches were
closed so that congregations and ministers could hear
Müller preach at the First Presbyterian Church.
Hundreds were unable to gain admittance and missed the
opportunity to hear Müller speak for an hour from
Lamentations 3 : 22–26. 'We have had a glorious meeting,'
a pastor told Müller at the close of the service. After a

series of meetings at Santa Cruz, they found time to visit California's famous 'Big Trees'.

More crowded meetings followed at San José; and an encouraging letter arrived from San Francisco. It was from a woman whose daughter had been converted at fifteen, but two years later had become tied up with spiritism to which she had remained attracted for nine years. At San Francisco, however, she heard Müller preach several times and was profoundly impressed by one particular sermon. 'You are the first person who has found the way to her heart for these nine years,' the woman wrote to Müller. '. . . she says she would not have lost that sermon for a hundred dollars.'

Numbers of friends repeatedly advised the Müllers not to leave California without making the trip to the celebrated Yosemite Valley; and after constant preaching at San José and Stockton Müller needed a break. They therefore decided to accept the suggestion, and never forgot their experience.

Though often told that travelling by Californian stage-waggon would prove an adventure never to be forgotten, scarcely were we prepared for the unpleasant jolting that now awaited us. Our coachman drove furiously. Rough and smooth, hill and dale, all were alike to him. Now we were driven over one great stone, and then came into collision with another; and as for a drag, going down hill, such a thing was never thought of. The man was doubtless an experienced driver, or at any rate he was a fearless one; but, being ourselves soberminded persons, unaccustomed to such 'go ahead' proceedings, we should have been thankful to take things more quietly; and besides this, desired greatly to reach our journey's end, with no bruises and without broken bones. Through the Lord's kindness, however, we reached Priest's Hotel in safety, where we alighted for the night; and after a journey of eleven hours and a half, retired immediately to rest.

After three days in the Yosemite Valley they rose at half-past four to set off for the return journey with ten other passengers in a stage-waggon drawn by five horses. At four in the afternoon a cart approached carrying a man and woman who drew up on one side of the road to let the larger carriage pass. Suddenly the woman jumped to her feet.

'Is that George Müller?'

'It is.'

'Then I must shake hands with you, sir. I have read your *Life of Trust*, and it has been a great blessing to my soul.'

Mr and Mrs Müller obliged by leaning out of the window to shake hands with the woman and her husband.

'Pray for me!' shouted the woman as the journey continued.

After a series of meetings in Sacramento, they set off on the Central Pacific Railway for Salt Lake City. Here, at the great stronghold of Mormonism, Müller preached the gospel in the 'plainest, clearest, most decided manner'. Lion House, the former home of Brigham Young, was pointed out to the Müllers. 'His body lies buried in a miserable, neglected piece of ground—a sort of back yard—and his grave is covered by a large, flat stone, bearing an inscription; but,' Mrs Müller added sardonically, 'what the epitaph upon it was, we did not care to ascertain.' They noted that the homes of Young's eighteen wives were also in the city. Müller preached a second time at the Methodist Church to a large congregation which included several Mormons.

In June the Müllers were back in Chicago where, on the Sunday evening, George addressed a large audience in Moody's Tabernacle. Numbers of people including the choir were accommodated on the platform.

Leaving Chicago more meetings were held at Cleveland, Washington and Gettysburg, until on Thursday, June 27th 1878, they boarded the *Adriatic* for Liverpool. Müller had spoken over three hundred times and travelled over nineteen thousand miles; the tour had lasted for a year. On July 8th they arrived back in Bristol,

and upon arriving in an open carriage at the top of Ashley Hill at half-past four, found a little army of the orphan boys and girls, with almost all our helpers at the Orphan-Houses, waiting to receive us. There, as we slowly drove along, the boys cheered heartily, and the girls waved their handkerchiefs, determined (as a by-stander remarked) to give us 'a right royal welcome'; and at the entrance of New Orphan-House No. 3, a crowd of children closed around us, with loving, friendly greetings.

CHAPTER TWENTY-ONE

Simply by Prayer

Over forty years had now elapsed since Müller first sought to demonstrate, by founding and maintaining an orphanage according to certain defined principles, that there is 'reality in the things of God'. During that period there had been many who were convinced by the demonstration and who had been brought from scepticism to faith. The response of others, who were already Christians, had often been to commit themselves more whole-heartedly to lives of prayer and service to God. Most remarkable of all, perhaps, was the effect that a knowledge of Müller's life had on a young Irishman, James McQuilkin, and subsequently through him, on the 1859 revival.

Soon after becoming a Christian in 1856, McQuilkin saw an advertisement for the first two volumes of Müller's Narratives. He managed to get hold of a copy in about January 1857 and was amazed and humbled by what he read.

'See what Mr Müller obtains simply by prayer,' he thought. 'Thus I may obtain blessing by prayer.'

The following autumn McQuilkin told a small group of young men who by now were praying regularly with him in Connor how God had blessed him through reading Müller's Narratives and how he had been led to realise the power of believing prayer; he suggested that they should pray regularly for an out-pouring of the Holy Spirit on their district. The revival which had begun in the States in 1857 was now known about in Ireland; and McQuilkin said to himself:

'Why may we not have such a blessed work here, seeing

that God did such great things for Mr Müller, simply in answer to prayer?'

In March 1859 these young men organised a series of meetings in Ahoghill, near Ballymena; on the 14th the crowds were so great that the meeting, in the First Presbyterian Church, was abandoned, and outside in chilling rain hundreds fell to their knees in the streets. This was to be typical of the revival which followed, as hundreds of thousands were to be convicted of sin by the Holy Spirit. In May the movement reached Belfast and began to affect churches of all denominations.

Before the end of 1859 the flame was spreading through Ireland, England, Wales and Scotland. In the centre of Dublin, Merrion Hall—designed like Spurgeon's Tabernacle and holding two thousand—was built and became one of the largest centres of the Brethren. The movement spread on through the Continent of Europe.

One result of the revival was that thousands of men and women felt called to become full-time evangelists. In England, one such was an Exeter shoemaker named George Brealey. Brealey was a fearless man who had achieved no mean reputation locally when he had rescued a drowning woman from the River Taw in full flood and later by entering a burning house in Exeter to rescue two children from the flames. The revival had filled him with a passionate zeal for souls and he had begun to work in the streets and slums of Exeter.

Later he devoted his life to preaching and working on the Blackdown Hills on the Devon and Somerset border; and, as his grandson Douglas has written, 'borne along by the Spirit of God, he swept through the hills like a flame of fire'. He built village chapels or re-opened older ones, carried on a consistent pastoral work and established Day Schools.

The schools which George Brealey and his son Walter established on the Blackdowns were—like so many other schools in Britain and throughout the world—financed by Müller's Scriptural Knowledge Institution.

The last of these schools—at Bishopswood—was not closed until 1947 when State education services finally made it redundant.

In the 1870s and early 1880s, the Scriptural Knowledge Institution entirely financed nearly eighty Day Schools for children and half a dozen Adult Schools; from five to ten schools were assisted. In the year 1879–80, the Institution was responsible for the education of over seven thousand children in seventy-six schools throughout the world as well as seven Adult Schools. Of these schools, there were fourteen in Spain, four in India, one in Italy and six in British Guiana; the rest were in England and Wales. In the same year nearly forty Sunday Schools were entirely financed and fourteen assisted by the Institution.

Another convert of the 1859 revival, later to become famous, was a young man from Manchester named Henry Moorhouse, who, in 1861, as a wild gambler and drinker rushed into a revival meeting at the Alhambra Circus in Manchester, looking for a fight, only to be arrested by hearing the name—Jesus; he 'who had entered to fight remained to praise and pray'.

He now spent his time, from morning to evening, distributing tracts, witnessing to individuals and, with his converted actor friend John Hambleton, preaching in the open air at local and national gatherings, including theatre services. (It was under Hambleton's preaching that Dr Barnardo had been converted.)

In 1867, Moorhouse met D. L. Moody in Dublin, and later Moody heard Moorhouse preach in Chicago.

Moody said, 'I have never forgotten those nights. I have preached a different gospel since, and I have had more power with God and man since then.' Moorhouse became a close friend of Moody and Sankey; it was said that Moorhouse was 'the man who moved the man who moved the world'; and that he taught Moody that God hates sin, but loves the sinner.

During the last years of his life, Moorhouse sold Bibles and tracts from a Bible carriage and conducted evangelistic campaigns with Richard Weaver in the industrial districts of Lancashire, Yorkshire and Leicestershire. In two years Moorhouse sold over one hundred and fifty thousand Bibles and Testaments, and gave away millions of books and tracts. All his literature was supplied by the Scriptural Knowledge Institution in Bristol.

On August 28th 1878 Moorhouse wrote to Müller from Blackpool:

Beloved Mr Müller, We are having a glorious time here, selling about one thousand copies of the New Testament a week, and preaching to thousands in the open air. Enclosed P.O.O. for £12 10s. Please send us three thousand twopenny Testaments. Many thanks for your kindness in giving them at half price to us. God bless you, dear Mr Müller.

In acknowledging receipt of the testaments sent, Moorhouse wrote again from Blackpool:

Beloved Mr Müller, The New Testaments have arrived safe from London. I thank you very much for giving them to me at one penny each. The expenses of the Gospel Carriage, for horses, lights and rent of ground, will average £3 a week; and I trust the sales of Bibles, etc. will cover this. I wish you could see the thousands of people listening to the preaching of the gospel in the open air, and sometimes hundreds of men weeping. You would say this is the Lord's Work. I wish there were a dozen more carriages out in the villages—I met a great many, in the States, who were much blessed by your ministry, out there; and many ministers told me how much they loved you. Again thanking you for your kindness, etc.

A letter the following October described how:

We were in Leicester last week, and in the fair sold five
hundred New Testaments, in six hours. A publican,
opposite whose place we stood, sent for the police to
remove us. He could scarcely get a customer into his
place. Of course the police could not interfere, as we
were breaking no law. The chief magistrate, in every
town we have visited, in almost every case, has stood
our friend, and given orders for us to have the best place
in the market for our carriage ... A lady in Leicester
has taken off her jewellery, and is going to sell it and
buy with it a Bible carriage for the county ...

Two years later, having visited factories in Oldham
with his Bible Carriage, Moorhouse wrote that: 'In many
mills, I am told, the girls are reading now the Scriptures
during the dinner hour, and the masters say these girls do
more work than those who are careless about better things.'
Four years earlier, in 1876, Moorhouse—who was
never strong—had been told by his doctors that his heart
was twice the size it ought to be; he had continued his
service in the same cheerful and energetic spirit as before.
In September 1880, Müller received his final letter from
Moorhouse:

Beloved Mr Müller, we have had a glorious time at
Darlington and Stockton-on-Tees. Tens of thousands
at the latter place have heard the glorious gospel of our
Lord Jesus. We took the carriage to the races, and never
had we such a week before at any place ... Could you
see the hundreds listening with upturned faces, and
many with tearful eyes, to the simple story of Calvary,
your heart would rejoice, and you would feel repaid for
all the loss you sustain in giving us the Scriptures and
the little Gospel books at so cheap a rate. May God
bless you, beloved Mr Müller. I enclose an order for
five thousand New Testaments and six hundred Bibles,
with many thanks for all your kindness and love.

A few weeks later, Henry Moorhouse was dead. In the year he died (1880), Müller's Scriptural Knowledge Institution sold nearly a hundred thousand Bibles and New Testaments at reduced prices and gave away over four thousand. As well as English the Bibles were in Welsh, Danish, Dutch, French, German, Italian, Portuguese, Spanish, Russian, Swedish, Ancient Greek, Greek and (The Old Testament and Psalms) Hebrew. In the same year (and the year was not untypical) the Institution circulated nearly three and a half million tracts and small books.

During Müller's life, the Institution which he had founded laid out nearly £500,000 on objects other than the orphan work. Of this nearly £115,000 was spent on the school work throughout the world, nearly £90,000 on the circulation of Bibles, Testaments, tracts and books, and over £260,000 on world-wide missionary work. In the peak years of the missionary work in the early 1870s, Müller sent £10,000 abroad annually to nearly two hundred missionaries. By the mid 1880s expenditure was running at about £5,000 a year and rather more than one hundred and thirty missionaries were supported. All this expenditure was quite apart from the sum of nearly £1 million which passed through Müller's hands during his life to be spent on the orphan work.

'See what Mr Müller obtains simply by prayer,' James McQuilkin had said, 'Thus I may obtain blessing by prayer.' And, as we saw, he did. There is indeed a simplicity in prayer—'Ask, and, it shall be given you; seek, and ye shall find; knock, and it shall be opened unto you: for every one that asketh receiveth; and he that seeketh findeth; and to him that knocketh it shall be opened.' This was the simple, yet profound, promise from Matthew 7:7 and 8, with which Müller began a sermon on prayer in 1880. 'Had it been left to us to make promises regarding prayer,' he said, 'I do not know that you or I could have done more than say, "Ask, and ye shall receive". Yet, while the promise is so full, so deep, so broad, so precious in every way, we have here,' he emphasised, 'as becomes us with other parts of the word of God, to compare Scripture with Scripture, because in other parts additions are made, or conditions given, which, if we neglect, will hinder our getting the full benefit of prayer.'

During the sermon Müller outlined a number of conditions upon which successful prayer depends. First, he said, our petitions must be according to God's will— I John 5:14. Second, we must not ask on account of our own goodness or merit, but 'in the name of the Lord Jesus Christ'—John 14:13 and 14. Müller was careful to remind his congregation, however, as he often did, of the verse in the sixty-sixth Psalm: 'If I regard iniquity in my heart, the Lord will not hear me.' 'That is,' he said, 'if I live in sin, and go on in a course hateful to God, I may not expect my prayers to be answered.'

The third condition was that we must exercise faith in the power and willingness of God to answer our prayers. 'This is deeply important,' Müller said. 'In Mark 11:24, we read, "What things soever ye desire, when ye pray, believe that ye receive them, and ye shall have them." "What things soever ye desire"—of whatever kind—"believe that ye receive them, and ye shall have them." I have found invariably, in the fifty-four years and nine months during which I have been a believer, that if I only believed I was sure to get, in God's time, the thing I asked for. I would especially lay this on your heart that you exercise faith in the power and willingness of God to answer your requests. We must believe that God is able and willing. To see that He is able, you have only to look at the resurrection of the Lord Jesus Christ; for having raised Him from the dead, He must have almighty power. As to the love of God, you have only to look to the cross of Christ, and see His love in not sparing His Son, in not withholding His only begotten Son from death. With these proofs of the power and love of God, assuredly, if we believe, we shall receive—we shall obtain.'

The fourth condition was that 'we have to continue patiently waiting on God till the blessing we seek is granted. For observe, nothing is said in the text as to the time in which, or the circumstances under which, the prayer is to be answered. "Ask, and it shall be given you." There is a positive promise, but nothing as to time . . . Someone may say, "Is it necessary I should bring a matter before God two, three, five or even twenty times; is it not enough I tell Him once?" We might as well say there is no need to tell Him once, for He knows beforehand what our need is. He wants us to prove that we have confidence in Him, that we take our place as creatures towards the Creator.

'Moreover, we are never to lose sight of the fact that there may be particular reasons why prayer may not at once be answered. One reason may be the need for the exercise of our faith, for by exercise faith is strengthened. We all know that if our faith were not exercised it would remain as it was at first. By the trial it is strengthened. Another reason may be that we may glorify God by the manifestation of patience. This is a grace by which God is greatly magnified. Our manifestation of patience glorifies God. There may be another reason. Our heart may not yet be prepared for the answer to our prayer. I will give an illustration . . .' Müller gave a number of illustrations from the lives of those known to him and then drew on his own vast experience.

'If I say that during the fifty-four years and nine months that I have been a believer in the Lord Jesus Christ I have had thirty thousand answers to prayer, either in the same hour or the same day that the requests were made, I should not go a particle too far. Often, before leaving my bedroom in the morning, have I had prayer answered that was offered that morning, and in the course of the day I have had five or six more answers to prayer; so that at least thirty thousand prayers have been answered the self-same hour or the self-same day that they were offered. But one or the other might suppose all my prayers have been thus promptly answered. No; not all of them. Sometimes I have had to wait weeks, months or years; sometimes many years.

'In November 1844, I began to pray for the conversion of five individuals. I prayed every day without one single intermission, whether sick or in health, on the land or on the sea, and whatever the pressure of my engagements might be. Eighteen months elapsed before the first of the five was converted. I thanked God, and prayed on for the others. Five years elapsed, and then the second was converted. I thanked God for the second, and prayed on for the other three. Day by day I continued to pray for them, and six years more passed before the third was converted. I thanked God for the three, and went on praying for the other two. These two remain unconverted. The man to whom God in the riches of His grace has given tens of thousands of answers to prayer, in the self-same hour or day on which they were offered, has been praying day by day for nearly thirty-six years for the conversion of these two individuals, and yet they remain unconverted; for next November it will be thirty-six years since I began to pray for their conversion. But I hope in God, I pray on, and look yet for the answer.

'Therefore, beloved brethren and sisters, go on waiting upon God, go on praying; only be sure you ask for things which are according to the mind of God. The conversion of sinners is according to the mind of God, for He does not desire the death of the sinner. This is the revelation God has made of Himself—"Not willing that any should perish, but that all should come to repentance." Go on, therefore, praying; expect an answer, look for it, and in the end you will have to praise God for it.'

Of the two individuals still unconverted at the time of this sermon, one became a Christian before Müller's death and the other a few years later.

CHAPTER TWENTY-TWO

The Scent of Honeysuckle

A highlight of the fifth preaching tour (September 1878
to June 1879), after Müller had held numerous meetings
in France and Switzerland, was the visit to a number of
the schools in Spain which for the last ten years had been
entirely supported by the funds of the Scriptural
Knowledge Institution. One, a school for about one
hundred and fifty boys, was in a poor district of
Barcelona; the Müllers found that the boys were 'quiet
and orderly'. Müller began to address them, speaking
very slowly so that the English director of the schools,
Mr Henry Payne, could translate: 'My dear children,' he
said, 'I love you all very much, and pray for you every
day. I long from my inmost soul to meet everyone of you
in Heaven; but, in order that you may go to that happy
place, as poor, lost, guilty sinners, you must put your
trust in the blessed Lord Jesus Christ, who was punished
in our room and stead; for His blood alone can cleanse us
from our sins.' He went on to tell them about the boys on
Ashley Down, and mentioned that some of them, about
the same age as they were, had already put their trust in
the Lord Jesus as Saviour.

Close to the boys' school was a school for girls, also
entirely supported by SKI. After Müller had spoken
similarly to these girls, and they had sung a hymn for
him, 'a pretty little girl, about six years old, with black
hair and very bright eyes, was mounted on a form, when
she repeated the 128th Psalm in Spanish with great ease,
and apparently without missing a word'. More recitations
followed before the Müllers moved on to visit a school

248

for infant girls, who could understand the Catalan dialect only. Thus, when Müller spoke to them, Mr Payne's Spanish translation had to be translated a second time into Catalan by the school governess. By this somewhat cumbersome process the children were told that the kind gentleman from England loved them, cared for them and was glad to see their bright, merry, little faces. The kind gentleman and his wife then gave the children a text to carry home to their parents: 'The blood of Jesus Christ His Son cleanseth us from all sin.' The couple visited ten schools in Barcelona, all of which were entirely supported by SKI.

On December 28th they rose at five and left Barcelona station for Saragossa. At midday (before the day of the restaurant car) all passengers got out at Levida for lunch; Mr and Mrs Müller walked up and down the platform giving away gospel tracts in Spanish. They were soon surrounded by a crowd of passengers all trying to get a tract for themselves. When their stock had been entirely distributed, the Müllers returned to their compartment followed by a large crowd of so far unsuccessful applicants. Fortunately more tracts were found in the carriage and handed out, but sadly—after George and Susannah had held up empty hands to show they had nothing more to give—a number of folk went away empty handed.

At Madrid Müller visited the five schools entirely supported by SKI and found them in a 'most satisfactory state'. Müller reported that:

when our schools in Madrid were established and a place was opened for preaching the gospel, a sign was placed outside over the entrance announcing that this was an evangelical place of worship for preaching the gospel. After this sign had existed for a considerable time, official directions were sent to Mr Fenn [who directed all the Madrid schools run by SKI] to have it painted over, so that the announcement might be obliterated. But the painter, who had done the work, being at heart grieved at having to destroy his own work, and sorrowful also, that these schools should be hindered instead of being encouraged by the Government, painted the sign over with water colours, so that still in a measure, what had been painted before could be seen.

With evident satisfaction Müller continued, 'Some time after also the rain made the former painting still more visible.' But sadly he had to record later that, 'Now the Government sent by night their own painter, to daub the sign thickly over with oil paint.'

After leaving Spain, some months were spent in the south of France, Müller preaching many times in French. At a church connected with an institution for mentally retarded and epileptic children, the director would not hear of an interpreter because, he said, *'Monsieur Müller est admirable.'*

The Müllers spent March in Menton and held meetings daily, at Eglise Française and the German Church. On Sunday mornings the little hall of the Free Church of Scotland was crowded, and its doors and windows left open; several people would sit outside on the balcony and listen to Müller in the spring sunshine. Among them on three Sundays was an Englishman in his middle forties, there for the benefit of his health: Charles Haddon Spurgeon. On several occasions, that spring, George and Susannah drove out with Spurgeon. One afternoon they drove along the Turin road leading to Castiglione, and winding slowly up a hill in an open carriage amid magnificent scenery Spurgeon said:

'When in the midst of landscapes such as these from the crown of my head to the sole of my foot, I feel as though I could burst out into one song of praise.' It is not known whether, in fact, he did so, or if he did whether Müller accompanied his friend.

Dr Henry Bennet was a Christian resident in Menton and during his convalescence Spurgeon was able to come and go in Bennet's garden as he pleased. That same spring, Spurgeon recorded that Mr and Mrs Müller spent a day with him there. 'Dr Bennet came up,' Spurgeon recalled, 'and I was amused to hear Müller teaching him the power of prayer, and recommending him to pray about one of the terraces which he wants to buy, but the owner asks a hundred times its value.'

'It is too trifling a matter to take to the Lord,' said Dr Bennet. 'You may very properly pray about your orphanage, but as to this terrace, to complete my garden—I could not make out a good case about it!'

'But,' said Müller, 'it encourages people in sin if we yield to covetous demands, and so I think you might pray that the owners should be kept from exorbitant claims.'

'As ignorant peasants,' replied Dr Bennet, 'they are in my opinion very excusable for trying either to keep their land, or to get all they can from an Englishman whom they imagine to be a living gold mine!'

Müller smiled. Spurgeon commented later that the 'spirit of both was good; but, of course, the simple, childlike, holy trust of Müller was overpowering. He is not a sanctimonious person; but full of real joy, and sweet peace, and innocent pleasure.' Charles Spurgeon junior once wrote in a letter that his 'Father declares himself far better able to "trust and not be afraid" through intercourse with Mr Müller.'

Their journey continued into Italy, with Müller holding meetings in San Remo, Florence and Rome.

On arrival at Naples, some English seamen from Bristol—hearing that Müller was in the area—invited him to address them, which he did in the harbour aboard the Bethel Mission ship. A number of meetings were held in Naples and the Müllers found time, too, to visit Pompeii, and the ruins of Herculaneum. They climbed Vesuvius and admired the famous view.

Travelling north again, they arrived in Venice, where, said Mrs Müller, 'instead of an omnibus, a gondola was waiting for passengers, in which we were rowed along several canals, to the Hotel Danieli'. On then to Milan and Turin for a series of meetings, before setting off on June 3rd for the final major event of the tour: an excursion through the Waldensian valleys. Here for centuries there had been congregations of believers calling themselves brethren, who later became widely known as Waldenses, or Vaudois, though they did not themselves accept the name. They traced their origin back to Apostolic times. In the quiet seclusion of their mountains they had remained unaffected by the development of the Roman Church.

In the two principal valleys of St Martin and Lucerne the members of the little churches, Mrs Müller wrote,

are obliged to walk many miles in order to attend the meetings. These Waldensian Christians are generally very poor, and many of them live in houses roofed with rough, flat stones loosely put together, instead of slates or tiles. In the windows, too, of a few of their abodes, paper occupied the place of glass. At Pomaret some of the people were standing at their doors to gaze at us, because our visit was expected; and as we drove along 'Monsieur le pasteur Georges Müller' had many respectful bows and salutations.

At five o'clock we reached the house of the pastor at Villa Sèche, and in the evening accompanied him to his church, a very ancient Vaudois place of worship, situated at a great height upon a mountain, many hundreds of feet above his residence. A steep, rugged, winding pathway, covered in places with loose stones, led up this mountain towards the church; and as some rivulets streamed over the ascent, it was difficult to avoid getting ankle-deep in water. The silence and solitude of the whole region, too, were striking. At length, warm, tired and almost breathless [Müller was now seventy-four], we reached the church, a large old-fashioned building, which was crowded with a rustic congregation, who (the meeting having been announced for five o'clock, though circumstances did not allow of our getting there till seven) had been sitting there two hours, patiently waiting our arrival. The service, which was in French, was opened with singing and prayer after which Mr Müller addressed the audience for an hour, throwing himself heart and soul into their circumstances. At the close of the meeting we distributed little French and Italian books amongst the people; shook hands with many of them; and soon after nine reached the pastor's cottage down below, a Swiss chalet, with a projecting roof, and two wooden galleries outside. In this mountain home the domestic arrangements were of the simplest, most frugal character possible, many of the comforts and conveniences of life (often considered indispensable) being wanting; but we were most kindly entertained, and greatly enjoyed our little visit.

They travelled on in a small open carriage to Perrier, La Perouse and eventually La Tour, the largest Vaudois settlement. In the evening at a school of St Jean (three miles from La Tour) Müller preached in French to a large congregation. At the close of the meeting the pastor prayed *'que le discours excellent de notre frère soit gravé sur nos coeurs'*; and another gentleman commented afterwards:

'Monsieur Müller nous a dit précisément ce qu'il nous faut; le sermon était admirable.'

Müller had ended his first tour of the United States with over a hundred written invitations to preach not yet accepted. Therefore, after spending ten weeks in Bristol following their return from Europe, the Müllers set sail again for the States aboard the *Germanic* on August 28th 1879.

Sunday evening, September 14th 1879, at the Methodist Episcopal Church, South Second Street, Brooklyn, the pastor introduces their guest preacher:

'My dear Friends, I rejoice to tell you that we are about to hear the gospel from the heart and lips of our venerable friend, who, though now aged seventy-four, has preached the gospel upwards of one thousand four hundred times during the last four years, in the various cities and countries he has visited. Hear this, you young men, and remember that he is no smoker, nor lover of alcoholic drink; but see how God can strengthen for His blessed service, those who trust in Him, and seek to live to His honour and glory. I have now great pleasure in introducing you to Mr George Müller, of Bristol, England.'

An introduction like that naturally assured Müller an attentive audience as he delivered a powerful address from Isaiah 3 : 10 and 11.

In December Müller was one of the speakers at a large conference in the Shaftesbury Hall, Toronto. On the first morning Müller spoke on 'The Inspiration of the Scriptures', and followed this later with another address entitled, 'Christ in all the Scriptures'.

On the second afternoon he spoke on the second coming of Christ, outlining the chief events which (in his view) would precede and accompany that event. He spoke for an hour and twenty minutes which meant that there was very little time for the Reverend Erdman to develop his subject 'No Millennium until Jesus comes'. After the delegates had sung 'with great animation':

> Down life's dark vale we wander
> Till Jesus comes . . .

the meeting ended.

In the evening Müller spoke again, this time expounding at great length the seventh chapter of Daniel. Once again, Müller had taken up so much time that poor Mr

Erdman was only able to say a very few words on the topic allocated to him. Fortunately, however, Mrs Müller was able to record that 'this dear brother in the Lord, possessed a gracious, Christ-like spirit' and that he stated from the platform:

'I rejoice that brother Müller should take the lead, for I feel like Timothy standing by the side of Paul.'

On the final afternoon Müller publicly replied to nine written questions one of which was as hotly debated then as it is in some quarters today. The question was: 'Are we to expect our Lord's return at any moment, or that certain events must be fulfilled before He comes again?' Hundreds of pulses beat a little faster as Müller rose to his feet to deliver his reply.

'I know that on this subject there is great diversity of judgment, and I do not wish to force on other persons the light I have myself. The subject, however, is not new to me; for having been a careful diligent student of the Bible for nearly fifty years, my mind has long been settled on this point, and I have not the shadow of a doubt about it. The Scriptures declare plainly, that the Lord Jesus will not come until the apostasy shall have taken place, and the man of sin, the "son of perdition" (or personal Antichrist) shall have been revealed, as seen in 2nd Thessalonians chapter 2. Many other portions of the Word of God distinctly teach, that certain events are to be fulfilled before the return of our Lord Jesus Christ. This does not, however, alter the fact, that the coming of Christ, and not death, is the great Hope of the Church, and, if in a right state of heart, we (as the Thessalonian believers did) shall "serve the living and true God, and—wait for His Son from Heaven".'

Müller's last sermon in Toronto was delivered to an immense congregation in the great Metropolitan Church. His subject was the indwelling and power of the Holy Spirit, and his scriptural passage (as often) was short: the words of Jesus in John 14:16 and 17, 'And I will pray the Father, and he shall give you another Comforter, that he may abide with you for ever; Even the Spirit of truth; whom the world cannot receive, because it seeth him not, neither knoweth him: but ye know him for he dwelleth with you, and shall be in you.' During this tour Müller had preached three hundred times.

They returned to Liverpool on Wednesday, June 16th, arriving at Ashley Down the following day. The children had all been assembled to greet them and as they caught their first glimpse of the couple, noisy hearty cheering broke out. A small girl stepped forward and presented Mrs Müller with an enormous bunch of honeysuckle while Müller stood beaming. Many years later (in 1939) that same girl, then in her sixties, wrote:

> I always follow the scent of honeysuckle, but have never yet found any to come near my memory of that bunch—each and every one looks smaller and much less lovely ... I've just returned from a fortnight's work in Wiltshire. I did so hope to have time to visit Bristol. Perhaps it is as well as I couldn't get time ... Perhaps the dear old home would have looked changed. It was so very beautiful, and my eleven years so very happy. I'd rather keep my memories.

George and Susannah, too, were glad to be back at the dear old home.

Müller had left North America with over one hundred and fifty invitations to preach unaccepted, and therefore in September 1880, the Müllers left again for Quebec. Müller held eight meetings aboard the *Sardinian*, led three Bible studies and distributed about two hundred small books to the passengers and crew.

One of Müller's most interesting recollections of his stay in the Boston area that year was a visit to Plymouth where he preached at the Church of the Pilgrims erected by the Pilgrim Fathers on arrival there in December 1620. They looked at the first house ever built in New England and 'at the Pilgrims' Hall we saw a number of interesting relics brought over to this country by the pilgrims in the *Mayflower* ... where they were obliged to take refuge from the persecution for Christ's sake, by which they had been assailed in their native land'.

At the end of November the Müllers arrived at New Haven, Connecticut, where Müller spoke several times to the staff and students at Yale University. Müller described this as, 'a service in which I take the deepest interest, from having been converted myself while a student at the University of Halle'.

On previous visits to the States, Müller had spent less time than he had wished in New York, and was determined during this tour to spend as long as possible in this city of about one and half million people. The couple therefore spent the winter months from December 1880 to March 1881 in New York. That winter was the coldest known in New York for thirty years and Mrs Müller recorded anxiously that:

> the many long drives my beloved husband took at night to Brooklyn and other places, seven, eight or nine miles from our hotel, when the weather was most severe, were very trying, especially as it was necessary to cross a ferry, where the ice was occasionally so thick, that it was with difficulty a passage could be forced through it by steamer. Constrained by the love of Christ, however, he persevered in a service, that would have been considered, by most persons of his age, an arduous undertaking; but though he felt the cold, was not allowed to suffer from it in the least.

During the period Müller held nearly one hundred meetings including thirty-eight in German trying to reach the half-million Germans in the New York–Brooklyn area.

More meetings were held in Port Chester and Pittsburgh before on May 21st the couple embarked for England aboard the *Britannic*.

The main interest of Müller's eighth missionary tour was the visit to Egypt, Palestine, Turkey and Greece. After spending some months in Europe, the Müllers left Marseilles for Alexandria towards the end of October 1881. Many meetings in English and German were held at Alexandria and Cairo, and in November the Müllers set off in an open carriage to see the Pyramids, and to explore the ancient burial places of Kings.

> Our walk to the Sphinx was oppressively warm, for the sun shone with a brightness that was dazzling. The heat and glare too from the sandy ground on which we trod, made the atmosphere around like the hot air issuing from an oven. Troops of Bedouin Arabs congregate in the neighbourhood of the Pyramids, who flock around strangers and volunteer their services as guides.

Before leaving Cairo the couple visited the Museum of Egyptian curiosities and were intrigued by the mummies; 'amongst them (it is said) is the mummy of that great oppressor of the Israelites, the Pharaoh, during whose reign they had so much to suffer, until delivered by Jehovah through His servant Moses'.

Aboard a Russian mail steamer bound for Jaffa, the Müllers came across about a hundred Russians on a pilgrimage to Jerusalem accompanied by their priests of the Greek Orthodox Church. 'These pilgrims performed their religious services on deck, where they bowed, crossed themselves repeatedly and turned their faces eastward towards the Holy Land. Each was supplied with a Bible in Russian by an Evangelist from Port Said who also acted as an agent for the British and Foreign Bible Society.'

At Jaffa they stayed at the Jerusalem Hotel, and Müller began to preach in the town to German and English congregations as well as with Arabic interpretation when neither of these languages was understood. During their walks they admired the orange and lemon plantations and the high, thick hedges of prickly pears and the varieties of cacti which flourished in the semi-tropical climate.

After twelve days in Jaffa they travelled south towards Jerusalem in an open Russian waggon, drawn by three horses. Going through the mountains of Judaea they found that the land, spoken of in the Old Testament as a 'land flowing with milk and honey', had grown barren, rocky and uncultivated and Mrs Müller decided that God's curse appeared to rest not only upon the Jews but upon their land also. (It is not clear whether her husband shared this view which would be strongly contested today.) But, she thought, 'at the return of the Lord Jesus, when Israel as a nation will be converted and restored, "The desert shall rejoice, and blossom as the rose".'

At the Mediterranean Hotel in Jerusalem they moved into a pleasant corner room on the first floor with a fine view of the Mount of Olives; and throughout their stay in the Holy City they took daily walks on the terrace on the flat roof of the hotel to admire the splendid panorama.

Müller held numerous meetings in Jerusalem preaching in English and German with interpretation into Arabic when necessary, and twice spoke to the patients at a hospital for lepers outside the city. The population of Jerusalem at that time was less than thirty thousand and included about eight thousand Jews living in the poorest part. 'At the present time,' Mrs Müller observed, watching for any signs of the fulfilment of biblical prophecy, 'there is no indication whatever of any gathering of Jews on an extensive scale from other countries to their own land.'

In December Müller (now in his seventy-eighth year) and his wife,

joined a party of English friends and rode on donkeys to Bethany, a mile and a half distant, the English clergyman kindly acting as our guide. On our way we crossed the Brook Kidron, saw the Garden of Gethsemane, now enclosed by a wall; and visited the cave, hewn out of a rock where it is supposed Lazarus was buried. An old ruined house, said to have been the dwelling place of Martha, Mary and Lazarus, was also pointed out. From the summit of the Mount of Olives the view embraced a portion of the Dead Sea, twenty-five miles distant, the plain of Jordan, the well-watered plain which Lot chose for himself, the Mountains of Moab in the distance, the neighbourhood of the Cave of Adullam and a small part of the river Jordan which flows into the Dead Sea. The weather was magnificent; after sunset the whole scene was lighted up by the full moon which shone brilliantly, and coming down the Mount of Olives, we had the finest view of Jerusalem that is to be obtained from any point. The Garden of Gethsemane, containing eight very old olive trees (considered by some, from their ancient characteristics to be coeval with the period of our Lord's history on earth), we passed both on our way to and from the Mount.

On the morning of December 9th we rode on donkeys to Bethlehem, six miles from Jerusalem; and, after lunching in a cloister of the Latin Convent, visited a church erected on the spot, where (according to tradition) the manger stood, in which after His birth our Lord was laid. During our stay in Jerusalem, we had opportunities also of visiting the various places of interest for which the city is celebrated. The Via Dolorosa, the Mosque of Omar (built on the site formerly occupied by Solomon's Temple), the Church of the Holy Sepulchre (erected, according to tradition, on the spot where our Lord was crucified), Absalom's Pillar, the Pool of Bethesda, the site of Herod's palace, the ruins of the Castle to which Paul was taken and the Pool of Siloam, were all visited in turn.

After over nine weeks in Jerusalem the Müllers returned to Jaffa for a week's stay before climbing into a small boat which, it was intended, should take them out to the Austrian steamship *Flora*, bound for Haifa and anchored some way from the shore. A heavy gale was blowing, and,

> after riding over heavy breakers, and getting clear of the rocks, our boat was tossed about upon the waves for nearly half an hour; and, after at last we reached the ship, a favourable opportunity of getting a footing on board (to be seized just at the right moment as the boat was lifted upwards by the waves) had to be closely watched for, when one after the other, at the risk of our lives, we had to spring on to the steep ladder stair-case, that led up towards the deck.

On arrival at Haifa after an experience only slightly less terrifying in another small boat, the undaunted travellers were met by some German brethren who drove them in an open waggon during torrents of rain to the Hotel du Mont Carmel. Müller's preaching at Haifa was the means of bringing about a spiritual revival amongst the large colony of German settlers there. In February they

> rode on donkeys to Mount Carmel, and when near its summit, alighted at a Monastery, where the monks entertained us with cups of black coffee without milk, and glasses of mulberry wine, flavoured with lemon juice. They afterwards showed us into a church containing (according to tradition) the cave in which Elijah dwelt, and finally led the way to a lighthouse standing on a rock, that we might see, from this elevated point, the magnificent prospect which extended far and wide ... Being favoured with bright sunshine, and a beautifully clear atmosphere, the whole scene was viewed under particularly favourable circumstances. The place where Elijah slew the false prophets of Baal, and by prayer brought down fire from heaven to consume his sacrifice upon the altar ... and, it was upon Mount Carmel he prayed, that Jehovah would again send rain upon the earth.

Twenty-one days of busy engagements at Beirut followed before the Müllers travelled on via Smyrna to Ayaslaloup, near Ephesus, where they inspected the ruins of the Temple of Diana; 'but the devastation there is so complete, that no trace whatever (as to form or outline) exists of the celebrated building which once occupied this site'.

On then to Constantinople where Müller preached many times, and from where they visited the barracks at Scutari, where Florence Nightingale and her helpers attended the sick, wounded and dying soldiers—victims of the Crimean war. And while walking a few minutes from their hotel, The d'Angleterre, they watched some dancing Dervishes.

There were eighteen performers altogether, who wore brown mantles, and high, round caps made of felt. At a particular signal, they all fell flat upon their faces; but afterwards rose, and walked a few times round the room, with folded arms, bowing and turning slowly many times. Their mantles were then suddenly cast off, when they appeared in long, full, bell-shaped petticoats and jackets, and, after stretching out their arms to the utmost, began gravely and deliberately to dance and revolve (that is, to spin round and round like a top) for about fifteen or twenty minutes, as rapidly as possible.

Athens was the next stop on the tour, and another busy programme for Müller followed. But time was found for the couple to visit to the Areopagus, or Mars Hill, and to stand on the spot where Paul preached his famous sermon. They explored the Acropolis, and saw the ruins of the many ancient idol temples which had so stirred the heart of the Apostle eighteen hundred years earlier.

And then home they came to Ashley Down via Corinth, Rome and Florence after a journey which had lasted over nine months.

CHAPTER TWENTY-THREE

Loved by Thousands

Every time he returned from a long preaching tour, Müller found that his son-in-law, James Wright, assisted by an efficient staff, was running Ashley Down well. Moreover when a problem arose during a foreign tour which required Müller's special judgment, Wright would include it in his frequent letters (sometimes he wrote more than once a week). Fears that donations would decrease in Müller's absence had been allayed in the third year after Müller had begun his work abroad when the total income received had been greater than in any previous year.

Müller had therefore no hesitation in setting off again with his wife in August 1882 for their ninth tour—of Europe. At Düsseldorf Müller was delighted to be greeted by the City Missioner whom he had met six years earlier (page 224) and to be told that from that time he had resolved to take Müller's advice and give himself more earnestly to prayer. Two months after Müller had left in 1876, five of the missioner's six sons had been converted and the sixth was now also thinking seriously about Christian things.

From Düsseldorf the Müllers travelled down the Rhine to Heidelberg, Mannheim and then to Vienna for a number of meetings. They visited Budapest and Prague before returning via Leipzig to Halberstadt where Müller had spent many of his school days. Here they wandered around the cathedral where Müller had taken communion for the first time sixty-two years earlier. Next morning they drove along the road to Kroppenstadt and Müller remarked that the road to his birthplace looked much the same as it had done when he was a boy, except that where there had been poplars on either side of the road, now there were fruit trees. It was the first time Müller had returned to Kroppenstadt since his childhood; he held two meetings in a large hall. The locals flocked to hear their most famous son give an account of his life and work: the building was crowded to overflowing. Müller was thrilled to find the house where he had been born still standing, and was able to show his wife the house in Heimersleben to which the family had moved when he was four.

From Heimersleben they travelled to Berlin for a number of addresses to large congregations as well as some—ever popular at this time—drawing-room meetings. Moving on to Danzig, Müller met two friends from his days as a student at Halle: both of them had been ministers for fifty years. At Königsberg on Christmas Day Müller addressed an immense congregation of three thousand people who had gathered that morning to hear him at half-past nine in the Tragheimer Kirche. In the afternoon he spoke again at the Moravian Hall, and hundreds were turned away for lack of room.

On December 29th they boarded a Prussian train bound for St Petersburg. They procured a comfortable sleeping compartment, heated with warm air, and containing two coaches, double windows and a little table. Next morning they awoke to find themselves travelling through a 'vast wilderness of snow'. At St Petersburg station, after a journey from Königsberg of nearly seven hundred miles, they were met 'very affectionately' by Her Highness the Princess Lieven and Colonel Paschkoff, an officer of the Imperial Guards, and wealthy nobleman whom Müller described as 'one of the most active Christians in the whole vast empire'. The Princess, whom Mrs Müller described as 'a beloved sister in the Lord', immediately pressed them to stay with her in her man-

sion; but, said Müller, 'as we rarely accept invitations to
stay with friends, because I require as much rest and time
to myself as possible, we declined the proposal, and went
to an hotel where we remained for two nights. Finding,
however, that the Princess greatly desired we should be
her guests, and that she would have been much disappointed if we had continued to refuse her kind offer of
hospitality, on Monday, January 1st, we went to her
mansion, and were most kindly entertained there, for
upwards of eleven weeks.'

The room set apart for the Müllers was known as the
Malachite Hall, because of its magnificent malachite
mantelpiece, pillars and cornices. The malachite—a hard
green stone, beautiful when polished—had been mined
near Ekaterinburg, on the eastern slopes of the Urals.
Despite the splendid luxury of the accommodation, however, Müller's stay at St Petersburg was to be neither idle
nor without its excitement. He preached sixteen times at
the British and American Chapel, in English; eight times
in German at the German Reformed Church, eleven times
in German at the Moravian Church; held three meetings
for the Swedes at the British and American Chapel, with
translation into Swedish, attended three pastors' meetings, held five large drawing-room meetings at Colonel
Paschkoff's mansion, conducted two at the residence of
Count Korff and held thirty-five at the home of Princess
Lieven. On top of this, he received visitors and enquirers
every day, and had about forty private interviews lasting
from between one to two hours each with very small
groups of Christian workers. He spoke in hospital wards
and children's institutions.

Tolstoy in his *Resurrection* captured the fascination St
Petersburg society had for drawing-room meetings in the
late nineteenth century. Nekhlyudov's aunt, Countess
Katerina Ivanova, is portrayed as a 'fervent adherent of
the doctrine which teaches that faith in the Redemption
is the essence of Christianity'. Tolstoy described the ele-

gant carriages which brought the faithful to a meeting
which had been arranged in the Countess's ball-room.

Ladies in silk, velvet and lace, with false hair, tightly
laced waists and padded figures, sat in the luxuriously
furnished ball-room. Between the ladies were men in
uniforms and evening-dress, and five or six from the
lower classes: two house-porters, a shopkeeper, a foot-
man and a coachman. Kiesewetter [the preacher], a
thick-set man with hair just turning grey, spoke in
English, and a thin girl wearing pince-nez translated
quickly and well. He said that our sins were so great,
and the punishment they deserved was so great and
unavoidable, that it was impossible to live, anticipating
such punishment.

It is thought that Tolstoy modelled his Kiesewetter on
Dr F. W. Baedeker, cousin of the 'Baedeker' of
Continental Guide-Book renown, and himself a con-
tributor to several of the Guides. Baedeker, whose home
was in Weston-super-Mare, had since the 1860s been a
close friend of Müller and also stayed with Princess
Lieven on his frequent visits to St Petersburg. He used
to tell of a long conversation he once had with Count
Tolstoy in Moscow about England and contemporary
Russian affairs; there seems no reason to doubt that it
was Baedeker who inspired Tolstoy in his somewhat unsympathetic portrayal of Kiesewetter.
    Through application by friends to the Minister of
the Interior Müller had obtained permission to preach at
the German churches in St Petersburg, and also to the
Swedes in the British Chapel. The document from the
Minister was in Russian, which neither Müller, nor his
friends who handed it to him understood, but they told
him that the desired permission had been granted.
    On the evening of Friday, February 9th, however, the
Müllers were startled to receive unexpected visitors at

the mansion. It was the police, with a summons for Müller to appear early next morning before their chief officer. He was charged with having held meetings with translation into Russian, for which no permission had been granted by the Minister of the Interior. The director of police treated Müller with great courtesy, shook hands with him and offered half an apology for acting as he did. From that time the services at Colonel Paschkoff's house were stopped but Müller was allowed to continue his other activities without hindrance.

Müller noted that during his stay he had frequent conversations, 'with persons of high rank, who I sought to benefit spiritually'. But, he emphasised, 'this was unsought for on my part; but the Lord opened deeply important service for me in this manner, which, I doubt not, will be found in the day of Christ to have been helpful not only to those dear Christians amongst whom I more particularly laboured, publicly and privately; but also, through them, to many others in the vast empire'.

A few years later, Colonel Paschkoff was exiled to Siberia by Tsar Alexander III for his persistent evangelising, drawing-room meetings and tract distribution. Once the Tsar allowed him to return to attend to his affairs, and soon heard new rumours about the Colonel's activities. He sent for Paschkoff.

'I hear you have resumed your old practices.'

'My friends have certainly called to greet me, and we have prayed and read the Word of God together.'

'Which you know I will not permit. I will not suffer you to defy me. If I had thought you would have repeated your offences, you would not have been allowed to return. Now go; and never set foot upon Russian soil again!'

St Petersburg lost a courageous Christian.

The Müllers found the cold, that winter, very severe and more intense than they ever found in Canada or the United States. However, they did not allow the weather to deter them in their search for a little adventure. In

March, they visited by sledge a small settlement of Laplanders encamped on the ice of the Neva. Mrs Müller recorded:

A party of Lapps (clothed in skins and furs, with the warm side turned inwards and looking as if sewn up in their thick garments) were standing near a tent. They wear no under linen (we were told), and never wash themselves nor change their clothes, except when they fall off from dirt and constant use. The interior of a Laplander's hut too, upon the ice, presented a miserable, uncomfortable appearance. It consisted of a tent made of skins, with the fur turned inwards, and had an opening at the top, which answered the double purpose of chimney and of window. An iron pot, containing soup, was suspended over a small fire in the centre of this tent, and the floor of ice in the hut was covered by rugs; but the domestic arrangements inside were of a most repulsive character . . .

They returned to England via Poland, where the highlight of their stay was Müller's success in touching the hearts of the citizens of Lódz, a large industrial town. After nearly a week of crowded services in the town, Müller received a note of which the following is a translation:

I, and almost the whole population of this town, in the name of the Lord Jesus, entreat that you will have the kindness to remain with us until after next Sunday. In the name of many thousands I thank you for your ministry.

The crowds at Müller's meetings continued to be as large as the German Baptist Church could hold, about one thousand two hundred people, and Mrs Müller noted that, 'the preaching too was the theme of conversation in the factories, public houses and in many private families'. They therefore prolonged their visit as long as possible.

Returning via Germany to England in May, Müller went immediately to London where he spoke seven times at a crowded Mildmay Conference.

Returning in June to Ashley Down after an absence of nearly a year, the hearty welcome from the huge crowd of children all but melted the Müllers to tears.

After fourteen engagements in Scotland in September, the Müllers left Tilbury in September 1883 aboard the *Siam* bound for Madras. Their stop at Malta was long enough to allow a drive to the beautiful Orange and Lemon Gardens of St Antonio, and at Ceylon there was time for a ride in an open 'bandy' through Colombo and its neighbourhood as well as to conduct a drawing-room meeting at Calton Lodge.

They set foot on Madras Pier at the end of October to stay with Robert Franck. Müller preached many times at Madras including an address to four hundred Hindus at the Free Church of Scotland. An Indian servant named Abraham had been engaged to travel with the Müllers throughout India, to look after their luggage generally and also because he could speak Hindustani, Tamil and Canarese. Meetings followed at Bangalore before the couple travelled by train and palanquin coach, drawn by bullocks, to Colar where they stayed at an orphanage founded by Miss Anstey.

In December a 'tonga'—a covered carriage on two wheels, drawn by ponies—took them up into the Nilgiri Hills to Coonoor. At Christmas, a busy period of engagements in Madras began, followed by visits to Calcutta and Darjeeling.

They travelled next to Benares, chief of the Hindu sacred cities, where their host was the Rev. John Hewlett of the London Missionary Society. Such was the heat that to explore the city an early start was necessary and on February 22nd they rose at five to set off in an open carriage for a drive through the city and its suburbs.

We visited a celebrated School of Philosophy, where numerous Brahmins, pundits and their pupils, were at work; embarked afterwards in a small steam-boat upon the Ganges, and from her deck had a full view of the city, as it extends along the river's banks, with its numerous bathing-ghâts, its burning-ghât, for consuming bodies of the dead, its Temples, Mosques, sacred Wells, etc. for which the city is so renowned. We . . . observed the dead bodies of three human beings floating down the Ganges, upon which crows were perched, pecking at their flesh, because the poor, who cannot afford to pay for the wood which is needed to consume the dead bodies of their relatives, throw them into the river instead of burning them.

Mrs Müller also recorded that:

before our departure from Benares, Mrs Hewlett conducted me . . . to visit a school for native girls, belonging to the London Missionary Society, situated in the Compound where the Mission House stands; and with these girls, most of whom were extremely poor, by means of interpretation I conversed. The delight with which they listened to a few particulars about our orphans, at the Five Houses on Ashley Down, Bristol, was great; and my brief interview with them was a most interesting one.

At Allahabad and Agra, from where they were able to visit the Taj Mahal, Müller's busy programme continued unabated. After a period staying at Government House in Lahore with Sir Charles Aitchison they travelled to Delhi and Poona.

In April, the Müllers took an early morning drive to Parbuttee a high hill four miles from Poona. Alighting from their carriage at the bottom of the hill, they walked to the top and admired the magnificent view. A temple stood on the summit containing a representation of the god Shiva, and other gods and goddesses. Their guide, a Hindu, was on the point of enlightening them about these deities when Mrs Müller, never a woman to mince her words, nor prone to see a great deal of light in other religions interrupted:

'We do not believe in Shiva in the least,' she said, 'but in the true and living God, who made heaven and earth, and who sent His Son to die for poor lost sinners, as revealed in the Holy Scriptures.'

'I, too, believe in a supreme Being,' said their guide.

'Did you ever hear of Jesus Christ?'

'Never!'

'Can you not then ask some kind missionary to teach you about Jesus, for without faith in Him you will never get to heaven.'

'I must try and learn about Him,' said the guide, 'I must try, I must try.'

A busy programme in Bombay brought the Indian tour to a close. Before they left Mrs Müller received a letter from the Rev. John Fordyce who was well-known in India at that time, which referred to Müller as 'loved by thousands in India, and I believe by hundreds of thousands in other lands'.

Early in May they bid Abraham, their servant, a reluctant farewell and boarded the *Indus* for Aden and home. On June 5th they caught an express from Paddington which made Bristol in two and a half hours, and returned to No. 3 House after a journey of over twenty thousand miles.

The next three tours were all in the British Isles.

The fourteenth tour took the Müllers (via the States) to countries which they had never previously visited. On January 23rd 1886 the couple sailed into Port Jackson harbour, Sydney, aboard the *Australia*; there they stayed—at Petty's Hotel—until March 3rd. Müller held a large number of crowded meetings. In mid February they were introduced by Sir Alfred Steven to Lord Carrington, the Governor of New South Wales and also called on Sir James Martin, Sydney's Chief Justice.

Next stops on the tour were at Bathurst and Melbourne, where Müller twice addressed audiences of three thousand at the Theatre Royal and on one occasion preached to about five thousand at Melbourne Town Hall. More meetings were held on a return visit to Sydney before moving on to Brisbane where the couple preferred the climate.

In August they boarded the *Dacca* bound for Java, where there was time for a little exploration before boarding the *Borneo* bound for Hong Kong. At Hong Kong they stayed at the Victoria Hotel and Müller held many meetings with translation into Chinese.

On then into the heart of China for meetings at Shanghai, Hankau and Nankin where they visited the great Temple of Confucius.

The feature of their stay in Japan, which was the next country visited, was the immense size of the audiences which turned up to hear Müller wherever he preached: it was the same story at Yokohama, Tokyo, Kobe, Kioto and Osaka.

On their return journey Müller delivered more addresses at Hong Kong and Singapore before travelling back to London via Nice and Switzerland. They rested for a few days in London, in June 1887, staying at the Charing Cross Hotel; after a journey which had kept them away from Bristol for twenty months the traditional cheers from the children on Ashley Down when they first caught sight of the intrepid travellers were almost deafening.

Mr and Mrs Müller's next tour (from August 1887 to March 1890) was their last beyond European shores, and—as it turned out—Müller was fortunate to arrive home alive. They travelled first, via the States to

Adelaide, Australia, where Müller held many meetings
during a stay lasting some months and which included a
visit to Keyneston. Müller also spoke at Mount Gambier,
where they enjoyed a visit to the lovely Blue Lake,
Narracoorte and Border Town before they travelled on to
Tasmania where Müller preached twenty times in Hobart
and a number of times in Perth (Tasmania).

Next they went to New Zealand where their tour began
with a series of meetings at Queenstown. Then, early in
1888, they travelled by train from Kingston to Dunedin.
Opposite them, in a long saloon carriage, sat a gentleman
with a newspaper in his hand,

> out of which [Mrs Müller recorded] he read aloud for a
> few minutes to his fellow passengers, that 'the Rev.
> George Müller of Bristol, England, was about to visit
> Dunedin', etc. etc.; adding—'I would give a great deal
> indeed to see *him*.' Upon being informed that Mr
> Müller was sitting just opposite him, he was delighted,
> took off his hat, shook hands with us both and entered
> into a long conversation, in which all our fellow pas-
> sengers seemed greatly interested.

At Dunedin they stayed at the Grand Hotel and all
Müller's meetings were crowded including those at the
large Garrison Hall, which held nearly three thousand.

The New Zealand tour took them on to Port Chalmers,
Oamaru, Timaru and Wellington. On Monday, February
27th 1888, one Wellington newspaper stated that,
'Yesterday evening the Rev. George Müller of Bristol,
England, preached at the Opera House to the largest congregation ever packed into that building, for not only were
all the seats crowded to the utmost, but hundreds of persons were obliged to stand.'

Next they visted Palmerston, Wanganui, Hawera, New
Plymouth and Auckland. Returning to Australia and, on
his third visit to Sydney, Müller preached eighty-six times

and publicly answered questions put to him at the Burton Street Tabernacle. After more meetings in Melbourne they left Australia, aboard the *Britannia* for Ceylon.

At the end of December they arrived in Calcutta for the start of their second visit to India. Once again they engaged an Indian servant to accompany them on their travels—this time, a native of Madras named John Nathaniel.

Müller worked hard in Calcutta, preaching many times, despite the heat which became intense even for India.

The mosquitoes, too, became increasingly trying, both by day and by night; and though large punkahs, in the drawing-room and dining-hall were worked continually by coolies, and in our own bedroom a great punkah was swinging rapidly all day and all night long, nothing could satisfactorily abate the intensity of the heat.

Müller was now in his eighty-fourth year and Mrs Müller grew alarmed for his health.

I persuaded my husband, therefore, to consult a physician with reference to the climate, who told him that we ought not, on any account, to remain a day longer in the city than was absolutely necessary, and that, if we did, so, it would be at the risk of our lives . . . On April 29th, therefore, we left Calcutta by the four-thirty p.m. train; but, soon after our departure from the railway station, my beloved husband—though an excellent traveller, and one amongst a thousand in his ability to endure fatigue—became so extremely unwell from exhaustion, produced by the amazing heat, that I was exceedingly alarmed, and feared that he might die suddenly in the train. I knew, too, that there were no hotels on the road, nor any railway stations at which we could stop with anything like comfort; so I persuaded him to lie down upon one of the long seats of the saloon compartment we occupied, in which,

happily, there were no other passengers besides ourselves; placed one of the pillows we carry with us, when
taking night journeys, under his head, and kept all the
windows down, so that we might not lose a single
breath of air. I fanned him repeatedly also with a large
fan, persuaded him to drink a little of the wine and
water, and to eat a few of the sandwiches we had with
us, and begged him, if possible, to try and sleep. When
the train stopped long enough at the stations, too, and
Nathaniel came to ask us if we wanted anything, I sent
him to fetch a cup of tea for Mr Müller, or a glass of
lemonade; and in answer to repeated, fervent prayer,
managed to keep life in him until we reached
Damookdea Ghât, where we arrived at nine in the
evening. There, finding that his pulse was good, I took
courage; we went on board the ferry-steamer immediately, where, seated upon a chair on deck, he found
the night breezes blowing over the Ganges exceedingly
refreshing; and, at Sara Ghât, we went on shore. At
that station, a comfortable sleeping compartment was
secured for us by Nathaniel in another train; at ten
o'clock we started, and after travelling all night, in the
course of which Mr Müller slept soundly for several
hours, the next morning (April 30th) at half-past eight,
we reached Siligari. From that station, we travelled by
steam tram-carriage up the Himalayan Mountains to
Darjeeling, and arrived there in the afternoon at half-
past four, when a jin-rickshaw conveyed my husband,
and I was carried in a *dandy* on the shoulders of
Nepalese coolies, up a very steep, long road to
Rockville, a large Boarding House, in a beautiful situation, with a fine view from it of the snow-covered
peaks of the Himalayan Mountains in the distance,
when the weather is clear. There, in a few days, Mr
Müller regained his ordinary good health, and I am
thankful to say that, through the Lord's kindness, he
became as well and as strong as usual.

CHAPTER TWENTY-FOUR

Admiring His Kindness

During some of our tours [wrote Müller] we have for many weeks together been exposed to cold from fifty to fifty-six degrees below freezing point; and at other times to heat from ninety to one hundred and ten degrees and upwards, discomforts which must have been experienced in order to know the full force of them. Then, on the sea, again and again, very heavy gales, and even a typhoon, have overtaken us, when the trials thus occasioned were severe. On the land we have had to travel, on a stretch, not merely for twenty or thirty hours uninterruptedly, but more than once we have been on the railway six days and six nights in succession. Though, on the whole, we have had excellent accommodation during our long journeys, yet sometimes we have been obliged to put up with the most trying and inferior kind. Twice, though in the best cabins, on board large, first-class steam-ships, we have been exceedingly tried by insects; in the United States, in New South Wales, in Ceylon, and in India, the mosquitos were most grievous; and in two first-class steam-ships, rats so abounded that they ran over us by night. Yet hitherto God has helped us and, we doubt not, will help us to the end.

And indeed He did. Within a few days of coming close to death on that train from Calcutta to Darjeeling, Müller was able to resume a typically busy schedule—preaching regularly at Union Chapel, delivering lectures at the Town Hall, conducting Bible readings at the Manse, preaching in the theatre in neighbouring Jellapahar and holding a meeting for the German population of Darjeeling. At the same time he was busy writing the fiftieth annual report of the Scriptural Knowledge Institution.

The Indian tour took them on to Simla, Mussourie, Dehra Dun, Agra, Cawnpore and Allahabad where Müller preached to seven hundred Indian Christians from five different churches who had gathered in the open air for a love feast.

At Jubbulpore, Müller was handed a telegram from his son-in-law, James Wright: Müller's only child Lydia Wright had died on January 10th 1890, in her fifty-eighth year. He had had no previous indication of her illness and he described the news, quite naturally, as a 'heavy blow'; but he took comfort from Romans 8:28: 'And we know that all things work together for good to them that love God, to them who are called according to his purpose.' The Müllers decided to return for England by the first suitable steamer from Bombay.

At Bombay—while waiting for the first ship to leave— Müller preached fifteen times in a large tent, and once in German to the sailors of a Prussian man-of-war, by courtesy of the commander. He arrived in London in March and preached at the Mildmay Conference Hall. Returning, then, to Bristol he had 'great cause for praise, that the whole work was going on so well under the direction of [the bereaved] Mr Wright'.

For more than four months in the summer of 1890 Müller worked on Ashley Down. He badly needed a rest, however, and for this reason he and Susannah left England in August for a river trip down the Rhine past Nenwied, Coblentz, Mayence and picturesque ruins set amid lovely wooded country. At Heidelberg, Müller, feeling rested and invigorated, preached four times at the German Evangelical Chapel. He began to receive numbers of invitations to preach in Germany and Switzerland

and therefore decided to extend his break into another lengthy preaching tour, and addressed large audiences in the two countries.

Travelling east Müller preached in Vienna at the Reformed Church, the Methodist and Baptist Chapels. It was in Vienna that year that he met up with his friend F. W. Baedeker and, according to Baedeker's biographer, Müller 'laid his hands on the head of Dr Baedeker, then a comparative youth of only sixty-eight summers, and "separated him to the special ministry to the banished brethren, committing him to the loving care of our Heavenly Father"'. In the previous year the Russian Orthodox Church had resolved that Baptists, Stundists and those following 'Paschkoffist heresies' should be sternly dealt with; Colonel Paschkoff was simply one of many thousands banished to Siberia, Transcaucasia or other remote parts of the Empire. Baedeker travelled right across Siberia and into Sakhalin Island, visiting and encouraging these groups of persecuted Christians.

Moving further south into Italy, Müller preached in Florence, Rome and Naples. In May the Müllers arrived back at Dover and proceeded straight to Ashley Down after an absence of twenty-one months.

The preaching tours were over. In seventeen years Mr and Mrs Müller had travelled about two hundred thousand miles; Müller was now in his eighty-eighth year. During the tours it had occurred to him that Mary, who had died in her seventy-third year, would not have had the strength to undertake such arduous travels. Susannah, on the other hand, while never taking any part in public, had been an ideal companion and had greatly assisted Müller in the circulation of tens of thousands of tracts in many different languages and large numbers of Bibles and Testaments. She had spoken privately to thousands about the Christian gospel.

The financial year that ended a few weeks after the

Müllers arrived back at Ashley Down—year ending May 26th 1892—was the second only in the history of the homes in which expenditure had exceeded income. The first occasion had been the year 1881–2 when the expenses of the children's work had exceeded income by nearly £500; but in less than a month after the opening of the new financial year a sum was received from the payment of legacies which was three times greater than the deficiency: and this had occurred before the publication of the annual accounts.

On this, the second occasion, expenditure was nearly £2,000 in excess of income. Sixteen legacies, however, which had been left were due and might be paid on any date, worth nearly £3,500. In addition there were between forty and fifty other legacies which had been left to the Homes, worth nearly £2,600, but the payment of which depended on the decease of the testators' widows or other relatives. Further, the five Houses on Ashley Down had been built and furnished at a cost of £115,000; none was encumbered by a mortgage. Finally, the Institution owned about nineteen acres of valuable building land worth thousands of pounds. On the strength of all this Müller had not the slightest difficulty in borrowing from the bank for a short period to cover the deficit.

On the other hand, however, Müller did not feel happy even to *appear* to be in debt. He wrote:

The Lord's dealings with us during the last year indicate that it is His will we should contract our operations, and we are waiting upon Him for directions as to how, and to what extent, this should be done; for we have but one single object in connection with this Institution, viz., the glory of God. When I founded it, one of the principles stated was, 'That there would be no enlargement of the work, by going into debt'; and, in like manner, we cannot go on with that, which already exists, if we have not sufficient means coming in, to meet the current expenses.

In the event, the only actual contraction of the work took place in the Day School activities: at the end of July 1892 it was announced that most home and foreign Day Schools would be closed on October 31st; and on the appointed date, the sad operation was duly carried out. The school at Purton in Gloucestershire, the premises of which were owned by the Institution, and where young teachers for Ashley Down were trained, carried on as usual. Also all the Spanish and Italian schools, as well as three United Kingdom ones, continued to exist independently of SKI, the Institution aiding them whenever it remained possible. Sunday Schools would be supported as usual.

With regard to the children's work, after some months of prayer, Müller and his staff finally interpreted God's will to be that the work should not expand further. Originally, Müller had purchased over ten acres of land on which he had planned to build two more Houses opposite Nos. 4 and 5. In March 1893, however, this land was sold at £1,000 an acre for £10,405.

By the end of the century, the social problem which Müller had sought to alleviate was itself easing. Leaders of national opinion such as Charles Dickens and the Earl of Shaftesbury had aroused interest in the care of children throughout the country. And others, besides Müller, had entered the field—Barnardo, Fegan, the Church of England Children's Society, etc. Following Müller's example, there was now none of the eighteenth-century style barriers to entry: and the system of admission by election of subscribers had, thanks to Müller, all but disappeared.

Müller's influence on the care of children was not now confined to the United Kingdom. In October 1893 he received the following letter from Japan:

Dear Mr Müller,

Having had the pleasure of meeting you in Japan, in which country I have been living for the last seven years, I should like to see you again, and tell you something about the orphanage, which Mr Ishii is now carrying on in Okayama, which is really one of the results of your visit, and of the accounts which you gave, while you were in Tokyo, of the wonderful way God has provided for your own orphans in Bristol.

The said Mr Ishii, a Japanese Christian, was acting on the same principles as were maintained on Ashley Down; he cared for some one hundred and fifty children.

Susannah Müller was now seventy-three. On January 13th 1894, Müller's journal notes without warning that,

It pleased God to take to Himself my beloved wife, after He had left her to me twenty-three years and six weeks. By the grace of God I am not merely perfectly satisfied with this dispensation, but I kiss the hand which administered the stroke, and I look again for the fulfilment of that word in this instance, that 'All things work together for good to them that love God' (Romans 8:28).

Thus Müller was again a widower.

My loneliness [he wrote] after sixty-two years and five months of a happy married life, has been great, and is great; but I continually praise God for what He gave me, for what He left me for a long time, and for what He has now taken; for it is all good for me. By constantly admiring the Lord's kindness to me in this very thing, and that He has now entirely freed my beloved departed one from all bodily and spiritual infirmities, and made her unspeakably happy in His presence; He overpowers my loneliness, and is doing more than merely supporting me.

With the last preaching tour over, Müller rarely left Bristol. Now that he was alone, he decided to give up No. 21 Paul Street and to move into a suite of rooms in No. 3 House on Ashley Down which became his home for the remaining years of his life.

In September 1985, on his ninetieth birthday, a presentation was made to him in Bethesda Chapel. Acknowledging it, he said that his voice was stronger than it had been sixty-nine years earlier, and that his mental powers were as good as ever. That same day he recorded in his journal that 'my mind is as clear and as capable of work, as when I passed my examination for the University in March, 1825 (seventy-one years since)'.

He still took regular part in the Sunday morning services at Bethesda, Alma Road and Stokes Croft Chapels. He no longer preached, however, at evening services, though he continued to play his normal part in the running of the Orphan-Houses. Indeed, he continued to write the Annual Reports until the edition for the period May 1896 to May 1897.

His passion for detail and accuracy never waned. On November 5th 1895, he recorded some of the articles of provision which had been sent to Ashley Down during the previous year:

9,455 quarterns of bread, whereby 100 sacks of flour have been saved, 141 lbs of butter, 13 very large cheeses and 24 lbs, 15 tons and 16 cwts of coal, 59 lbs of tea, 239 lbs of bacon, 709 lbs of meat, 20 boxes of soap, 29 large pots of jam, 72,648 apples [who counted them?] 7,037 pears, 240 lbs of cherries, 3,362 plums, 4,174 buns, 22 cases of oranges, a large quantity of potatoes, carrots, turnips, flour. There were also two living oxen sent to be killed for meat for the Institution.

CHAPTER TWENTY-FIVE

Precious Prospect

Early in the summer of 1897 Charles Parsons visited Müller in his study at No. 3. 'He received me with a cordial handshake,' Parsons recorded, 'and bade me welcome.'

'You have always found the Lord faithful to His promise?' Parsons asked.

'Always,' replied Müller with great earnestness, 'He has never failed me! For nearly seventy years every need in connection with this work has been supplied. The orphans, from the first until now, have numbered nine thousand five hundred, but they have never wanted a meal. Never! Hundreds of times we have commenced the day without a penny in hand, but our Heavenly Father has sent supplies by the moment they were actually required. There never was a time when we had no wholesome meal. During all these years I have been enabled to trust in God, in the Living God, and in Him alone. £1,400,000 have been sent to me in answer to prayer. We have wanted as much as £50,000 in one year, and it has all come by the time it has been really needed. No man on earth can say that I ever asked him for a penny. We have no committees, no collectors, no voting and no endowments. All has come in answer to believing prayer. My trust has been in God alone; He has many ways of moving the hearts of men to help us all over the world. While I am praying He speaks to this one and another, on this continent and on that, to send us help. Only the other evening, while I was preaching, a gentleman wrote me a cheque for a large amount for the orphans, and handed it to me when the service was over.'

'I have read your life, Mr Müller, and have noticed how greatly, at times, your faith has been tried. Is it with you now as formerly?'

'My faith is tried as much as ever, and my difficulties are greater than ever. Besides our financial responsibilities, suitable helpers have constantly to be found, and suitable places have to be provided for scores and hundreds of orphans who are constantly leaving the Homes. Then often our funds run very low; we had come nearly to the end of our supplies: I called my beloved helpers together and said to them "Pray, brethren, pray!" Immediately, £100 was sent us, then £200, and in a few days £1,500 came in. But we have to be always praying and always believing. Oh, it is good to trust in the living God, for He hath said, "I will never leave thee, I will never forsake thee." Expect great things from God, and great things you will have. There is no limit to what He is able to do. Praises for ever be to His Glorious Name! Praise Him for all! Praise Him for everything! I have praised Him many times when he has sent me sixpence, and I have praised Him when He has sent me £12,000.'

'I suppose you have never contemplated a reserve fund?'

Müller answered with much emphasis: 'That would be the greatest folly. How could I pray if I had reserves? God would say, "Bring them out; bring out those reserves, George Müller." Oh no, I have never thought of such a thing! Our reserve fund is in heaven. God, the living God is our sufficiency. I have trusted Him for one sovereign; I have trusted Him for thousands, and I have never trusted in vain. "Blessed is the man that trusteth in Him".'

'Then, of course you have never thought of saving for yourself?'

'I shall not soon forget,' Parsons wrote, 'the dignified manner with which I was answered by this mighty man of faith. Hitherto, he had been sitting opposite me, with his knees almost close to mine, with clasped hands, and eyes that betokened a calm, quiet and meditative spirit.

Most of the time he leaned forward, his gaze directed to the floor. But now, he sat erect, and looked for several moments into my face with an earnestness that seemed to penetrate through my very soul. There was a grandeur and majesty about those undimmed eyes, so accustomed to spiritual visions, and to looking into the deep things of God. I do not know whether the question seemed to him a sordid one, or whether it touched, shall I say, a lingering remnant of the old self to which he so often alludes in all his discourses. Anyhow, there was no shadow of doubt that it aroused his whole being. After a brief pause, during which his face was a sermon, and the depths of his clear eyes flashed fire, he unbuttoned his coat and drew from his pocket an old-fashioned purse, with rings in the middle separating the character of the coins. He placed it in my hand, saying, "All I am possessed of is in that purse—every penny! Save for myself! Never! When money is sent to me for my own use I pass it on to God. As much as £1,000 has thus been sent at one time, but I do not regard these gifts as belonging to me; they belong to Him, Whose I am, and Whom I serve. Save for myself! I dare not save; it would be dishonouring to my loving, gracious, all-bountiful Father." '

Parsons handed the purse back to Müller, who told him the sum it contained.

Parsons asked him if he spent *much* time on his knees.

'More or less, every day. But I live in the spirit of prayer. I pray as I walk about, when I lie down and when I rise up. And the answers are always coming. Thousands and tens of thousands of times have my prayers been answered. When once I am persuaded that a thing is right and for the glory of God, I go on praying for it until the answer comes. "George Müller never gives up!" '

The words were spoken in an exulting tone. There was a ring of triumph about them, and his countenance was all aglow with holy joy. He had got up from his seat while uttering them, and had walked round to the side of the table. He went on: 'Thousands of souls have been saved in answer to the prayers of George Müller. He will meet thousands, yea, tens of thousands in heaven!'

There was another pause, but Parsons made no remark, and Müller continued: 'The great point is never to give up until the answer comes. I have been praying for fifty-two years, *every day*, for two men, sons of a friend of my youth. They are not converted yet, but they will be! How can it be otherwise? There is the unchanging promise of Jehovah, and on that I rest. The great fault of the children of God is, *they do not continue in prayer; they do not go on praying; they do not persevere*. If they desire anything for God's glory, they should pray until they get it. Oh, how good, and kind, and gracious, and condescending is the One with Whom we have to do! He has given me, unworthy as I am, immeasurably above all I had asked or thought! I am only a poor, frail, sinful man, but He has heard my prayers tens of thousands of times, and He has used me as the means of bringing tens of thousands into the way of truth. I say tens of thousands, in this and other lands. These unworthy lips have proclaimed salvation to great multitudes, and many, very many, have believed unto eternal life.'

Parsons' record continues:

' "I cannot help noticing the way in which you speak of yourself," I said, conscious that I was approaching a subject at once tender and sacred, and closely allied with his deepest spiritual moods and personal relationship to God, that I half reproached myself as soon as the words were uttered. He disarmed all my fears, however, by exclaiming, "There is only one thing George Müller deserves, and that is—hell! I tell you, my brother, that is the only thing I deserve. I am indeed, a hell-deserving sinner. By nature I am a lost man, but I am a sinner saved by the grace of God. Though I am by nature a sinner, I do not live in sin; I hate sin; I hate it more and more; and I love holiness; yea, I love holiness more and more."

'I said to him, "I suppose through all these long years in your work for God, you have met with much to discourage you?"

' "I have met with many discouragements," he answered; "but at all times my hope and confidence has been in God. On the word of Jehovah's promise hath my soul rested. O, it is good to trust in Him; His Word never returns void. He giveth power to the faint, and to them that have no might He increaseth strength. This applies also to my public ministrations. Sixty-two years ago I preached a poor, dry, barren sermon, with no comfort to myself, and, as I imagined, with no comfort to others. But a long time afterwards I heard of nineteen distinct cases of blessing that had come through that sermon."

'. . . Mr Müller fetched from another room a copy of his life, in which he inscribed my name. His absence afforded me an opportunity of looking round the apartment. I observed that the furniture was of the simplest and plainest description, and such as was useful. All seemed in harmony with the man of God who had been talking to me. It is a great principle with Mr Müller that it does not become the children of God to be ostentatious in their style, or appointments, or dress, or manner of living. Expensiveness and luxury are not seemly in those who are the professed disciples of the meek and lowly One, Who had not where to lay His Head. On the desk there lay an open Bible, of clear type, without notes, or references.

'This, then, I thought, is the abode of the mightiest man, spiritually, of modern times—a man specially raised up to show to a cold, calculating, selfish age the realities of the things of God, and to teach the Church how much she might gain, if only she were wise enough to take hold of the arm of Omnipotence.

'I had been with the Prince of Prayer one whole hour, and only once there came a knock at his door. It was opened by Mr Müller, and there stood one of his orphans,

one of the largest family on earth, a fair-haired maiden.
"My dear!" said he, "I cannot attend to you just now.
Wait a while, and I will see you." '

That summer, Müller's ninety-second, also marked the
Diamond Jubilee of Queen Victoria's long reign. On June
16th, he recorded the arrival on Ashley Down of a gift
from the Mayor of Bristol of £50, a sum allotted to the
Institution out of the City Jubilee Fund, 'for the purpose
of providing treats for the orphans, in commemoration of
the sixtieth year of the happy and prosperous reign of
Her Most Gracious Majesty the Queen'. The money was
spent by arranging for the children from the five Houses
to visit Clifton Zoo—a treat which, Müller said, they
greatly enjoyed. 'Besides inspecting the interesting and
instructive collection of animals, the children were
supplied with tea and an abundance of suitable provisions.' The balance of the sum was taken to provide
special treats for the very youngest infants who were too
small to walk to Clifton.

June 20th 1897, was Jubilee Sunday, and, for once,
Müller broke his recently self-imposed rule by preaching
at the evening service at Bethesda. How eagerly the large
congregation watched as the tall, erect figure mounted
the pulpit stairs and turned to address them! This was to
be a sermon from the man who had founded his Scriptural
Knowledge Institution three years before the teenaged
Princess had become Queen and who had begun to care
for thirty children in No. 6 Wilson Street, fourteen
months before her accession. In the sixty years that had
elapsed his name had become a byword for faith throughout the world; this was the man who claimed, in a letter
to the British and Foreign Bible Society, to have read the
whole Bible through 'considerably more than one
hundred times ... with prayer and meditation'. This
would be a sermon worth listening to.

'Our meditation this evening,' he began, 'as the Lord

may help us, will be on the short but precious 23rd Psalm, "The Lord is my Shepherd; I shall not want." ' He expounded the Psalm verse by verse and concluded: 'Now comes the last verse, "Surely goodness and mercy shall follow me all the days of my life, and I will dwell in the house of the Lord for ever." The poor one has been invited as a guest by the Rich One. He goes, and finds it very pleasant there, and is happy. All that is just what he desires naturally. Now, what conclusion does he come to? "I find it so very pleasant to be here, I will remain here, I will not go away any more." This brings before us what the child of God finds, in acquaintance with Christ. Not merely entering into what God has given him in Christ Jesus; not merely having to say, "My cup runneth over; I am brimful of happiness." But, "I have almost more than I can bear. I find it so pleasant, so exceedingly pleasant, this way of going on, I can never get into another position any more. I will remain in the house of my Heavenly Father for ever."

'That is the position into which we are brought as believers in Christ! And as assuredly as we are honestly walking in the ways of the Lord, and truly surrendering the heart to God, this is the result to which we come. We find it so pleasant, so precious, even for this life, that we have no desire to depart from the ways of the Lord. In our natural, worldly condition, we seek after happiness; but we do not get it. Nothing but disappointment is the result, for after a few hours all this worldly happiness is gone. But the position into which we are brought by faith in the Lord Jesus Christ not only ensures us happiness for a few days, or a few months, or a few years, but for ever and ever. So that our heart says, "I will remain in this way; I am so happy in this way; I will never forsake this way."

'Not merely so. But "Goodness and mercy shall follow me all the days of my life." I shall now be for ever and ever a happy man, and I will remain in the presence of my Father; I will not leave His House any more, because I have found it so very, very precious to be a child of God.'

Dr Pierson records that to one who asked him the secret of his service, Müller replied, 'There was a day when I died, utterly died'; and, as he spoke, he bent lower and lower until he almost touched the floor—'died to George Müller, his opinions, preferences, tastes and will—died to the world, its approval or censure—died to the approval or blame even of my brethren and friends—and since then I have studied only to show myself approved unto God.'

Whatever the secret, service for God was a passion with Müller. During that summer he was persuaded to take a few weeks' rest at Bishopsteignton; on the evening of his arrival he asked:

'What opportunity is there here for service for the Lord?'

It was suggested to him that he had just come from continuous work, and that this was a time for rest. Müller promptly replied that, being free from his usual labours, he felt he must be occupied in some other way in the service of God; for to glorify Him was his object in life. Meetings were accordingly arranged and he preached to attentive congregations at Bishopsteignton and Teignmouth.

Müller then returned to Bristol; the leaves on Ashley Down turned golden and then fell. Summer gave way to winter. In his rooms in No. 3, Müller continued to work and pray; as the weather grew colder he still ventured out from time to-time to preach in Bristol. One week-day evening that winter, a huge crowd assembled to hear him in Old Market Street Chapel. His text was an unusual one: Lamentations 3:22, 'It is of the Lord's mercies that we are not consumed, because his compassions fail not.' It is said that, as he spoke, he seemed full of the Holy Spirit. Towards the end of his address, he said:

'While all things change here below, the precious Jesus our Friend, is "the same yesterday, and today, and for ever" What He was millions of years since, He is now. What He was when He walked through Judea, Samaria and Galilee, He is now—His heart full of tenderness, of pity, of compassion.

'Though you be the greatest, the oldest, the most hardened sinner, though you have sinned again and again against light and knowledge, if you now trust in Christ, you will for His sake be forgiven, for there is power in the blood of Christ to take away the greatest sins.

'Learning in itself gives no happiness—no real, true happiness. Christ, and Christ alone, gives real, true happiness. I know seven languages, and with all this I should have gone to hell if it had not been that I knew Christ, Christ, Christ. Oh! the blessedness of being a disciple of the Lord Jesus!

'I am a happy old man; yes, indeed, I am a happy old man! I walk about my room, and I say, "Lord Jesus, I am not alone, for Thou art with me. I have buried my wives and my children, but Thou art left. I am never lonely or desolate with Thee and with Thy smile, which is better than life itself!" '

Sunday morning, March 6th 1898: the sea breezes above the Avon gorge seemed just a little less chilly; the residents of Clifton watched for signs of the approaching spring. At Alma Road Chapel, latecomers at the morning service quickly noticed: Bristol's most distinguished citizen was present. Fervently, they hoped he would take part. He did. Shortly before the time when it was customary to 'break bread', the aged saint rose to his feet.

'May we read from Isaiah, chapter six.' He read the chapter and then asked the congregation to turn with him to the gospel of John chapter twelve. He read verses 37–41: 'These things said Esaias, when He saw His glory, and spake of Him' (verse 41). 'This last verse,' said

Müller, 'settles the matter, that what we were reading in Isaiah 6 all refers to the glory of our adorable Lord Jesus Christ. In the whole of divine testimony we do not find a single portion which speaks more of His majesty and glory. We will now read it once more, verse by verse, in reference to our precious, adorable Lord Jesus.'

In his own inimitable style, Müller read the passage again, making clear, concise comments on each verse: drawing lessons where there were lessons to be drawn, but never imposing on the text unintended meanings. He concluded, 'O how pitifully, how mercifully, how tenderly, how graciously the Lord has been dealing with us in Christ Jesus! And what He has been doing and is doing, He will continue to do to the end of our earthly pilgrimage—He will not leave us nor forsake us, and a little while, and then He takes us home to Himself. O the bright, glorious prospect which we poor, miserable sinners have through faith in Christ Jesus! And at last taken home to be for ever with the Lord, and to see that lovely One who laid down His life for us, ourselves being permitted to kiss His feet, ourselves being permitted to kiss His hands! O the precious prospect that awaits us! . . . O the precious blood of Christ!'

Müller sat down. The bread was broken and passed, reverently, one to another. The wine poured out and drunk—the perfect sacrifice remembered, once more, once less.

Müller spent the afternoon with one of his closest friends, Benjamin Perry. During their conversation, Müller mentioned that a week or two earlier he had paid a visit to two mutual friends of theirs, both eight or ten years younger than himself, but both unable any longer to play an active part in the Lord's work. 'I came away,' Müller told Perry with a smile, 'feeling myself quite young in comparison. Oh, how very kind and good the Lord has been to me! Now in my ninety-third year I am still without rheumatism, or an ache or pain, and I can still do my ordinary work at the Orphan-Houses with as much comfort to myself as seventy years ago.'

And so he did. Next day, Monday, he was at his desk again at No. 3 working as usual. In the evening he travelled to Bethesda for the prayer meeting. After the meeting, Mr Fred Bergin introduced two friends to him who had just arrived from Barnstaple, one of whom brought greetings from Robert Chapman.

'Dear Mr Chapman,' said Müller, 'give him again my love; he is the oldest friend I have.' They had enjoyed sixty-eight years of close friendship.

On the Tuesday Müller worked as usual. Next morning, Wednesday, Müller felt weak as he got up and found it necessary to rest three times as he dressed. James Wright suggested that in future he ought to have an attendant in his bedroom to help him dress. 'After tomorrow,' said Müller.

Later in the day, he remarked, 'I feel quite myself again.' In the evening he led the usual weekly prayer meeting in No. 3, giving out the hymns 'The countless multitude on high', and, 'We'll sing of the Shepherd that died'. After the singing of the last verse:

> We'll sing of such subjects alone,
> None other our tongues shall employ;
> But better His love will be known
> In yonder bright regions of joy.

Müller wished Mr Wright 'Good night' and climbed the stairs to his bedroom.

Close behind, but not knowing who was ahead of her, a young student teacher, then living in No. 3, ran up the stairs, singing, 'I know not what awaits me, God kindly veils my eyes'.

'On nearing the top of the first flight,' she recalled later, 'I was conscious of a dark figure standing quite still. It was Mr Müller on the way from the prayer meeting to his bedroom. He waited until I reached him, and then, shaking hands with me, said:

' "I am so glad to see you so happy, but you must not run up the stairs two at a time, you may hurt yourself." '

Müller retired to his room. For some time, he had been in the habit of taking some nourishment during the night, and as usual that evening, a glass of milk and a biscuit had been put on his dressing table, should he need it. Next morning he awoke between five and six o'clock. He got up and walked towards the dressing table.

And then, in a moment, that bright prospect of which he had spoken just four days earlier became—for him—a glorious reality. George Müller saw the lovely One.

CHAPTER TWENTY-SIX

A Final Assessment

At about seven on the Thursday morning, Müller's attendant knocked at his door with a cup of tea. On entering, she found him lying dead on the floor beside his bed.

The news created a sensation in Bristol. On the Sunday there was scarcely a pulpit in the city, Anglican or non-conformist, from which reference was not made to the city's late philanthropist and preacher; in some churches, the Dead March was played.

Next day, Monday, March 14th, was the day of the funeral. It is said that nothing like it has been seen in Bristol before or since. Firms closed or gave their employees time off to witness the event: thousands of people lined the route of the procession; on Bristol cathedral and other churches flags flew at half mast and muffled peals were rung; in all the main streets black shutters were put up or blinds drawn. The city mourned.

After a short service at No. 3 House, a procession formed to walk to Bethesda for the main service. Amongst the column were four of the occupants of Müller's first home in Wilson Street, who remembered the day in June 1849, when they had marched up to Ashley Down to see their spacious new quarters.

Hundreds were unable to gain admission to the service at Bethesda. Among those who did squeeze into the main area of the chapel and its galleries were a number of clergymen and dissenting ministers. After the two addresses, hymns and F. S. Arnot's closing prayer, nearly a hundred carriages including the mayor's state coach joined the procession across the river to the cemetery.

At about two o'clock the procession reached the main gates inside of which a vast crowd of about seven thousand people had gathered. With considerable difficulty, a way was cleared for the bearers to carry the coffin up the hillside to the spot under a yew tree where Mary and Susannah had been buried. The service at the graveside concluded with the massive open-air congregation joining to sing the last hymn which Müller had chosen at the prayer meeting less than five days previously—ending, as he would have wished, not in sadness, but in anticipation of those 'yonder bright regions of joy'.

Obituary articles appeared in most national and local newspapers; one of the longest and most detailed—in *The Times*—has already been quoted in chapters fifteen and sixteen, and will be further cited below. Several newspapers contrasted the unequivocal facts of Müller's life with the rationalism of the age. 'Mr Müller,' said the *Bristol Evening News*, 'occupied a unique position among the philanthropists of the nineteenth century. In an age of agnosticism and materialism, he put to a practical test theories about which many men were content to hold profitless controversy.' The *Liverpool Mercury*, noting that thousands of children 'have been fed, clothed and educated out of funds, which have poured in without any influential committee or organisation, without appeal or advertisement of any sort', asked: 'How was this wonder accomplished? Mr Müller has told the world that it was the result of "Prayer". The rationalism of the day will sneer at this declaration; but the facts remain, and remain to be explained. It would be unscientific to belittle historical occurrences when they are difficult to explain, and much juggling would be needed to make the Orphanages on Ashley Down vanish from view.' *The Daily Telegraph*, in similar vein, said: 'Mr Müller's life and example, by their eloquent and touching beauty, cannot fail to impress even a sceptical and utilitarian age.' Writing of Müller's far-reaching social achievements, the *Telegraph* noted that he had 'robbed the cruel streets of thousands of victims, the gaols of thousands of felons, the workhouse of thousands of helpless waifs'.

In a sense, the tributes of the Bristol press are of greater significance than those of the national papers. For it was in Bristol that Müller sought to demonstrate that God answers prayer. Hundreds of Bristolians were or had been permanently employed at the Homes; many more worked there temporarily teaching, nursing, carrying out repairs or making deliveries; others took the weekly opportunities to visit the five Homes. Had Müller's principles failed, the truth could scarcely have been shielded from Bristol's watchful eyes. The West Country has never lacked its sceptics nor the nineteenth century its cynics. The news of under-fed, ill-clothed or cruelly treated children would have quickly travelled from Ashley Down to the heart of Bristol and beyond. And yet the *Bristol Times*, devoting its first leader as well as a separate news item and obituary article to Müller's passing, commented: 'It may be taken as substantiated that nearly all which has been said about Mr Müller is absolutely true.' The paper spoke of Müller's 'rare and stupendous intellectual gifts' and genius, and concluded he was 'raised up for the purpose of showing that the age of miracles is not past, and rebuking the sceptical tendencies of the time'.

How are we to assess George Müller eighty years after his death?

Some of his personal qualities were by themselves unusual, and when combined in one man, are rare to say the least. We may point, in the first place, to the outstanding administrative ability of the man (himself the son of a civil servant) who founded a home for thirty children and over the years undertook to expand the operation, becoming responsible for the welfare and education of ten

thousand children and the direction of a full-time staff of
several hundred people. That same man, as a director of
the Scriptural Knowledge Institution, controlled the expenditure of hundreds of thousands of pounds to aid and
encourage missionary work overseas, and to provide education for children and adults at home and abroad in
schools financed and often directly run by the Institution.
His supervision of all this activity was characterised by a
consistent attention to detail: he maintained accurate accounts of every aspect of his work; he was renowned—
even when the work was at its peak—for his knowledge of
many of the children by name (in the early days he knew
them all); he took a similar personal interest in the affairs
of the members of his large congregation at Bethesda and
in the missionaries all over the world whose activities he
supported. In his decision-making as the work grew he
was scrupulously correct: whether the decision was to
move or not to move from Wilson Street, to expand or
not to expand, whom to appoint to his staff, he would
carefully set out the pros and cons in true managerial
style—but with this in addition, long hours would be
spent in thoughtful prayer. And yet with all his attention
to detail, he was, as we have seen, neither inflexible nor
lacking in vision.

Then we may point to the man's remarkable energy,
which he demonstrated as a student in Halle and London
by regularly working for between twelve and fourteen
hours a day, and in his seventies and eighties by travelling
about two hundred thousand miles to preach and work in
thirty countries.

Müller was an individualist. He preferred to direct than
to be directed, to be the employer rather than the em-
ployee. His early connection as a trainee with a London
Missionary Society did not last: he found their restrictions unacceptable and preferred to go his own way—
though the break was friendly enough. But there was a
master whom he delighted to obey, and it was in the ser-

vice of Christ that he found his life's work. From that summer in Devon when, as he put it, he 'found his all in God', his life was one of total commitment to Him. 'Honour, pleasure, money,' he wrote, 'my physical powers, my mental powers, all was laid down at the feet of Jesus.'

He was not, therefore, a selfish individualist. The evidence corroborates his testimony that there was a day when he died, 'died to George Müller, his opinions, preferences, tastes and will'. His energy and abilities were directed into selfless channels in the service of God and his fellow human-beings. (It is known that during his life he received about £93,000 for his personal expenses: of this he gave away over £81,000; and at his death his sole estate was valued at about £160, including household furniture.)

Combined with the undoubted stubbornness of the Prussian, there was a surpassing graciousness of character which won him the affection and loyalty of friends and staff, the love and admiration of hundreds whom he met on his preaching tours, and the obvious respect of the citizens of Bristol. Charles Parsons, who knew him well, recorded: 'In himself George Müller was one of the most lovable of men: his heart overflowed with love. To the orphans whether singly or in groups he spoke in the tenderest manner imaginable. Said one of the schoolmasters to me one day, himself brought up as an orphan in the Homes, "Mr Müller is more than a father to us all." ' No one who has read his journal could deny the marked absence of harsh or caustic comment: as shrewd a judge of character as any, for Müller it was the good and wholesome aspects of men which were worthy of note; as for the rest he was content to be silent.

There will be those who will say he was narrowminded. It is true that he appears to have thought of 'the world' as *disordered* and in the grip of the evil one—a view that he would no doubt have defended on the basis of both observation and Scripture—probably calling in aid verses like 1 John 5:19, 'And we know that we are of God, and the world lieth in wickedness'. Twice after his conversion, he went to the theatre (except to preach) and once to a concert, but felt 'that it was unbecoming for me, as a child of God, to be in such a place'. Even had he been fond of the normal forms of entertainment, there would have been little time for this amid his busy life— or, perhaps, he would have achieved less. Narrow-minded or single-minded?—the reader must decide. His attitude to the world did not prevent him from devoting the last years of his life to going 'into all the world' to preach the gospel. And as for his attitude to Christians who held differing views from his, we saw that one of his aims on these tours was to discourage sectarian attitudes amongst Christian denominations and, as he said, to 'preach amongst all' (chapter 19).

The reference in the *Bristol Times* to Müller's 'rare and stupendous intellectual gifts' is somewhat surprising. There is no doubt that he was gifted intellectually: he shone at school, despite his wild life; he left Halle with a good degree; and spoke seven languages. But on the whole he was happier in the field of action than in the realm of ideas. When he taught Christians, his ministry was mainly either *practical* (how they might live the Christian life, find reality and know definite answers to prayer), or such as would inspire his hearers to greater commitment. This interested him far more than rather abstract theological debate: it was only with reluctance (and of necessity) that he was drawn into the controversy in the 1840s on the humanity and sufferings of Christ. It is clear that he well understood the issues involved: indeed, his comments on the debate are strikingly penetrating; but he refused to indulge in unedifying tract warfare on the subject.

His most notable intellectual quality was his ability to *think clearly*. In 1839, for instance, when a separation threatened at Bethesda over a dispute on points of church order, Müller and Craik went into retreat for a fortnight, to think, study and pray. They returned to Bethesda for a series of meetings at which they explained their findings. The paper which Müller produced containing the substance of what they said is something of a masterpiece of concise, logical thought. It outlined their findings on eldership, discipline and the Lord's Supper, carefully distinguishing between what could be 'expressly proved from Scripture', and what Scripture seemed 'rather in favour of'. (In the latter case, it was particularly emphasised that 'mutual forbearance ought to be exercised' where churches differed.) Primarily a man of action rather than a philosopher or controversialist, Müller was nevertheless capable of sustained and objective thought. It is noteworthy that *accuracy* was the feature that struck him about Newton's later writings.

What has intrigued and inspired people for over a century now, is not so much what George Müller *was* as what he *did*: if his personal qualities were unusual, his achievements were in one respect unique, perhaps since apostolic times and possibly even since Elijah's finest hour on Carmel (see 1 Kings 18). For Müller embarked on his project with the stated aim of demonstrating God's reality, and of proving to those who cared to observe that God answers prayer. There have always been those who would claim to have proved this power for themselves or who have trusted in God alone to support them; Müller's uniqueness lies not in his exercise of faith, or in the importance he attached to prayer, but in his announcement, as he embarked on the undertaking, that he was setting out to demonstrate that God is real. In 1837, recalling the reasons which led him to establish his first home (in 1836), he wrote:

Now, if I, a poor man, simply by prayer and faith, obtained *without asking any individual*, the means for establishing and carrying on an Orphan-House: there would be something which, with the Lord's blessing, might be instrumental in strengthening the faith of the children of God, besides being a testimony to the consciences of the unconverted, of the reality of the things of God.

So Müller issued his challenge to unbelievers to watch the work he had begun and see whether there was a God who would finance it; he invited believers not only to see what God would do, but to consider their response if He proved faithful.

The preceding pages have told what happened. In brief: during the next sixty-three years, Müller received nearly £1,500,000 (to be precise: £1,453,513 13s 3d); and the many branches of his work included the care of some ten thousand children. He claimed that neither he nor his staff ever issued an appeal for funds or asked any individual to support his work. No evidence has been produced to disprove this. (There was once an allegation that Müller had prayed publicly that God would send money to the Homes; Müller described this as 'entirely false'.) According to Müller, for over sixty years God provided the means—and thus demonstrated His reality.

What will be the reaction to this in the closing years of the twentieth century?

It would be foolish to claim that the events of Müller's life constitute scientific proof either of the existence of God, or, if He exists, of His willingness or ability to answer prayer. It is the view of the author, however, that what Müller described as 'the Lord's dealings' with him constitute—not proof of these things—but evidence which deserves to be taken seriously.

Leaving aside for a moment the issue of *how* the money was raised, the reader can verify the visible facts of the case by taking a trip to Bristol. Those five great buildings still stand on Ashley Down. Now used by Bristol Polytechnic, No. 3—where the founder lived and died—is clearly marked and suitably named: *Müller House*. When in Bristol, the reader may care to visit the other

Müller House, at Cotham Park, headquarters of the work today, to enquire whether Müller's principles have stood the test of time. There has been no departure from them.

The sceptical reader, while readily agreeing with the *Liverpool Mercury* that 'much juggling would be needed to make the orphanages on Ashley Down vanish from view' may raise a number of objections to Müller's explanation as to their financing. We have allowed Müller to reply to some of the objections put forward in his day in chapter thirteen—including the argument that it was simply the publication of annual reports which produced the results. (We do not repeat Müller's reply here.)

Müller believed that God exists; that in the nineteenth century, He was still the Living God; that this Living God answered his prayers and 'put it into people's hearts' to give to the work which he directed. Perhaps the argument of those who do not believe in God, or who are doubtful and remain unconvinced by Müller's attempt to demonstrate His reality, would run something like this:

   (i) It may well be true that George Müller never appealed for funds, but it is a fact that he publicly announced his intention of founding a home for children;

  (ii) He clearly had a large number of Christian friends, many of them in the Brethren movement, who would have been anxious that his attempt to demonstrate God's reality should succeed;

 (iii) Seeing the value of what he was doing, and the obvious extent of the need, they therefore gave generously to his work;

 (iv) His refusal to appeal for funds, so the critic may argue, was a convenient device to spare him indignity and embarrassment.

Just as we have stated that the events of Müller's life do not *prove* the existence of a God who answers prayer (rather they constitute evidence that deserves to be taken seriously), so it must be said that none of these objections *disproves* Müller's contention. But, in Müller's defence, it may be noted:

(a) In answer to (i) above, Müller's concept of trust in God rarely involved *doing nothing*. This attitude he described as the 'counterfeit of faith'. Once he had satisfied himself that it was God's will to found a Home, it was necessary to *act* and to act correctly: therefore the meeting to outline his plans was arranged (a collection, of course, being deliberately excluded). Also three statements in the Bristol press summarised his proposals and gave certain details of eligibility, and so on. Without considering the practical difficulties of proceeding in the absence of some publicity, this also may be added: it required courage for Müller to make no secret of his intentions at the outset. For this way, if ever his principles failed, he knew that his God would be publicly discredited;

(b) In answered to (ii) above. It is true that, as the years passed, Müller's circle of friends increased. But in 1836, when his first Home was founded, he was relatively unknown even in Bristol. Indeed, he had lived in England for barely seven years;

(c) In answer to (iii) above. It is not only the total amount of money that Müller received which is striking, but the timing of its receipt—for periods the income being consistently adequate but no more than adequate (discussion of this below);

(d) In answer to (iv) above. This is an assertion capable neither of proof nor disproof. Even if it were true, it would not explain why and how the funds came in.

To argue that God did not answer Müller's prayers, as

he believed, or that there is and was no God to support his work, is to say that he was deluded. (This assumes that he sincerely believed that God was providing for him: an alternative view—though more difficult to sustain—that he was a deceiver is discussed below.) The view that Müller was deluded can be held without malice, and can be maintained alongside an admiration, even affection, for the man: he was a good, perhaps a great man of considerable achievement—but he was wrong, sincerely wrong. It is the conviction of the author, however, that the evidence of Müller's life lends no support to this position. The evidence points not to a deluded or disillusioned man, but to someone who daily had his faith confirmed and strengthened.

It is true that Müller's faith was tried. Chapters 9 and 10 described the period from 1838 to 1846 when—although the children knew nothing of this—there was rarely an excess of funds. The need was supplied by the day, even by the hour. Just once during this period, as we saw, Müller became—in his words—'tried in spirit' (chapter 9). 'For the first time, the Lord seemed not to regard our prayer.' But an hour or so later, having been handed a gift by a visitor from London who had been staying for several days next door to the Boys' Home in Wilson Street, and who had been entrusted with this donation by her daughter in the metropolis, Müller was able to 'burst out into loud praises and thanks the first moment I was alone'. In Müller's view the fact that 'the money had been so near the Orphan-Houses for several days without being given, is a plain proof that it was in the heart of God to help us, but because He delights in the prayers of His children, He had allowed us to pray so long; also to try our faith, and to make the answer so much the sweeter'.

Müller apparently regarded this early period as a test of his obedience, and of that of his helpers. 'It can only be ascribed to the especial mercy of God, that the faith of

those who were engaged in this work did not altogether
fail, and that they did not entirely grow weary of this way
of carrying on the Lord's work, and go, in despair of help
from God, back again to the habits and maxims of this
evil world.' It was a period when his character was
moulded, prepared for his life's work. And can we not
agree that the very fact that for long periods enough was
sent but no more than enough was evidence of the hand
of God? Is not this as remarkable in itself as the total
receipt of £1,500,000? Does not a rejection of Müller's
version of the events, involve the acceptance of an incredible alternative? It would mean that for sixty or so
years, his sympathisers, for various reasons excluding
actual divine intervention, not only sent him sufficient
funds in total to enable the vast expansion of his work,
but also for periods—particularly in the early years—sent
just enough to supply the need, but never, even for one
day, too little.

We have noted that an alternative to the view that
Müller was deluded is that he was a deceiver; in other
words that, despite his assertions to the contrary, there
were periods when the children were in need. But this
view is almost impossible to reconcile with Müller's
popularity in Bristol, and the respect which, as we have
seen, the citizens of that city—with the evidence before
them—held for him.

If, as the author believes, there is little evidence to
support the hypothesis that Müller was either deluded or
a deluder, there is even less to suggest that, as the years
passed, he grew disillusioned. He never struck his contemporaries as a man who was anxiously striving to preserve a myth, or who had reason to doubt that the needs
of over two thousand persons would be met. 'A peaceful
and stately demeanour ... without a care' was the testimony of a West-Country farmer. 'The twenty-third Psalm
seemed written on his face!'

Müller's longevity itself is surely consistent with his

profession of an inner peace: a delight in God cradled in the experience of answered prayer. 'I cannot tell you,' he told a friend, 'how happy this service in which I am engaged makes me. Instead of my being the anxious, careworn man so many persons think me to be, I have no anxieties and no cares at all. Faith in God leads me to roll my burdens, all my burdens, upon God. Not only burdens concerning money, but burdens concerning everything, for hundreds are my necessities besides those connected with money. In every way I find God to be my helper, even as I trust in Him for everything, and pray to Him in child-like simplicity about everything ... I have found invariably, during my long life as a believer, that if I only believed, I was sure to get in God's time the thing I asked for.'

The incident, described in chapter 20, when—anxious to honour an engagement in Quebec—Müller prayed successfully for fog to be lifted, is, while almost certainly authentic, not typical of the man.

We do not pretend to miracles [he wrote at another time]. We have no desire that the work, in which we are engaged, should be considered an extraordinary, or even a remarkable one. We are truly sorry that many persons, inconsiderately, look upon it as almost miraculous. The principles are as old as the Holy Scriptures. But they are forgotten by many; are not held in living faith by others; and by some they are not known at all; nay, they are denied to be scriptural by not a few, and are considered wild and fanatical.

The particular relevance of the 'fog incident' to our present discussion is Müller's comment to the ship's captain, 'for fifty-two years, there has never been a single day that I have failed to get an audience with the King'. This, surely, was the confidence of a man in the habit of seeing his prayers answered.

Another illustration of his calm assurance that God would meet the needs of his children, was his readiness to send thousands of pounds abroad to missionaries and lay out large sums on his educational work in England and in various parts of the world. He did not think it necessary to put every penny he received to the Ashley Down account. It is the contention of the author that this was the confidence of a man who had discovered that his God was a rich God.

The obituary writer in *The Times* was struck by the loyalty that Müller commanded in his staff. 'His reliance upon a Higher Power in the great crises of life was regarded on the part of many as simple fanaticism; but the results he obtained were marvellous; and though mis-understood in some quarters, he was able to kindle in those around him a devotion and an enthusiasm which was as extraordinary as they were unique.' Cannot the explanation of this 'extraordinary enthusiasm' be that these people, like Müller, had discovered for themselves, the reality of the things of God?

The Times observed, and Müller frequently conceded, that there were those who dismissed his principles as (in Müller's words) 'wild and fanatical'. The dictionary defines a fanatic as a 'person filled with excessive and mistaken enthusiasm, especially in religion'. Was Müller a fanatic? Not according to the *Western Daily Press*:

> Never was there a philanthropist with less of fanaticism and more of method. His bearing and his speech were not those of an emotional enthusiast who would incur heavy liabilities with a light heart; indeed, had he been such a man, his life would have been less surprising than it was; it was his calmness and confidence, associ-ated with the most careful watchfulness over expendi-ture and most business-like habits, that presented a combination of qualities altogether unique and wholly surprising.

And, of course, Müller himself denied it: 'I am not a fanatic or enthusiast, but, as all who know me are well aware, a calm, cool, quiet, calculating businessman.' And will not most businessmen agree that a man who successfully raised £1,500,000 at nineteenth-century values, and directed its outlay, cannot easily be dismissed as 'filled with . . . mistaken enthusiasm'?

Müller was not, of course, a political reformer and did not, like Lord Shaftesbury, seek to improve social conditions by influencing legislation in Parliament. Nor, like F. D. Maurice and the Christian socialists, did he strive to awaken the social conscience of Victorian Christians. He was, though, an interested member of the 'Reformatory and Refuge Union' of which the President was Lord Shaftesbury, and Quintin Hogg (ancestor of the present Lord Hailsham) a prominent member. It was perhaps in this connection that Shaftesbury visited Ashley Down. Müller's diaries indicate an awareness of the findings of official Reports on poverty, of conditions in the work-houses and prisons. But his main concern was to do what he could by direct action to offer children a better start in life rather than seeking to reform the existing Poor Law Institutions. His reaction to the revelation in an official Report that there were six thousand young orphans in the prisons of England was to say: 'By God's help, I will do what I can to keep poor orphans from prison'; he was content—in the main—to leave to others the attempt to change the system itself.

It may be that the reaction of some to the re-telling of the Müller story will be to wish that they themselves were similarly gifted with faith. To any such, let this be said: Müller denied that the faith which enabled him to found his Orphan-Homes was a special gift. He wrote: 'It is not true that my faith is that gift of faith which is spoken of in 1 Corinthians 12:9.' (In this verse Paul includes faith in a list of spiritual gifts, others mentioned being healing,

miracle working, prophecy and tongues.) Müller spoke of
his faith in these terms (in 1869): 'It is the selfsame faith
which is found in *every believer*, and the growth of which
I am most sensible of to myself; for, by little and little, it
has been increasing for the last forty-three years.' He
continued: 'Oh! I beseech you, do not think me an extraordinary believer, having privileges above other of God's
dear children, which they cannot have; nor look on my
way of acting as something that would not do for other
believers. Make but trial! Do but stand still in the hour
of trial, and you will see the help of God, if you trust in
Him.'

Müller's answer to those who asked him how they
might have their faith strengthened was as follows. He
would begin by quoting James 1 : 17: 'Every good gift and
every perfect gift is from above, and cometh down from
the Father of lights, with whom is no variableness, neither
shadow of turning.' Then he would point out that as the
increase of faith is a good gift, it must come from God,
and therefore He ought to be asked for the blessing. But,
in addition, he recommended four steps which those who
wished to see their faith increased could take to help the
process along.

First, he advised 'the careful reading of the word of
God, combined with meditation on it'. This, he said, is
how the believer learns more of the nature and character
of God and 'thus sees more and more, besides His holiness and justice, what a kind, loving, gracious, merciful,
mighty, wise and faithful Being He is', and therefore
when difficulties arise 'will repose upon the *ability* of God
to help him', having 'seen instance upon instance in the
Holy Scriptures in which His almighty power and infinite
wisdom have been actually exercised in helping and delivering His people; and he will repose upon the *willingness* of God to help him, because he has not only
learned from the Scriptures what a kind, good, merciful,
gracious and faithful being God is, but because he has

also seen in the word of God, how in a great variety of instances He has proved Himself to be so'.

Secondly, he warned that 'it is of the utmost importance that we seek to maintain an upright heart and a good conscience, and, therefore, do not knowingly and habitually indulge in those things which are contrary to the mind of God ... All my confidence towards God, all my leaning upon Him in the hour of trial will be gone, if I have a guilty conscience, and do not seek to put away this guilty conscience, but still continue to do things which are contrary to the mind of God. And if, in any particular instance, I cannot trust in God, because of the guilty conscience, then my faith is weakened by that instance of distrust; for faith with every fresh trial of it either increases by trusting God, and thus getting help, or it decreases by not trusting Him; and then there is less and less power of looking simply and directly to Him, and a habit of self-dependence is begotten and encouraged.'

Thirdly, he advised those who wanted their faith increased not to shrink from situations where their faith might be tested and thus strengthened. 'In our natural state we dislike dealing with God alone ... This cleaves to us more or less, even after our regeneration. Hence it is, that, more or less, even as believers, we have the same shrinking from standing with God alone—from depending upon Him alone—from looking to Him alone—and yet this is the very position in which we ought to be, if we wish our faith to be strengthened.' It is in trying situations, depending on God alone, that Müller said the believer 'may see the hand of God stretched out on his behalf'.

Finally, Müller said it is important that 'we let God work for us, when the hour of the trial of our faith comes, and do not work a deliverance of our own ... However weak our faith may be, God will try it; only with this restriction, that as, in every way, He leads on gently, gradually, patiently, so also with reference to the trial of our faith ... God never lays more upon us than He is willing to enable us to bear. Now when the trial of faith comes, we are naturally inclined to distrust God, and to trust rather in ourselves, or in our friends, or in circumstances. We will rather work a deliverance of our own somehow or other, than simply look to God and wait for His help ... Would the believer, therefore, have his faith strengthened, he must especially, *give time to God*, who tries his faith in order to prove to His child, in the end, how willing He is to help and deliver him, the moment it is good for him.'

To those who have never yet embarked on a life of faith, two brief sentences on the theme of 'Christianity' written by Müller one hundred and thirty-five years ago bear repeating today: 'There is life,' he wrote, 'and power, and reality in our holy faith. If you never yet have known this, then come and taste for yourself.'

Let those who seek reassurance that the God of the late twentieth century is the God in whom George Müller delighted, note his declaration: 'The Living God is with us, whose power never fails, whose arm never grows weary, whose wisdom is infinite and whose power is unchanging. Therefore today, tomorrow and next month, as long as life is continued, He will be our helper and friend. Still more, even as He is through all time, so will He be through all eternity.'

CHAPTER TWENTY-SEVEN

Eighty Years On

The warm sunny days of early September 1980, were especially welcome after a summer which, on the whole, had been dull and wet. But when the author visited Weston-super-Mare one weekend that September, there was scarcely a cloud in the sky.

It was not my first visit to the large late nineteenth-century house a few hundred yards from the sea, and I knew I should enjoy it. Except for the barking of the dogs, the house was quiet as I arrived and was welcomed by the Houseparents' teenage daughter. The children—less one who had a Saturday job—were on an outing organised by the local Round Table for several Müller's and local authority Homes in Weston and Clevedon.

Over tea with the Housemother I chatted about the problems and rewards of running a modern 'family group' home. Children in care today are rarely orphans. In most cases they come from broken homes where there may have been a long history of marital conflict and disharmony before the final breakdown of the marriage; or they may have come into care as a result of a court appearance. Such children bring with them deep-seated emotional problems because of their experiences, and may be suffering the effects of what the experts call 'maternal deprivation': they have not known the continuing security of a mother's love. It is the task of the Houseparents and their assistants first of all to love and care for the children, and then to help them come to terms with their experiences and circumstances. They will try to rebuild a feeling in the child that he or she is a worthwhile person, and that he does matter, whatever may have happened.

Our conversation is interrupted as the family arrives home: five boys (including one who is the Houseparents' own), four girls and one resident young lady assistant. The average age of the children is about ten to twelve. Most of them have met the author before and they talk excitedly about their adventures on the outing and how they have spent their precious pocket-money. Saturday tea is informal—even chaotic—taken buffet-style in the large kitchen as anecdotes and reminiscences of the day's excursion to the Wild Life Park at Cricket St Thomas are exchanged in a cacophony of sound and laughter.

Early Saturday evening is bath time and, as a highly-popular film is to be shown on the television, there is no time to be lost. One by one dressing-gowned figures gather in the comfortable lounge and settle in front of the colour television, their wet hair drying in the warm evening air. Several join me on the sofa and show me a scrap book recording some recent highlights in their lives: the day they visited London for the mammoth children's party in Hyde Park—there are the Queen and Prince Philip mingling with the children, there is a London bobby, there are the parachutists who landed in the park, that's my friend eating an ice-cream, there we are having a picnic; the day they went to Land's End; a letter from a former member of the family; and so on, and so on.

One of the girls produces two presents she has bought and some wrapping paper and instructs me to wrap them for her. She explains that one is for her dad and the other is for Mark: I must hurry, she says, because Mark—who will be thirteen tomorrow—will shortly be emerging from the bathroom. My good deed is done and, with little time to spare, Mark appears.

The film is not watched in silence. Its merits and shortcomings are discussed, and subtleties of the plot are explained to those who need such enlightenment. At intervals, members of the audience are summoned to another room: tomorrow is the Sunday School prize-giving. The Housefather is the superintendent and is auditioning candidates to do the Scripture reading. No one demurs at missing a part of the film, knowing that on return he or she will be brought fully up to date. There is just the slightest tension when the successful candidate is announced and the Housefather's own son observes a little tetchily that he could read better; but the observation is hardly noticed and quickly forgotten. The auditioning over, the Housefather settles on the floor in the lounge and himself receives a briefing on the story so far.

Just before ten, the film ends and the instant obedience which follows the command 'Bed!' staggers the author, and I consider the possibility of sending my own son here for a course of treatment! Over a bedtime drink the Housefather tells me how things have gone since we last met. Once his wife had come close to breaking point as the strains and stresses had almost overwhelmed her—but now she was well again. Shortly after that, a girl assistant had left them without warning and for several months they had been without help. But there had been encouragements too: several of the children had responded well to the love and attention they had received and the summer holiday had been a great success.

My bedroom is tucked away at the top of the house. It has a basin with hot and cold water, but although I fancy I can smell the salt air I do not have a sea view. The children are asleep in their rooms beneath posters of pop-stars and football idols, and dreaming I suppose of unlikely film dramas occurring in darkest Somerset.

Sunday is another glorious day and before eight I am strolling across Weston's massive beach, watching the early-morning sun light up the elegant houses of the Royal Crescent and Atlantic Road at the north end of the seafront. I return for breakfast—taken on Sundays at the civilised hour of nine-thirty—with a hearty appetite. The meal is a little more formal than Saturday tea, the family sitting around an enormous table in the dining-room. As we bow our heads briefly I reflect on the special significance of a grace at Müller's—where the considerable financial needs are made known only to God in prayer. We tuck in to a breakfast which does ample justice to the demands of growing children and hungry adults.

It is Mark's birthday and, although he will have to wait until tea for his party and presents, the cards he has received are passed around for us all to read. One is somewhat inappropriately chosen and another is a little cheeky—but no one has forgotten his special day. Before we leave the table after breakfast, the Housefather commits us all to God in prayer; and then the birthday boy receives the inevitable bumps. A small group gather round the piano while I play choruses as requested. Later everyone piles into the minibus (which today all Müller's family groups are proud to own) for the combined morning service and prize-giving at the local church the family attends. As her husband manoeuvres the vehicle out of the drive, the Housemother recalls the occasion when the whole family drew up at a filling station for petrol. As he filled the tank she had noticed the attendant looking distinctly puzzled. Unable to restrain his curiosity he asked her husband, 'Are they all yours?' 'Yes,' came the reply without a moment's hesitation, 'second time around!'

At lunch we are joined by my wife and three-year-old son of whom a great fuss is made. They soon feel as at home as I do. It is difficult to remember what we have been told about emotional problems and maternal deprivation: for the moment there are no such signs and we are enriched by being a part of this happy family. We have to leave after lunch, but before we go the Housefather takes us into his delightful walled garden and proudly cuts us an enormous bunch of grapes from a vine in his greenhouse and picks us some tomatoes. Timothy is presented with crisps and an orange to eat on his long journey home, and we wave sadly goodbye.

And so the work continues. There are eleven Homes like this looking after ten or so children in each house at Bristol, Weston-super-Mare and Clevedon. More recently, a Day Care Centre has also opened. Its objectives are to look after children of two to five years, whose home circumstances are, for various reasons, not conducive to a healthy upbringing, either mentally, physically or emotionally, and to create an environment at the Centre where advice and practical help can be given to parents, as well as the good news of the gospel. This is an exciting new aspect of the work which may well be expanded in future years.

Much has changed since Müller's day. The vast buildings on Ashley Down have been sold (although they remain very much alive serving the needs of higher education); the quaint uniforms have been relegated to the Müller House Museum; the children mix with their contemporaries at local schools; and their accommodation is more luxurious and homely.

But in all the change there is a certain continuity. The Homes still meet a major social need: in Müller's day the need was that of children who had lost their parents often as the result of tuberculosis; today, it is that of children who are the casualties of the disintegration of family life in our society. And in meeting this pressing social need, George Müller's objective of demonstrating to the world the 'reality of the things of God' remains. As they meet every day without fail for prayer at the Bristol headquarters of the work, the directors and staff are very conscious that people still look to the Homes for a visible proof that God answers prayer. Every year as the Annual Reports are published, faith is strengthened as people read of God's continued provision for the work. But in providing this demonstration of God's reality, the directors are anxious that the work should not continue in existence just for the sake of it, but that it should meet real needs.

Traditionally, social workers in many parts of the

country frequently recommended that children should be placed in a Müller's Home. They were impressed by the Christian principles on which the Homes are run, and by the relative stability offered where Houseparents and their young assistants tend to stay for longer periods than in comparable local authority Homes. But with the current emphasis on fostering and the improvement in local authority care there is some tendency for applications for places to decrease.

And so the work is continually adapting to the needs of the day. As well as an expansion of the Day Care Centres, future possibilities include: an Evangelical Centre, to which parents would be free to come at any time for help which would, in particular, be unashamedly spiritual—'getting at the root of the problem' as one of the directors put it; a Community Centre for particularly disturbed children, providing education in the Centre and having a high staff/student ratio; a Home for physically handicapped children some of whom might come on a short-term basis and then return to their own parents; and a school—not for children in the Homes who are integrated into local schools—but for other children to receive a Christian education. All these options remain speculative at present, and the last one may be totally unrealistic even though it would be well within the mainstream of the Müller tradition. Many schools were supported in the last century, and well into this century children at Müller's Homes were taught on Ashley Down.

The present directors attach great importance to the spiritual results of the work, and see the Homes as sowing the foundation truths of the gospel in young lives. Sometimes the reaping is done quickly: although pressure for conversions is deliberately avoided, every year some children become real Christians. Sometimes it is done many years later, and by others perhaps far away from the Homes.

A typical example is that of Carl Laurie who died in

1979 and who left the Homes prior to the First World War. Apprenticed to a farmer in South Wales, he intensely disliked farming and the farmer, and ran away to sea as a stowaway. He eventually arrived in California where he settled and lived for the rest of his life. During his life he amassed a great deal of wealth. He was married and had three sons and two daughters. During the latter years of his life he got into the habit of returning to England every year or two. He would visit the headquarters of the work in Bristol, but always, it seemed, to criticise the Homes and everything that had been done or, as he felt, not done for him while he was in care. He insisted that the spiritual instruction he had received had been wasted, and prided himself on being a self-made man.

And then in October 1977, one of the directors received a letter from Carl which included the following *volte-face*:

Lately I've begun to realise God's goodness in His wisdom in guiding me to the orphanage in my early days, and the participation in the religious instruction, and clean living (giving me a long life—86) and still good health. Only lately have I begun really to understand and appreciate His goodness, and feel Him in His quiet way telling me to come to Him, understanding in these later days, His great love, and how He has taken care of me. Bless Him and His Holy Name. With the help of the pastor of the church, things have gradually been made clear to me, and now I can say, 'Thank-you Lord, and I'm sorry for all my sins.' What patience He must have to have put up with me throughout my life from the early days when sitting in Bethesda Chapel and seeing both Mr Müller and Mr Wright together in the pulpit.

The other objectives of the Scriptural Knowledge Institution, founded by George Müller and Henry Craik in 1834 are still upheld: gifts are sent at regular intervals to missionaries in many parts of the world; home evangelists are helped and the Bible warehouse, which Müller commenced in 1849, has been enlarged in size and scope. Evangelical Christian Literature is the familiar name of well-stocked and busy Christian bookshops in Bristol and Bath run by the Homes, which also supply well over one hundred church bookstalls. The profits are channelled abroad to missionaries.

Since 1958, the Homes have been under the wise direction of Mr J. J. Rose, ably assisted in recent years by his associate director and social worker Mr J. Cowan. In June 1978, Mr Bernard Cooper, associate director and accountant, died and is sorely missed. The future of the work is in God's hands. Mr Rose wrote recently of the pressures to which modern children are subjected—'an ugly age of drugs, licence and abounding immorality, which presents a challenge to us'. He continued, 'In spite of these things and the quickened pace of decline, we lift our banner and declare afresh the utter faithfulness of God. The times may be difficult and unstable, but we are heartened and strengthened in the knowledge that our Lord is, "The same yesterday, and today, and forever" (Hebrews 13:8). He is unchangeable. It is the Lord, Himself, who declares: "I am the Lord, I change not" (Malachi 3:6) ... This is the anchor of our faith and trust (Hebrews 6:13–20) as we step out into a future all unknown.'

You may obtain further information about the Homes from:

The Honorary Director
The Müller Homes for Children
Müller House
7 Cotham Park
Bristol BS6 6DA